Clergy Sexual Abuse

The Northeastern Series on Gender, Crime, and Law
Editor: Claire Renzetti

For a complete list of books available in this series, please visit www.upne.com

Claire M. Renzetti and Sandra Yocum, editors, *Clergy Sexual Abuse: Social Science Perspectives*

Taryn Lindhorst and Jeffrey L. Edleson, *Battered Women, Their Children, and International Law: The Unintended Consequences of the Hague Child Abduction Convention*

Edward W. Gondolf, *The Future of Batterer Programs: Reassessing Evidence-Based Practice*

Jessica P. Hodge, *Gendered Hate: Exploring Gender in Hate Crime Law*

Molly Dragiewicz, *Equality with a Vengeance: Men's Rights Groups, Battered Women, and Antifeminist Backlash*

Mary Lay Schuster and Amy D. Propen, *Victim Advocacy in the Courtroom: Persuasive Practices in Domestic Violence and Child Protection Cases*

Jana L. Jasinski, Jennifer K. Wesely, James D. Wright, and Elizabeth E. Mustaine, *Hard Lives, Mean Streets: Violence in the Lives of Homeless Women*

Merry Morash, *Women on Probation and Parole: A Feminist Critique of Community Programs and Services*

Drew Humphries, *Women, Violence, and the Media: Readings in Feminist Criminology*

Gail A. Caputo, *Out in the Storm: Drug-Addicted Women Living as Shoplifters and Sex Workers*

Michael P. Johnson, *A Typology of Domestic Violence: Intimate Terrorism, Violent Resistance, and Situational Couple Violence*

Susan L. Miller, editor, *Criminal Justice Research and Practice: Diverse Voices from the Field*

Jody Raphael, *Freeing Tammy: Women, Drugs, and Incarceration*

Kathleen J. Ferraro, *Neither Angels nor Demons: Women, Crime, and Victimization*

Michelle L. Meloy, *Sex Offenses and the Men Who Commit Them: An Assessment of Sex Offenders on Probation*

Amy Neustein and Michael Lesher, *From Madness to Mutiny: Why Mothers Are Running from the Family Courts—and What Can Be Done about It*

Jody Raphael, *Listening to Olivia: Violence, Poverty, and Prostitution*

Cynthia Siemsen, *Emotional Trials: Moral Dilemmas of Women Criminal Defense Attorneys*

Lori B. Girshick, *Woman-to-Woman Sexual Violence: Stories of Women in Prison*

Karlene Faith, *The Long Prison Journey of Leslie van Houten: Life Beyond the Cult*

Jody Raphael, *Saving Bernice: Battered Women, Welfare, and Poverty*

Neil Websdale, *Policing the Poor: From Slave Plantation to Public Housing*

Lori B. Girshick, *No Safe Haven: Stories of Women in Prison*

Social
Science
Perspectives

Clergy Sexual Abuse

Claire M. Renzetti
and Sandra Yocum,
editors

Northeastern University Press BOSTON

Northeastern University Press
An imprint of University Press of New England
www.upne.com

Manufactured in the United States of America
Typeset in Minion Pro and Optima by Integrated Publishing Solutions

Hardcover ISBN: 978-1-55553-810-1
Paperback ISBN: 978-1-55553-809-5
Ebook ISBN: 978-1-55553-811-8

University Press of New England is a member of the Green Press Initiative. The paper used in this book meets their minimum requirement for recycled paper.

Library of Congress Cataloging-in-Publication Data is available upon request.

5 4 3 2 1

For the victims and the survivors

Contents

Preface

The idea for this book developed from our work on an eighteen-month lecture series, "The Wounded Body of Christ: Sexual Abuse in the Church," held at the University of Dayton beginning in 2003. We were members of an interdisciplinary committee tasked with identifying topics and speakers, and as we discussed and debated the issues with our fellow committee members, it quickly became clear that there is a multitude of lenses through which the problem of sexual abuse in the Roman Catholic Church can be viewed. Perhaps of greatest importance were the perspectives of victims and survivors, who, we recognized, were not a homogeneous group, despite media reports that often presented them in that way. Their experiences were diverse, as were the consequences of those experiences in their lives and their feelings about how offenders should be (or should have been) handled. There was, of course, the official perspective of the Church, but others associated with the Church—clergy and religious, pastoral counselors, lay religious leaders, and parishioners—had their views as well. We also identified academics and professionals who had studied the problem, or some aspect of it, and whose analysis or experience contributed to the public debate. Included were psychologists and therapists, theologians, historians, and lawyers and legal scholars. But our goal with the lecture series was not to blend a cacophony of voices, each trying to convince all present of the value and correctness of its perspective. Instead, we wished to create a safe space for dialogue: an environment in which individuals with differing, often conflicting, views and experiences could come together to think, silently and out loud; to learn from one another; perhaps receive support, maybe even some relief from their pain; and ultimately arrive at a better understanding of what happened, why it happened, and how it can be prevented from happening again.

We will never know how close we came to achieving our goal. Every lecture was well attended, not just by faculty members and students, but also by members of the larger Dayton community who had little or no direct affiliation with the university. We received a great deal of positive feedback from people who attended some or all of the lectures, and we also received suggestions and requests for additional programming. For many months after the lecture series ended, we discussed the possibility of publishing several of the talks in a single volume to reach a larger audience. That task proved daunting for several reasons, not the least of which were the difficulties in deciding which talks to include and in presenting them coherently without editing out the greatly disparate views and analyses the authors presented. We gave up, but we never abandoned our commitment to continuing analysis and public discussion of the crisis of clergy sexual abuse in an effort to redress past wrongs and prevent future ones.

It was Phyllis Deutsch, editor in chief at the University Press of New England, who suggested that we concentrate on social science perspectives on the crisis. In taking Phyllis's suggestion to heart, we made the project simultaneously more narrow (by excluding other disciplinary points of view) and more comprehensive (by including the analytical lenses of multiple social science disciplines). What we have lost in breadth of coverage, we believe we make up for in coherency. We realize some readers may disagree, and we take full responsibility for this decision. But we wish to take this opportunity to thank Phyllis for her support of the book, as well as her insight, knowledge of publishing, and incredible editorial skill—all of which have been invaluable to us. One of us—Claire—has worked with Phyllis for several years on the Gender, Crime, and Law book series, and I would like to add a special word of thanks: Phyllis, in collaborating with you on the series, I've learned about editing and publishing from one of the best in the business. Among the lessons you've taught me is that patience, good humor, and a periodic indulgence in gelato are as important as correct punctuation and grammar. I'm grateful for our friendship.

We also wish to thank our colleagues at the University of Kentucky and the University of Dayton, especially those at Dayton who served with us on the lecture series committee: Fr. Chris Wittmann, SM; Dennis Doyle; and Kelly Johnson. Our many hours of conversation and reflection together over the two years of planning and implementation of the lecture series were stimulating and made work that was at times depressing and at other times frustrating not just bearable, but rewarding.

We are, of course, grateful to the contributors to the book. None of them was a participant in the lecture series. Each responded enthusiastically to our invitation to write about the problem of clergy sexual abuse from the perspective of her or his respective social science discipline, and their enthusiasm for the project did not appear to wane even after we asked for revisions or for attention to the tedious details of citation and reference formatting—or at least they were gracious enough not to express to us any reductions in their enthusiasm. We and the contributors benefited from the comments of two reviewers of an earlier draft of the manuscript, Patrick Donnelly and Nancy Nason-Clark. Their generous gifts of time and knowledge undoubtedly improved the book, and any deficits that remain are the products of our errors in judgment and not their oversight.

Claire M. Renzetti

1 An Introduction to Social Science Perspectives on the Problem of Clergy Sexual Abuse

The headlines are familiar: "Diocese Enters Plea in Sex Case" (*Denver Post*, November 21, 2003), "Catholic Church's Costs Pass $1 Billion in Abuse Cases" (*New York Times*, June 12, 2005), "Philadelphia Church Official Sentenced to 3 to 6 Years for Covering Up Child Sex Abuse" (*New York Times*, July 24, 2012). Indeed, as Mary Gordon (2004) has pointed out, so much media attention has been given to clergy sexual abuse in recent years that one might expect the American public to be experiencing "atrocity fatigue" by now. Although there is evidence that some people, including Catholics, know little about the scope of the Catholic clergy sexual abuse scandal (see, for example, Gray and Perl 2006), most studies show that among Catholics and non-Catholics alike, reports of clergy sexual abuse, particularly of children, continue to evoke strong reactions of shock, anger, and dismay. Such violations represent a severe breach of trust: between the perpetrator and the individual who has been victimized, who may be a powerless child; between the perpetrator and the church, at both the corporate level and the local level of the parish, congregation, school, or other religious community; and, in light of the way such cases are often handled—or mishandled—by church officials, between the official church and its members.

Given the numerous articles and books that have been published in the wake of the Catholic clergy sexual abuse scandal, one may justifiably ask what more is left to say about clergy sexual abuse. The purpose of the present volume is not to document the extent of the abuse. That task has been ably accomplished by others, whose research shows that the abuse probably occurs even more frequently than available data indicate (see, for example, France 2004; John Jay College 2004, 2006; Plante and McChesney 2011). Moreover, although the spotlight in recent years has focused on sexual abuse perpetrated by Roman Catholic priests, sexual abuse by clergy is not a problem unique to the Catholic Church. There is ample research showing that clergy of nearly all faith traditions, and in many countries, have been accused by both youth and adults of sexual abuse (Fortune 1995; Keenan 2012; Neustein 2009; Otterman and Rivera 2012; Thoburn and Baker 2011). Much of the work on clergy sexual abuse, however, approaches the problem from a pastoral counseling perspective and/or focuses largely on the pathology of perpetrators (for example, poor impulse control, intimacy deficits, weak psychosocial development, and substance abuse). The purpose of this book is to examine clergy sexual abuse in the United States through the prism of social science interdisciplinarity, with a focus on the cultural, institutional, and structural factors that contribute to the problem and therefore must be understood to address it effectively. Our objective is not to discount the importance of pastoral counseling or the role of individual or personal factors, but rather to nest these within a broader framework that includes cultural, contextual, organizational, and structural factors as well (Heise 1998). Few, if any, problems are unidimensional; the complexity of social problems demands an interdisciplinary analysis that, in turn, suggests multilayered solutions.

As the book's subtitle makes clear, this volume brings social science perspectives to bear on the problem of clergy sexual abuse. The authors draw on research—their own and that of colleagues—from sociology, criminology, religious studies, anthropology, psychology, social work, and law. Rather than each chapter having a distinct disciplinary focus, the authors often blend work from all of these fields—and others—to enrich our understanding of the causes and consequences of, and therefore potential remedies for, clergy sexual abuse.

In chapter 2, Karen Terry, the lead investigator on the studies commissioned by the US Conference of Catholic Bishops, presents some of the major findings from those studies. The first study, covering the period 1950–2002, collected data to measure the extent of clergy sexual abuse in the Catholic Church and to identify characteristics of perpetrators and victims and the circumstances in which abuse occurred. Terry and her colleagues found that allegations of sexual abuse had been made about 4,392 priests; these priests represented 4 percent of all priests in active ministry during the fifty-two-year period the researchers examined. These allegations had been brought by 10,667 individuals, 81 percent of whom were men or boys. More than half of these men and boys had been victimized when they were between the ages of eleven and fourteen. Incidents of abuse peaked during the 1970s and early 80s. Most were perpetrated by diocesan priests, which in itself is not a surprising finding, given that there are about twice as many diocesan priests as there are priests affiliated with a specific religious order. Most of the priests who were accused were also serving as pastors or associate pastors, a point that Terry notes is important, since priests in these roles are subject to less oversight. And although most of the accused priests (56 percent) victimized a single individual (although often multiple times), a small group (3.5 percent) was responsible for the abuse of 26 percent of all the victims. Terry refers to this group as "career criminals"; I would characterize them as serial predators.

The nature and scope study is enlightening, although given what we know about victims'—especially male victims'—reluctance to disclose sexual abuse (Finkelhor 2008; London, Bruck, Ceci, and Shuman 2005), the findings regarding abuse incidence are very likely a gross underestimation, a problem of which the researchers are not unaware. But the central question raised by the nature and scope study is why does the abuse occur? The primary purpose of the causes and context study, as Terry points out in her chapter, was to answer this question. The study analyzed data from seven different sources, covering 1950–2010. The researchers sought data that could help situate the abuse in a historical and cultural context, and they also examined case data; court documents; and data from abuse survivors, victim advocates, bishops, and priests, among others. As Terry reports, the analysis not surprisingly showed that a variety of factors—individual, situational, and organizational—are related to sexual abuse by Catholic clergy. For instance, the researchers found that priests who were ordained during the 1940s and 1950s were significantly more likely to be named as abusers than priests ordained during other periods included in the study. Terry notes that this was a time when seminary enrollments were high, but the seminary curriculum was weak with regard to the subject of personal formation as a priest, especially in terms of issues of sexuality and preparation to adhere to the mandatory vow of celibacy. And although few of the abusive priests were diagnosed as pedophiles, they typically had other psychological problems as well as substance use disorders, emotional and psychosexual immaturity, and financial problems.

But there were two other aspects of the causes and context study that generated the greatest commentary and concern; in fact, it might be more accurate to describe the widespread negative reaction to the report as a firestorm. First, although there is substantial evidence in the report indicating that members of the Church hierarchy badly mismanaged the cases brought to their attention, some observers argue that the report downplayed what amounted to complicity on the part of the bishops, whose attitudes and behavior—for example, transferring accused priests to other parishes or settings where they would continue to have contact with children, prioritizing damage control for the Church over the welfare of victims, relying on confession and prayer instead of the criminal justice system to sanction perpetrators, and failing to comply with a set of principles adopted by the US Conference of Catholic Bishops in 1992 regarding how to proactively address clergy sexual abuse—were major contributors to the continuation of the abuse over many years (Voice of the Faithful [VOTF] 2011).

Terry makes clear in her chapter in this volume that there are important differences between the responses of bishops who came to their positions before 2000 and those of bishops who reached their positions after 2000. As she points out, prior to 2000, the bishops typically treated clergy sexual abuse of minors as a sin rather than a crime that harmed a child, a point to which I will return shortly and that will be taken up by other authors in this book. After 2000, however, bishops were more likely to emphasize social problems and faulty seminary instruction as causes of the abuse and, more important, to acknowledge the harm done to the victims. Still, relatively few cases (9.3 percent) were brought to the attention of police, and fewer still resulted in criminal charges being filed and the perpetrators being convicted. The cases that were successfully prosecuted were much more likely to be the especially heinous ones involving serial predators, who victimized numerous children over a long period of time. Terry emphasizes that one of the primary reasons for the low rate of criminal justice involvement was the lengthy delay in reporting by victims. Often victims did not publicly disclose the abuse or bring a complaint to the police until decades after the offense occurred. (Several authors in this book discuss explanations of victims' prolonged silence.) These delays frequently meant that by the time a police report was made, the statute of limitations had expired, and criminal legal action was no longer possible (but see Goodstein and Eckholm 2012). But Terry also states that another major reason for lack of criminal justice involvement was that when bishops were made aware of allegations against one of the priests under their authority, they preferred to help him (for instance, by sending him for treatment), rather than involving the criminal justice system to investigate and eventually punish him.

The second aspect of the causes and context study that generated considerable controversy was what quickly became labeled the "blame Woodstock excuse." This charge refers to the aspect of the study that sought to identify the larger social and historical context in which the bulk of the abuse incidents appeared to have occurred. More specifically, the study found that clergy sexual abuse of minors rose dramatically from the mid-1960s to the mid-1980s. In the larger society, this was a period of rapid and seismic social change—what some sociologists might label a period of anomie—during which social norms were in flux and there was a greater openness to experimentation with behavior, including sexual behavior and the use of drugs, previously defined as inappropriate, deviant, or even taboo. The divorce rate and the crime rate climbed during this period, too. Seminaries, religious communities, and parishes were not immune to these wider social changes; for instance, priestly and seminary life became far less constricting, but at the same time, resignations from the priesthood increased substantially. The causes and context study ties the spike in clergy sexual abuse of minors to this broader historical and social context, which led some observers to respond with the criticism that the researchers were trying to deflect responsibility from the Church and blame the so-called swinging sixties for the problem.

Elsewhere, Terry (2011) notes that even though the causes and context study identifies a confluence of factors that contributed to the spike in Catholic clergy sexual abuse of minors from the mid-1960s to the mid-1980s, the media and other social commentators zeroed in on only one of these factors, and the phrase "blame Woodstock" was cited in connection with the report more that 14,000 times in the two days following its release, in May 2011. Other criticisms of the report include its focus on too limited a time period, producing the impression that clergy sexual abuse was rare or nonexistent prior to 1950. To this charge, Terry (2011) responds that although the researchers recognize that sexual abuse has always occurred in the Catholic Church, it would have been too difficult for practical and methodological reasons to try to study the problem prior to 1950.

Although Terry strongly defends both John Jay College studies in her chapter in this volume and elsewhere (2011), the heated criticism those studies have provoked is not easily rebutted. For example, Voice of the Faithful (VOTF), an organization of Catholic lay people established in the wake of the Church's sexual abuse crisis to support survivors and "priests of integrity" as well as to lobby for progressive change in the Church, acknowledges that the findings of the causes and context study "support a consistent set of conclusions" (2011, 1). Nevertheless, VOTF argues that "conspicuously absent from the researchers' analysis and conclusions is any clear reference to clericalism (the lived belief that clergy are different, separate and exempt from the norms, rules, and consequences that apply to everyone else) as an influence, much less a major one, in explaining why priests sexually abused minors and the hierarchy enabled it to continue" (2011, 8). The role of clericalism is addressed from several different perspectives in the remaining chapters in this book.

In chapter 3, John Gonsiorek maintains that despite the lack of reliable data on clergy sexual abuse, it does not appear that clergy perpetrate such abuse against children or adults any more than individuals in other helping professions do. But Gonsiorek, a clinical psychologist who has studied male sexual abuse and sexual abuse perpetrated by healthcare professionals, notes that since the late 1970s there has been a noticeable shift in the organizational culture of healthcare such that denial and tolerance of such behavior have largely been replaced by uniform and active prohibition and sanction. This does not mean, of course, that sexual abuse by health professionals no longer occurs, but Gonsiorek states that it appears to have measurably declined. As he looks at cases of clergy sexual abuse, however, he is less optimistic that recent efforts by the Church to stem the problem will be as successful as those in healthcare have been. He attributes this likely failure to organizational or institutional dysfunction in the Church. Granted, Gonsiorek writes, there are individual (idiopathic) factors that contribute to the propensity of some priests to perpetrate sexual abuse, but in his chapter he focuses primarily on "idiosyncrasies of church structure and organizational culture, especially the culture and structure of church leadership." He argues that an individual propensity to sexually exploit others is not sufficient for abuse to actually occur; such individuals must also have opportunities to abuse others. Church structure and the relatively persistent unwillingness of Church leaders to aggressively and effectively respond to sexual abuse by clergy—in fact, the leaders' typical choice to cover up such incidents instead—create an environment that not only allows clergy sexual abuse to occur, but is de facto complicit in the abuse.

Gonsiorek reviews what he considers to be the most salient features of the Catholic Church in terms of contributing to clergy sexual abuse. He observes first that compared with other helping professionals such as psychologists and therapists, clergy play a role that is more intense and "boundary strained." A priest, for instance, is expected to fulfill liturgical duties that involve some of the most personal and private aspects of his parishioners' lives, such as premarital counseling and praying with family members as a loved one is dying. At the same time, with these same people, the priest raises money, teaches, coaches, manages parish finances and staff members, and socializes. All of these interactions occur in the context of an institutional culture that explicitly condemns all forms of sexual expression, except sexual relations between husband and wife—and even married couples are expected to have sex only within certain prescribed constraints. The institutional culture of the Catholic Church also denigrates women, while it simultaneously elevates priests to the level of the divine through the claim of ordination as ontological transformation. (This latter point is taken up as well by Sandra Yocum in chapter 5.) Women, even women religious (nuns), are regarded as naturally unfit for leadership roles in the Church. Consider, for example, a document issued by the Vatican in 2010 codifying Church administrative procedures for trying and disciplining priests accused of sexual abuse. The document, which still does not require bishops to report sexual abuse incidents to state or local criminal justice authorities, nevertheless provides a list of "more grave delicts" (sins or offenses) that ranks the ordination of women to the priesthood as comparable to pedophilia (Donadio 2010). And although the Vatican steadfastly refuses to hold bishops accountable for abuse by priests under their authority, in 2012 it appointed a US bishop to reform the largest and most influential group of Catholic nuns in the country, the Leadership Conference of Women Religious, which the Vatican reprimanded for disagreeing with or challenging the bishops, "who are the church's authentic teachers of faith and morals"; for challenging Church teachings on homosexuality and the male-only priesthood; and for promoting "radical feminist themes" (Goodstein 2012).

Although such statements and actions, and the attitudes that underlie them, may appear arrogantly self-destructive, Gonsiorek would no doubt see them as quite rational, even if perversely so, when viewed from the aristocratic vantage point of Church leaders. He characterizes the Catholic Church as a "true aristocracy," which devalues those outside the leadership: their central purpose is to serve Church leaders. This aristocratic hierarchy is to be maintained at all costs, with the power of those at the very top preserved, if not extended.

Some readers may take issue with a number of Gonsiorek's assertions—for instance, his claim that most Roman Catholic clergy "fake" celibacy; it is a state to which most aspire but typically fail to attain. But his insights into the organizational structure and culture of the Catholic Church are instructive for understanding how macro-level factors intersect with individual traits and experiences to generate specific problems and varied responses to them. Although Gonsiorek is a clinical psychologist, I don't think he would mind my saying that he demonstrates the power of the sociological imagination (Mills 1959) in his analysis of the intimate connections between "personal troubles" and "public issues."

The criminologist Paul Steele continues this theme in chapter 4, noting that much criminological theorizing and research has been of a "dispositional" nature, focusing on the personal traits and pathologies of individuals—and specifically, in terms of the problem at hand, of individuals who perpetrate child sexual abuse. Though not disavowing the importance of examining individual variables, Steele emphasizes the inadequacy of a dispositional approach alone for explaining crimes such as clergy sexual abuse of children. For one thing, actual or potential perpetrators are not the only social actors whose traits and characteristics must be taken into account; the traits and characteristics of actual or potential victims and of those charged with guarding or protecting them are also relevant to understanding criminal offenses such as child sexual abuse. One must examine the traits and characteristics—that is, emotional states, knowledge, capacities, values, and motives—of all the social actors involved: offender, victim(s), and guardian(s). In addition, Steele emphasizes the need to analyze contextual and situational variables: physical, temporal or historical, and ecological environments; social network, community, and institutional contexts; and situational precipitants to action. Unlike dispositional theories, then, situational theories require the study of the synergistic contribution of all of these elements to the criminal event.

In examining child sexual abuse perpetrated by clergy from the point of view of a situational theorist, Steele identifies important similarities and differences between cases involving clergy and other cases with regard to all of the relevant elements. For instance, he notes that clergy offenders are typically better educated, have stronger communication skills, and are less likely to come from disorganized or chaotic home environments than other child sexual abuse perpetrators. Child victims of clergy sexual abuse also differ in important ways from child victims of nonclergy sexual abuse: they are somewhat older, and the majority are boys. Moreover, unlike child victims of nonclergy sexual abuse, child victims of clergy sexual abuse are less likely to live in disrupted or disorganized homes; ironically, in fact, their families' integration into the church community and involvement in church activities increase the children's risk of being victimized by a clergy offender. These characteristics also inhibit a child victim's willingness to disclose the abuse to his parents, let alone to teachers or the police. Parents' trust of and respect for the clergy offender, as well as their respect for the Church's authority, also inhibit them from involving the criminal justice system if their child does disclose the abuse to them.

Steele also distinguishes between contextual risk factors and precipitants. A contextual risk factor is an environmental characteristic that influences the likelihood that a criminal event will occur at that specific location. But, as Steele points out, an individual may be predisposed to offending and in an environmental or contextual setting favorable to committing the offense (for example, a private place, affording easy access to a potential victim), but no crime may occur because there is no stimulus that prompts the potential offender to act. One precipitant that Steele notes was identified by Terry and her colleagues (2011) in the causes and context study is the use of alcohol or drugs by the offender, the victim, or both. Steele discusses several ways that substance use can precipitate child sexual abuse. Although most people realize that alcohol and drugs may impair judgment and lower inhibitions—both of which are obvious precipitants for many forms of deviant behavior—Steele cites research showing that alcohol may precipitate some forms of deviance, such as aggressive behavior, only when the imbiber believes that the alcohol will induce such behavior. Consequently, some offenders may intentionally use alcohol or drugs and provide them for their potential victims in the belief that these substances will impair judgment and increase willingness to participate in the sexual encounter; thus, when the abuse occurs, it is a form of self-fulfilling prophecy. Substance abuse may also facilitate deviance disavowal, such as "I'm not a child abuser. I'm an alcoholic; I have a disease that causes me to do things I wouldn't normally do. Therefore, I am not responsible for my actions; I am not to blame."

Although substance use may be an unintentional precipitant in some cases of clergy sexual abuse, there is considerable evidence that, as Steele puts it, clergy abusers are quite strategic in their selection of a victim as well as a location to perpetrate the abuse. The extensive "grooming" of victims, as well as their guardians or protectors, also belies the notion that much clergy sexual abuse is unintentional. As Steele and other contributors to this book define it, grooming involves a careful, gradual escalation of events and situations over time, designed by the perpetrator to gain access to the victim, win the victim's trust and the trust of the victim's guardians, and ensure that the victim will not disclose abuse or will not be believed if he (or she) does disclose it. The perpetrator uses this time to get the victim comfortable with being alone with him, and to desensitize the victim to touch and conversations about sexual topics. The perpetrator may give the victim or the victim's family gifts or special favors. Essentially, the grooming primes the victim for the sexual abuse, but it can also be used by the perpetrator to justify his behavior and/or to deny any wrongdoing.

Most child sexual abuse researchers think of grooming as a process that takes place between offender and victim, but there are ways that organizational culture may also groom victims and their families for clergy sexual abuse. Both Gonsiorek and Steele discuss the special authority conferred on priests through ordination, which is recognized and respected not only among themselves, but also—perhaps, especially—by the laity. In chapter 5, Sandra Yocum explores how the religious education of young Catholics may groom them, in a sense, for clergy sexual abuse by instilling in them beliefs about the supernatural powers of priests. Her central argument is that we must understand Catholic culture in order to understand abusive priests and the people who protect and defend them, and to determine the best ways to help those they victimized.

Yocum presents an analysis of the *Baltimore Catechism*, the textbook used in Catholic schools and religious education classes from the 1940s through the 1960s—the period, readers will recall, when seminary enrollments were rising and that marked the start of what the John Jay College studies identified as the peak of sexual abuse incidents. Multiple editions of the catechism were published for instruction of very young children as well as for adolescents and adults, and even for non-Catholics. The format, as Yocum notes, is question and answer, with each edition written at a level supposedly appropriate for the intended audience, but all covering the same essential topics. Yocum analyzes the specific sections of the catechism that offered instruction on the roles of priests and how lay Catholics should regard priests and interact with them. In the examples she provides, quoted directly from different editions of the catechism, one is left with little doubt that the priest, through ordination, essentially becomes transformed into the embodiment of Jesus Christ. Moreover, catechists are explicitly instructed that priests receive supernatural powers through ordination: they can literally change ordinary bread and wine into Jesus's body and blood; they can condemn you to spend eternity in hell or forgive you your sins and thereby assure that you will spend everlasting life in heaven. Catholic students are also directed to cooperate with their priests and bishops, to be deferential in interactions with them, and to always act and speak in ways that will reflect positively on the Church.

Yocum's analysis has a strong personal resonance for me, because I attended Catholic elementary school and received my religious instruction through the *Baltimore Catechism*. In fact, to this day I can recite many of the questions and their answers—not all that surprising, given that we were drilled on them daily. I have quite vivid recollections of the images in the catechisms. For instance, I recall one drawing of a milk bottle in which the milk was tainted with black spots. This image, I was told, represented my soul when it was blackened by sin. On the next page, though, was a child in a confessional box, confessing his sins (yes, the child was a boy) to a priest, who subsequently assigned the child penance (usually, prayers that needed to be said) and then absolved the child of his sins. The following image was of a milk bottle filled with white milk; confession had gotten rid of the offending spots (the sins). I was instructed that only with a pure soul would I be permitted entry into heaven, and that only forgiveness through absolution by the priest in the sacrament of confession would restore my soul to a pure state. This series of drawings was actually one of the less frightening ones; images of tortured people, their faces distorted in agony and their bodies surrounded by flames, were not uncommon.

The catechisms played on the imaginations of young Catholics, and Yocum asks readers to use their imaginations, too; she asks us to imagine being instructed daily by this catechism, being sexually abused by a priest, and then trying to disclose this abuse to one's parents or another adult, especially another Catholic. Keep in mind that sex was rarely, if ever, discussed openly in Catholic households; recall Gonsiorek's point that probably few other denominations are as ill at ease with sex as Catholics. If discussion of sex is frowned on, to put it mildly, then disclosure of sexual misconduct with a priest is surely taboo. And, as Yocum argues, such allegations would not only threaten to dethrone a single offending priest, but the entire system—the Church itself. The victim, therefore, who seeks help, even if only to get the abuse to stop, is viewed as evil; he or she is the one to be reviled, for damaging not only the priest (the embodiment of Jesus Christ) but also "God's holy Church."

Though the discussion thus far has focused almost exclusively on sexual abuse of children, particularly boys, by Catholic clergy, chapters 6 and 7 of this book remind us, as I noted at the outset, that sexual abuse is perpetrated by clergy and religious leaders of other faith traditions as well, and that adults may also be victimized. Diana Garland reports on her research with adult female victims of sexual abuse, most of whom were victimized by non-Catholic clergy. One aspect of the women's experiences that I find most interesting is the similarities to the experiences of the child victims discussed in earlier chapters. Clearly, for example, these women were groomed for victimization by their clergy abusers. And the grooming tactics used were not unlike those used by clergy perpetrators of child sexual abuse, especially manipulating potential victims' faith and spirituality, citing religious teachings, praying with potential victims or meeting with them under the pretext of counseling, and singling them out as "special."

Another similarity between the child sexual abuse discussed in earlier chapters and the adult sexual abuse described by participants in Garland's study is the lack of belief in and support offered to victims by others who discover the abuse or to whom the victim discloses it. Indeed, the women themselves did not at first label their experiences abuse. The clergy perpetrators so skillfully constructed these relationships as "mutual," loving, and a gift from God that the women's trust in the abusers overrode their own perceptions that the interactions were somehow wrong, inappropriate, or just off.

The majority of the perpetrators and victims in Garland's study were heterosexual adults, which sets them apart from the clergy abusers and child victims in the Catholic sexual abuse scandal. As Garland points out, these characteristics—the perpetrators' and victims' heterosexuality and adult status—lead many observers, even help providers such as social workers and psychologists, to also describe the relationship as consenting. The widespread perception is that the women make a conscious choice to accept or reject the advances of the clergymen; they are not relatively powerless, as children are. Consequently, these abusive relationships are mislabeled "affairs," even by victims, who at least initially blame themselves for what happened; the coercive nature of the relationships is ignored. Further contributing to this mislabeling is the fact that victims and others have no cognitive categories to correctly define and understand what the clergy abuser is doing. Victims' struggles to label and respond to the clergyman's behavior as abuse, Garland adds, are also undermined as they succumb to what she calls the "culture of niceness"—that is, a concern with hurting a good, well-intentioned person's feelings and, of course, the fear of being wrong and accusing an innocent man of serious misconduct. But although most of the victims in Garland's study were adult women abused by adult clergymen, 5 percent of the perpetrators were women, which she notes is somewhat startling given that there are far fewer female than male clergy. As she emphasizes, this finding is particularly important because it underlines the point that clergy sexual abuse is an abuse of power, not an abuse of sexuality.

As in cases of clergy sexual abuse of children, the women in Garland's study suffered a range of personal consequences coupled with the reverberating negative effects within their families and congregations. We will return to the issue of healing momentarily, but for now another critical question that observers often raise, particularly with regard to adult victims of clergy sexual abuse, must be addressed: Why didn't she just call the police or sue him? In cases involving child victims, the law is quite clear: children are vulnerable, easily manipulated, and incapable of consenting to sex with an adult. Consequently, as Brad Toben and Kris Helge state in chapter 7, all fifty states and the District of Columbia have criminalized child sexual abuse, and there is no exception or loophole that allows clergy to escape punishment if convicted of this crime. In cases involving adult victims, however, Toben and Helge discuss in detail the legal limitations, both civil and criminal, that prevent victims from successfully suing their abusers or pursuing criminal prosecution of them.

Although clergy are no longer protected by the benefit of clergy doctrine, Toben and Helge review the many other ways that the law, in effect, functions to protect clergy who sexually abuse adults. For instance, most states do not have laws that specifically require clergy perpetrators to pay adult victims for damages caused by their abuse, and only thirteen states and the District of Columbia have laws that support the criminal prosecution and punishment of clergy engaged in sexual misconduct with adult congregants or parishioners. Usually, these laws require that the misconduct or abuse occur in the context of a counseling relationship, and they categorize clergy as psychotherapists or counseling professionals. But as Toben and Helge point out, and as Garland's participants revealed, these requirements are problematic because much abuse occurs outside a counseling context. Adding to the difficulty in civil suits and criminal prosecutions involving adult perpetrators and victims is the requirement that the interaction or relationship in question between the clergy and the congregant or parishioner be secular in nature to avoid "entangling" the court in religious matters, which would constitute a violation of the First Amendment's Establishment Clause. In fact, the lion's share of Toben and Helge's analysis of the limitations of civil and criminal legal remedies for adult victims of clergy sexual abuse focuses on First Amendment entanglement issues.

But Toben and Helge's goal is not simply to highlight the limitations of current laws. Rather, it is to propose a constitutionally sound criminal statute that overcomes the many existing legal barriers to successful civil suits against and criminal prosecutions of clergy perpetrators of adult sexual abuse. All the contributors to this volume emphasize the clergy's special position of authority. Toben and Helge's model statute is based on the theory of positional authority, which centers on how a clergy member, because of his position of authority, has knowledge of an adult congregant's or parishioner's emotional dependence or vulnerability and then takes advantage of his position of authority to engage in sex or have sexual contact with the adult congregant or parishioner. As Toben and Helge point out, their model statute does not focus on religious or faith-based aspects of the relationship between clergy and the congregant or parishioner, so it avoids any potential First Amendment violations inherent in other laws, but it still manages to cover clergy abuse situations that occur outside of a secular counseling relationship. The authors discuss an Arkansas law that uses the theory of positional authority to criminally prosecute clergy perpetrators of adult sexual abuse, and they cite a 2006 case in which the law withstood a challenge to its constitutionality in part on the ground that it violated the Fourteenth Amendment's Equal Protection Clause.

All the contributors to this volume offer recommendations for improving responses to clergy sexual abuse perpetrators and their victims. All the authors would like to see clergy perpetrators—and the people who protect and defend them—held accountable for their behavior, and most see the criminal and civil legal system as one of the best means for achieving this objective and for attaining protection and justice for child and adult victims of clergy sexual abuse. Although I, too, wish to see offenders brought to justice and to send a strong message that clergy are not above the law, I would add a word of caution gleaned from recent research with the victims of sexual assault and intimate partner violence. Sometimes, the process of seeking justice through the legal system results in further trauma for victims. For a variety of reasons, many victims do not wish to involve, or to become involved with, the legal system (see, for example, Goodmark 2012). They wish instead to tell their stories and be believed, to exercise autonomy and have some control over the disposition of their cases, to have the abusers understand the harm they have caused, and—especially—to have the abusers stop victimizing. But our society offers these victims few options for seeking the type of justice they desire; they seem to be presented with the possibilities of only formal legal action or no action at all. One alternative that has been suggested is a restorative justice model. Susan Miller—who has studied restorative justice programs in the United States, Australia, and New Zealand—draws on the work of Howard Zehr, one of the founders of the restorative justice movement, to distinguish restorative justice from traditional criminal justice:

> In the traditional criminal justice model, crime is a violation of the law and is committed against the state. Breaking the law means that guilt must be determined through the adversarial system, and punishment must be imposed; the focus is on offenders receiving the penalty deserved for their harmful actions. However, in the contest between the offender and the state, victims' voices and needs are peripheral to achieving justice for the offender. In contrast, the restorative justice model sees crime as a violation of people and relationships. This violation creates obligations to make things right; the focus is on meeting victims' needs and facilitating offenders' responsibility in order to repair the harm. (Miller 2011, 7)

The idea is not to replace the criminal and civil legal system with restorative justice programs; to be sure, criminal and civil procedures are in many cases both necessary and effective. Rather, it is to provide restorative justice programs alongside the traditional legal system as an additional vehicle for achieving justice or as an alternative for victims who seek one.

Miller (2011) and others (see, for instance, Ptacek 2009; Umbreit, Vos, Coates, and Brown 2003) examine a variety of innovative restorative justice programs that have been implemented in the United States and abroad for addressing the "needs-rights" of crime victims, including child victims of sexual abuse (see Gal 2011). These programs, not surprisingly, are controversial and have been roundly criticized, especially by those who see them as reprivatizing crimes such as sexual abuse and for being more lenient on offenders than the traditional legal system is (see, for example, essays in Strang and Braithwaite 2002). More research is obviously needed to rigorously evaluate restorative justice models, particularly in terms of victims' assessments of the programs' responsiveness and effectiveness. Yet such programs, I suggest, are worth exploring because of their promise of a victim-centered approach to justice in cases of clergy sexual abuse, an approach that clearly has not characterized the handling of such cases by either religious or secular authorities.

Although the present volume addresses many issues, it is hardly a comprehensive treatment of the problem of clergy sexual abuse. The chapters address abuse by Christian, and primarily Catholic, clergy only. The discussion is also limited to clergy sexual abuse in the United States. And although many social science perspectives are offered here, the research from some (such as history) is discussed only in passing, and from others (such as economics) is not mentioned at all. But our main objective was to focus the social science lens on the problem of clergy sexual abuse and, by doing so, add to the growing body of scholarship on this problem, moving the discussion beyond the level of individual pathology to the macro level of structure, organization, and culture. We invite researchers from other disciplines, in other countries, and with an interest in other denominations and faith traditions to join us in the effort to peel back the multiple, complex layers of clergy sexual abuse and seek more effective responses to both perpetrators and victims.

References

Donadio, R. 2010. "Vatican Revises Abuse Process, but Causes Stir." *New York Times*, July 16.

Finkelhor, D. 2008. *Childhood Victimization: Violence, Crime, and Abuse in the Lives of Young People*. New York: Oxford University Press.

Fortune, M. M. 1995. "Is Nothing Sacred? When Sex Invades the Pastoral Relationship." In *Breach of Trust: Sexual Exploitation by Health Care Professionals and Clergy*, edited by J. C. Gonsiorek, 29–40. Thousand Oaks, CA: Sage.

France, D. 2004. *Our Fathers: The Secret Life of the Catholic Church in an Age of Scandal*. New York: Broadway.

Gal, T. 2011. *Child Victims and Restorative Justice: A Needs-Rights Model.* New York: Oxford University Press.

Goodmark, L. 2012. *A Troubled Marriage: Domestic Violence and the Legal System.* New York: New York University Press.

Goodstein, L. 2012. "Vatican Reprimands a Group of U.S. Nuns and Plans Changes." *New York Times*, April 19.

Goodstein, L., and E. Eckholm. 2012. "Church Battles Efforts to Ease Sex Abuse Suits." *New York Times*, June 14.

Gordon, M. 2004. "Unholy Orders: A Journalist Revisits the Pedophilia Scandal in the American Catholic Church." *New York Times Book Review*, January 25.

Gray, M. M., and P. M. Perl. 2006. *Catholic Reactions to the News of Sexual Abuse Cases Involving Catholic Clergy.* Washington: Center for Applied Research in the Apostolate, Georgetown University.

Heise, L. 1998. "Violence against Women: An Integrated, Ecological Framework." *Violence Against Women* 4:262–90.

John Jay College. 2004. *The Nature and Scope of Sexual Abuse of Minors by Catholic Priests and Deacons in the United States, 1950–2002.* Washington: US Conference of Catholic Bishops.

———. 2006. *The Nature and Scope of Sexual Abuse of Minors by Catholic Priests and Deacons in the United States, 1950–2002: Supplementary Data Analysis.* Washington: US Conference of Catholic Bishops.

Keenan, M. 2012. *Child Sexual Abuse and the Catholic Church: Gender, Power, and Organizational Culture.* New York: Oxford University Press.

London, K., M. Bruck, S. J. Ceci, and D. W. Shuman. 2005. "Disclosure of Child Sexual Abuse: What Does the Research Tell Us about the Ways That Children Tell?" *Psychology, Public Policy, and Law* 11:194–226.

Miller, S. L. 2011. *After the Crime: The Power of Restorative Justice Dialogues between Victims and Violent Offenders.* New York: New York University Press.

Mills, C. W. 1959. *The Sociological Imagination.* New York: Oxford University Press.

Neustein, A., ed. 2009. *Tempest in the Temple: Jewish Communities and Child Sex Scandals.* Waltham, MA: Brandeis University Press.

Otterman, S., and R. Rivera. 2012. "Ultra-Orthodox Shun Their Own for Reporting Child Sexual Abuse." *New York Times*, May 9.

Plante, T., and K. McChesney, eds. 2011. *Sexual Abuse in the Catholic Church: A Decade of Crisis, 2002–2012.* Santa Barbara, CA: ABC-CLIO.

Ptacek, J., ed. 2009. *Restorative Justice and Violence against Women.* New York: Oxford University Press.Strang, H., and J. Braithwaite, eds. 2002. *Restorative Justice and Family Violence.* Cambridge: Cambridge University Press.

Terry, K. J. 2011. "The Report on the U.S. Catholic Priests' Sex Abuse: What the Critics Got Wrong." *Inside Criminal Justice*, June 23. http://www.thecrimereport.org.

———, et al. 2011. *The Causes and Context of Sexual Abuse of Minors by Catholic Priests in the United States, 1950–2010*. Washington: US Conference of Catholic Bishops.

Thoburn, J., and R. Baker, eds. 2011. *Clergy Sexual Misconduct: A Systems Approach to Prevention, Treatment, and Oversight*. Carefree, AZ: Gentle Path.

Umbreit, M. S., B. Vos, R. B. Coates, and K. A. Brown. 2003. *Facing Violence: The Path of Restorative Justice and Dialogue*. Monsey, NY: Criminal Justice.

Voice of the Faithful [VOTF]. 2011. *Voice of the Faithful's Conclusions about the John Jay College Report, "The Causes and Context of Sexual Abuse of Minors by Catholic Priests in the United States, 1950–2010."* October 11. http://www.votf.org.

Karen J. Terry

2 Understanding the Response to Sexual Abuse of Minors by Catholic Priests

A Criminal Justice Perspective

Introduction

Sexual victimization of children is a serious and pervasive issue in society, and it is particularly prevalent in institutions where adults form mentoring and nurturing relationships with children and adolescents. Such institutions include churches, schools, sporting organizations, and child-care settings. Much of the media focus on child sexual abuse within institutions in the last decade has focused on the Roman Catholic Church. Though the crux of this media attention came in 2002 with reports about a serial predator, John Geoghan, the first high-profile priest-abuser came to the attention of the Catholic Church and the nation in the mid-1980s.

In 1983, it emerged that Gilbert Gauthe had allegedly sexually abused over a hundred children in his parish in Lafayette, Louisiana. He was convicted in 1985 and served nearly ten years in prison. As a result of the Gauthe case, the US Conference of Catholic Bishops (USCCB) began discussing the problem of abuse for the first time at its national meetings. In 1993 James Porter was reported to have abused over a hundred young boys and girls in parishes across Massachusetts. He was subsequently dubbed by the media as Boston's first "predator priest" and was sentenced to eighteen to twenty years in prison.

It was John Geoghan, however, whose actions led to widespread and sustained media attention on the issue of sexual abuse by priests. Geoghan was a priest in the Boston Archdiocese who was accused of abusing more than a hundred children over three decades. He was processed through both the canonical system (the laws adopted by the ecclesiastical authority) and criminal justice system. The Church eventually laicized him, defrocking him and removing him from ministry, and the criminal justice system convicted him of indecent child assault and incarcerated him. He was murdered in prison by a fellow inmate, illuminating the level of indignation against such offenders. The *Boston Globe* published a special series on abusive priests for nearly a year as Geoghan's abuses were coming to light (Boston Globe Spotlight Team 2004). The media attention to this topic led to a substantial increase in reporting of abuse cases; approximately one-third of all cases reported by the end of 2002 had been reported in that year alone. This explosion of reporting led to the understanding of what is referred to today as the sexual abuse crisis in the Catholic Church.

In June 2002, at the height of this flood of reporting, the USCCB created a charter that aimed to understand and address this problem (see US Conference of Catholic Bishops 2002). Among other things, the charter called for empirical studies of the sexual abuse of minors by Catholic priests. The Office of Child and Youth Protection and the National Review Board, two entities formed as a result of the charter, commissioned researchers at John Jay College to conduct two studies: *The Nature and Scope of Sexual Abuse of Minors by Catholic Priests and Deacons in the United States, 1950–2002* (John Jay College 2004, hereafter referred to as the *Nature and Scope* study), and *The Causes and Context of Sexual Abuse of Minors by Catholic Priests in the United States, 1950–2010* (Terry et al. 2011, hereafter referred to as the *Causes and Context* study). The research team released a report of their descriptive *Nature and Scope* findings in February 2004 and a supplementary report in 2006 (John Jay College 2006). The *Nature and Scope* study provided information about the extent of the abuse crisis, the distribution of offenses throughout the country and over time, the priests against whom allegations were made, the minors they abused, the Church's response to the allegations, and the financial impact of the crisis (John Jay College 2004, 2006). The *Causes and Context* study, released in May 2011, analyzed the conditions that permitted abusive behavior in the Catholic Church to persist, integrating research from sociocultural, psychological, situational, and organizational perspectives (Terry et al. 2011).

This chapter provides an overview of the key findings from these two studies, including the diocesan and criminal justice responses to abuse. Few priests with allegations of abuse were arrested, charged, convicted, and incarcerated for their crimes, and this chapter outlines the priests who were processed through the criminal justice system and how they differ from those who were not.

Sexual Abuse in the Catholic Church: The John Jay Studies

Prior to 2002, few researchers had empirically studied the problem of child sexual abuse by clergy. The studies that did exist were limited in scope because of small sample sizes or because they were based on information from a single parish or diocese or on clinical samples from a single treatment center. The *Nature and Scope* report is based on reports from the universe of records for all priests and deacons in the United States from 1950 to 2002. The *Causes and Context* report is based on multiple sources of data, including official documents; clinical data; and surveys and interviews with diocesan leaders, priests (some accused of abuse, some not), and victim advocates. Together, these data provide a wealth of information about what happened and when, and what factors contributed to the sexual abuse crisis in the Catholic Church.

Nature and Scope *Study*

The mandate for the *Nature and Scope* study was to determine the extent of the sexual abuse of minors by Catholic priests in the United States from 1950 to 2002. The John Jay College research team developed three separate surveys and sent them to all dioceses (districts of the Catholic Church that are supervised by bishops) and eparchies (eastern orthodox districts that are similar to dioceses) in the United States, as well as 140 religious orders of men. The first survey requested information about the diocese, eparchy, or order; the second requested information about every priest who had allegedly sexually abused a minor; and the third requested information about each victim of abuse and the incidents of abuse. Identities of all priests and victims were kept confidential, and the researchers employed a double-blind procedure to ensure the anonymity of the subjects. Overall, 97 percent of all dioceses and eparchies (representing 99 percent of all diocesan priests) and 63 percent of all religious communities (representing 84 percent of religious priests) responded.

The results of the *Nature and Scope* study showed that the total number of priests who allegedly sexually abused minors from 1950 to 2002 was 4,392, which was equivalent to 4 percent of priests in ministry during that time. The number of individuals who made allegations of sexual abuse was 10,667. Abuse incidence peaked in the 1970s and early 1980s. This distribution was consistent across all regions of the Catholic Church in the United States, as well as in all sizes of dioceses (the US Catholic Church is divided into fourteen regions, av-

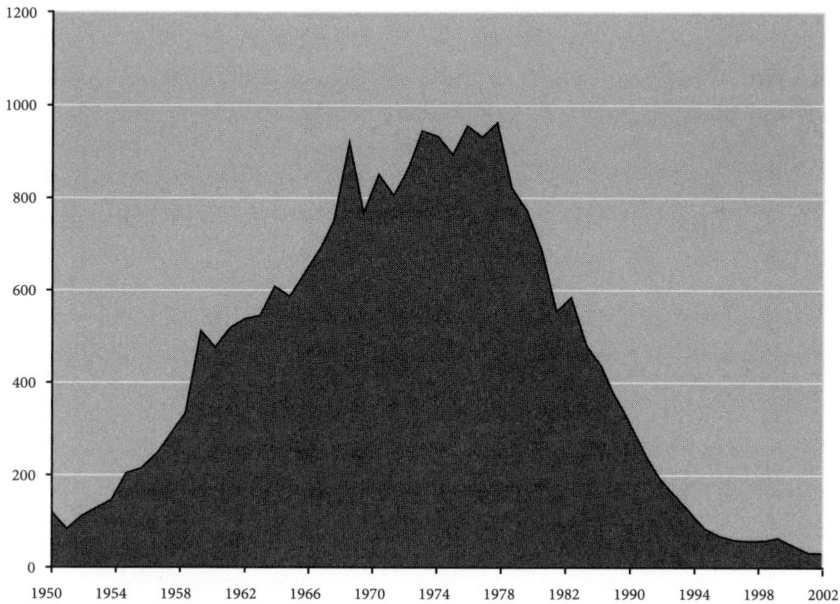

Figure 1. Distribution of incidents from 1950 to 2002.

eraging just over a dozen dioceses per region). Figure 1 shows the distribution of abuse incidents from 1950 to 2002.

There was a significant delay in reporting of offenses, and many victims waited decades to report their abuse to the dioceses. In the years of the high-profile cases of abuse that were published in the media—Gauthe in 1985, Porter in 1993, and Geoghan in 2002—reports increased, with the largest number of cases reported in 2002. Though many reports are still being made, most of the abuse being reported occurred decades ago. The peak of abuse cases that are being reported today remains in the 1970s. Therefore, most cases reported today are beyond the statute of limitations for reporting in the criminal justice system.

Of those abuse cases reported by 2002, the majority of abusers (69 percent) were diocesan priests. Of all priests in ministry from 1950 to 2002, 4.3 percent of the diocesan priests had allegations of abuse, and 2.7 percent of religious priests had allegations of abuse. Most abusers were serving as a pastor (25 percent) or associate pastor (42 percent) at the time of the abuse. This is important because pastors and associate pastors generally have high levels of discretion in their parishes and little direct supervision of their day-to-day activities, and they usually live alone in a parish residence. The majority of priest abusers (56

Figure 2. Distribution of victims by age and gender.

percent) had one victim (often with multiple incidents of abuse), though 3.5 percent of abusers were responsible for abusing 26 percent of the victims. These career criminals were unusual in the number and types of victims they abused as well as in the duration of their abusive careers. The majority of all victims (81 percent) were male, and most victims (51 percent) were between the ages of eleven and fourteen. Figure 2 shows the gender and age distribution of the victims.

The priest-abusers committed numerous and often multiple types of sexual offenses, ranging from touching outside the clothes to penetration. Abuse occurred most often in the home of the priest (41 percent of incidents), though it also occurred frequently in the church (16 percent), the victim's home (12 percent), a vacation home (10 percent), school (10 percent), and cars (10 percent).

As of 2002, nearly 40 percent of priests with allegations of sexual abuse had participated in some type of treatment program. Those with more than one allegation of abuse were more likely to have participated in treatment, regardless of the severity of the offense(s) committed. The types of treatment programs included programs specifically for sex offenders, spiritual counseling, psychotherapy, and general treatment programs. The Church also responded in a variety of other ways, such as reprimands, administrative leaves, and occasionally laicization. More details about these responses are presented later in this chapter.

Causes and Context *Study*

Although the *Nature and Scope* study provided a snapshot of the problem of sexual abuse of minors by Catholic priests, it did not explain what factors were associated with the abuse crisis or why there was a surge in abuse incidents in the 1970s and early 1980s. The *Causes and Context* study provided a unique opportunity to collect robust, rich, and multifaceted data from a variety of sources on the sexual abuse of minors over a sixty-year period. The researchers analyzed data from the following sources:

- Existing longitudinal data sets of various types of social behavior (including crime, divorce, and premarital sex) over the time period to provide a historical framework (see Gfroerer and Brodsky 1992; Goldstein 1999; Hofferth, Kahn, and Baldwin 1987; Norton and Moorman 1987).
- Seminary documents outlining the history and development of a curriculum on human formation (that is, personal formation as a priest, with an emphasis on sexuality and preparation for celibacy).
- Surveys of various groups within the Catholic Church, including bishops and other diocesan leaders; vicars general; victim assistance coordinators; priests with allegations of abuse and a comparison sample of priests in active parish ministry who had not been accused (the identity and behavior survey); and a group of "priests with integrity" who served in some capacity to assist victims of abuse.
- Primary data from a 1971 survey on the psychology of US Catholic priests. These study data, collected by researchers at Loyola University, are based on a representative sample of 271 priests (who were not known to be abusers) in ministry in 1970. These data served as a normative baseline for understanding the psychological characteristics of men in the priesthood around the peak time of incidence of sexual abuse of minors.
- Clinical data from files at three treatment centers. The sample included priests with allegations of abuse against minors, priests with allegations of other sexual misconduct, priests with behavioral or mental health problems, and a normative sample. The files included psychological history and testing data, as well as information from in-depth clinical interviews.

The findings of the *Causes and Context* study indicate that there is no single cause of the sexual abuse crisis and that instead it was caused by a complex interaction of psychological, developmental, organizational, cultural, and situational factors. Consistent with literature about sex offenders in the general population, the *Causes and Context* data showed that priests who sexually abused minors constituted a heterogeneous population. The clinical data showed that priests with allegations of sexually abusing minors were not significantly more likely than other priests to have personality or mood disorders, and there were no significant differences in IQ between abusers and others who were treated (all groups of priests in the sample had above average intelligence). The clinical data also showed that few abusers were driven by sexual pathologies; in the two clinical samples with sexual disorder data, 5 percent of the priests with allegations of abusing children were diagnosed with pedophilia. The clinical history data as well as the identity and behavior survey and interview data indicate that the priests' personal vulnerabilities, in combination with situational stresses and opportunities, increased the risk of abuse. Many of the abusers had poor psychosexual development or other weaknesses (such as emotional congruence with children or adolescents), had intimacy deficits (including having few close peers and only weak family bonds), experienced increased stressors from work (for example, having recently received more responsibilities, such as becoming a pastor), and had opportunities to abuse (such as unguarded access to minors in their role as pastors). The clinical data also showed that most priests (80 percent) who abused minors also participated in sexual behavior with adults, and sexual identity did not predict abuse of a minor.

Access to victims played a critical role in victim choice. Few significant differences were found between the locations and situations in which boys and girls were abused, but priests had more access to boys until recently (primarily because parishes permitted girls to be altar servers only after 1983). Priests who abused minors exhibited behavior consistent with abusers who were not priests. In particular, the abusers "groomed" their victims (enticed them to participate in the abuse through gifts and other benefits, or through emotional or spiritual manipulation), and they justified and excused their own behavior, often shifting responsibility to the victims or others.

The decade of ordination also had a significant impact on patterns of abusive behavior. The majority of abusive priests were ordained prior to the 1970s, and more abusers were educated in seminaries in the 1940s and 1950s than at any other time period. There was a significant expansion of seminaries in this postwar period, and the educational curriculum for priests has developed significantly since that time. In particular, seminary education prior to the 1970s had almost no human formation component and instead focused primarily on spiritual development. Thus, seminarians were not being adequately prepared to live a life of chaste celibacy. Human formation training evolved from the 1980s onward, and although there is no indication that this is a cause of the decrease in abuse of minors, it is consistent with the drop in allegations of abuse.

Most of the abuse incidents that have been reported occurred decades ago. Though abuse does still occur in the Catholic Church, analyses show that it takes place at a significantly lower rate now than at the peak of the abuse crisis in the 1970s. Most of the incidents of sexual abuse of minors by priests that are being reported today continue to fit into the distribution of abuse incidents concentrated in the mid-1960s to mid-1980s. This lag in reporting has led to a complex understanding of the diocesan and criminal justice responses to abuse behavior.

Responses to Abuse

In addition to addressing the scope and causes of the abuse crisis in the Church, the two John Jay College studies chronicled the responses to abuse throughout the time period investigated. Responses to abusive behavior by priests can be broadly divided into two categories: from the Church (both diocesan and canonical) and from the criminal justice system. In all cases where abuse is reported to the dioceses, there is information on the Church response—or lack of response—to the abuse. However, only a small percentage of cases have been processed through the criminal justice system. The diocesan responses to abusive priests changed substantially over the period of time addressed in these studies. For example, abusive priests were less likely to be returned to active ministry and more likely to be placed on administrative leave during more recent years. Criminal justice responses, on the other hand, depended largely on the number of years it took to report the abuse behavior.

Diocesan Responses

The *Causes and Context* study assessed the diocesan responses to abuse from 1985 onward. It was in 1985 that the high-profile Gauthe case led to national discussions about sexual abuse, and by 1985 nearly every diocese in the United States had experienced cases of sexual abuse of minors by priests. The questions of how to understand the act of sexual abuse of a minor by a priest and how to respond to the victim, the family, and the parish were presented for regular discussion in bishops' meetings from that point onward. Legal advisors and insurers counseled the development of explicit policies, but in many dioceses, there was not a thorough recognition of the problem or an implementation of policies. Based on written documents from that time, the bishops were focused primarily on the well-being of the priests who had abused, not on the harm they had caused their victims.

Bishops responded to surveys for the *Causes and Context* study that asked about their dioceses' responses to abuse from 1985 onward. The survey responses from more recently appointed Catholic bishops differed from the responses from bishops who were in leadership positions between 1985 and 2000. Bishops who held positions through the early 1990s stated that they had made several efforts to remove abusive priests from ministry, but many of these efforts had not been successful. In particular, they noted that some of the psychological treatments for abusive priests were not always successful, the Church had inadequate processes to help priests leave the priesthood, and the canon law processes for suspension were complex and took years to complete. Very few bishops discussed criminal justice options for the abusive priests; rather, they were focused on canonical processes or helping the priests overcome their problems through rehabilitative approaches. Generally, until the 2000s the abuse of minors seemed to be viewed through the lens of human failure and sin rather than as a criminal act that caused harm to a child.

Those bishops who came to their positions after 2000 explained the sexual abuse crisis and the Church response to it in a far wider and evolving framework. They were more likely to focus on societal issues and faulty seminary teaching and formation programs as contributors to the sexual abuse crisis. They were also more likely to acknowledge that the earlier diocesan protective focus on the priest-abuser eclipsed the most serious dimension of clergy abuse: harm done to the victim.

Based on the survey results from all diocesan leaders, as well as documentary evidence of the diocesan responses to abuse, it is possible to trace the evolution of diocesan responses to the sexual abuse of minors. Most of the responses to abuse were internal (not involving the criminal justice system); however, this evolution over more than fifty years shows how diocesan leaders' understanding and perspective on abuse shifted from being entirely abuser-centered to eventually becoming victim-centered.

In 1947 an international religious community called the Servants of the Paraclete opened a spiritual retreat center for troubled priests; in 1959 the group opened a second such center. These centers were meant to assist priests with various problems, preparing them to return to ministry. By the 1960s, psychological treatment of priests with behavioral problems became as common as, or more common than, spiritual treatment alone. After 1960 several centers were either founded specifically for the psychological treatment of Catholic priests and religious community members or incorporated psychological treatment into their regimens.

Though sending a priest to treatment was the most common response to allegations of abuse, the bishops had several possible responses and often took multiple actions with priest-abusers. The responses to reports of sexual abuse of minors made before 1985 differed greatly from reports brought to dioceses by the mid-1990s. More than 80 percent of pre-1985 reports of sexual abuse were made to the diocese within a year of the incident, and three-quarters of the reports were made by the victim or a family member. Documents show that the most common request from the victims or victims' families was that help be provided for the priest-abuser. Many families did not want publicity, nor did they wish to confront the priest. In other cases, however, families were pressured by church leaders to keep the incident confidential, often while ensuring that the priest would be helped. Prior to 1984, many bishops believed that sexual misbehavior by the priests in their dioceses was psychologically curable and could be spiritually remedied by recourse to prayer.

On October 18, 1984, a Louisiana grand jury indicted Gilbert Gauthe for a long list of sexual crimes against children. The Diocese of Lafayette had received multiple reports of Gauthe's abusive acts for seven years before he was indicted. Gauthe had been repeatedly cautioned about his behavior, but he was not removed from ministry until 1983, when—following another report of abuse by a parent who demanded action—he was sent to a treatment center in Massachusetts called the House of Affirmation. The specifics of the Gauthe case were shocking: Gauthe had not only raped and sodomized dozens of boys, he had used his status as a priest to justify his actions to the victims and to intimidate them into silence. Gauthe caused significant physical and psychological harm to his victims, with some requiring hospitalization and others years of psychological treatment. The criminal case and related civil litigation filed by the families of the victims drew national and international press attention and became the first high-profile case of sexual abuse of a minor by a Catholic priest. Much of the media focus was not only on Gauthe's actions but also on the failures of the diocese in response to them. Diocesan leaders hesitated to remove Gauthe from ministry even after he admitted to the abuse, and they failed to redress the harm he had done to the child victims and their families. The leaders were preoccupied with controlling negative publicity and so were not forthcoming with information to the affected parishes. Such failures on the part of the Diocese of Lafayette were to be repeated by leaders of some other dioceses, many of which were nationally prominent, in subsequent years.

Reports about the Gauthe case, combined with information emerging in dioceses in other parts of the United States about incidents of sexual abuse of minors by priests, prompted the National Conference of Catholic Bishops (NCCB, the body that later became the USCCB) to address the issue of sexual abuse in its national meeting in the summer of 1985. The body of bishops revisited this issue annually for the next decade. Prior to the 1985 meeting, a resource paper and proposal for action on the issue, titled "The Problem of Sexual Molestation by Roman Catholic Clergy: Meeting the Problem in a Comprehensive and Responsible Manner," was circulated to the bishops (Mouton and Doyle 1985). This was written by Father Michael Petersen, a psychiatrist at the Saint Luke Institute; Father Thomas Doyle, a canon lawyer on the staff of the Apostolic Delegation (the Vatican's equivalent of an embassy) in Washington, D.C.; and Raymond Mouton, the attorney who had represented Gauthe (though only Mouton and Doyle appear as authors of the final document). These three men, acting from specific knowledge of the Gauthe case, worked collaboratively to craft a document that would provide a basis for understanding the problem of sexual abuse of minors. They also proposed an action plan that would designate a response team, track all cases, and work from a uniform strategy in all dioceses. Specifically, the proposal advocated the formation of a committee, which would then elect four bishops with knowledge of civil or canon law to serve as a Group of Four. This group, supervised by committee members, would be charged with implementing all necessary aspects of the project. Additionally, the Group of Four would also be responsible for recruiting a variety of consultants with legal, clinical, and religious expertise to form two subgroups, the Crisis Control Team and the Policy and Planning Group.

The three authors provided several clinical articles about pedophilia along with the resource paper. This background information about the problem of sexual abuse of minors was to be supplemented by a series of presentations made directly at the bishops' meetings by clinical psychologists. Though the document and proposal presented by Petersen, Doyle, and Mouton was distributed to all bishops in the United States, the proposed action plan was not adopted. Diocesan leaders cited various reasons for the lack of implementation of this plan, including concerns about the appropriateness of a single response group for 190 dioceses, concerns about the authors, and the absence of a clear financial outline of the costs. Whether or not these concerns were legitimate, the failure to adopt this plan led to the perception that the bishops were not doing anything, or were not doing enough, to address the problem of abuse.

In the years after 1985, the staff counsel for the NCCB worked with diocesan leaders to promote a direct course of intervention when reports of incidents of sexual abuse were made. Prompt psychological treatment for the priest was generally considered to be the best course of action and became the primary intervention for abusive priests. Notably absent in the policies for responding to abuse were criminal justice actions, and none of the intervention policies at this time focused on the need to address the harm caused to the victims. Most of the early policies focused on the actions that should be taken in regard to the priest-abusers.

Treatment was the most common response for abusive priests. Data from the *Nature and Scope* study showed that 1,624 priests received treatment between 1950 and 2002 for sexually abusing minors, and most of those priests received more than one type of treatment. In total, there were 3,041 instances of treatment. The peak decade for treatment was the 1980s, though there was a sharp decline in treatment thereafter. This rise in the use of treatment in the 1980s, particularly in specialized treatment programs for sex offenders, is consistent with the response to sex offenders in the general population. It was also in the 1980s that there was a rise in cognitive-behavioral treatment programs for sex offenders, particularly those employing relapse prevention techniques.

Treatment was not the only action taken, however. Table 1 shows data from the *Nature and Scope* study about the diocesan responses to priests accused of sexual abuse of minors (though it describes only actions taken with priests who were alive and not retired at the time the abuse was reported). The table shows the types of actions clustered by the decade in which the report was made (as opposed to when the abuse actually occurred). The actions are not mutually exclusive, and in some cases multiple actions were taken with an individual priest. Of importance, however, is the change in response by decade. Before 1980 a reprimand and return to duty was as likely as a referral for evaluation by a professional. Beginning in the 1980s, the likelihood of a reprimand and return to duty decreases, and the likelihood of being put on administrative leave or suspended increases. The elevated percentages for the category of "no action taken" were most often a result of accusations against priests who were not in active ministry at the time of the report. Because of the delay in reporting, the later the decade of the report, the more likely the priest-abuser was no longer in active ministry.

The likelihood of a priest being reprimanded and returned to the parish or reinstated after an accusation changes from 35 percent for priests first accused

Table 1 Diocesan Response to Priests Who Abused Minors, by Decade

Diocesan responses	*Distribution by decade of first report*				
	1950–79	1980–89	1990–99	2000–2003	1950–2003
Reprimanded and returned to duty	34.8%	12.4%	4.8%	3.8%	8.8%
Referred for evaluation	33.0	50.7	45.6	28.0	40.4
Suspended	6.4	7.6	6.8	8.1	7.3
Put on administrative leave	6.0	8.9	11.9	16.3	12.0
Resigned or retired	5.2	4.8	8.7	11.6	8.5
Reinstated	3.0	1.7	1.6	1.4	1.7
Given treatment	2.2	4.6	3.6	2.2	3.2
No action taken	3.7	2.4	6.5	14.7	7.7

before 1985, to 18 percent for reinstatement and 5 percent for reprimand and return for those first accused after 1985. Spiritual retreats and medical leaves also declined by more than 50 percent after 1985. This trend may reflect the growing understanding of the harm caused to children by sexual abuse; it also may reflect the effect of policies implemented as the extent of the problem of clergy sexual abuse was becoming known.

Though treatment was a common response, particularly in the 1980s, it was often not the first course of action in response to abuse. Additionally, most priests (more than 75 percent) who were sent to a specialized center for residential treatment had previously participated in outpatient forms of therapy. The priests who were sent to residential treatment facilities specializing in sex offender treatment were more likely to have longer histories of offending. Overall, the use of treatment for priests with allegations of sexual abuse declined in the 1990s, which may reflect concerns about relapse and re-offense. During the 1990s, when the Ad Hoc Committee on Sexual Abuse was meeting to discuss types of evaluation and treatment in the various treatment facilities, some of the optimism about the value of treatment had waned. Though this committee had reasonable intentions for identifying appropriate paths to evaluation and treatment for priests with allegations, fewer priests were actually being treated by the mid-1990s than had been treated previously.

A pressing question from the mid-1980s to the early 1990s was whether and under what circumstances a priest should be reassigned to a parish after treatment for the sexual abuse of a child. The NCCB sought professional guidance from experts in the treatment of sexual abuse. These presentations, made in executive session (closed to all but NCCB members) at annual meetings, included discussions of pedophilia and related behaviors, the prospects for treatment, the question of reassignment and other canonical options, the risks of liability resulting from failure to supervise a priest with a history of abusive behavior, and theological and pastoral considerations. Again absent from the discussions was the role of the criminal justice system in prosecuting abusive behavior.

During these meetings, many bishops offered their firsthand experiences with supervision of abusive priests and their perspectives on responses to victims and affected parishes. In June 1992 a commission of the Archdiocese of Chicago established by Cardinal Joseph Bernardin released its report and recommendations for an adequate diocesan response to the issue of sexual abuse by priests. The commission recommended that a priest involved in sexual misconduct with minors not be returned to parish ministry or other ministry with access to minors, although it left open the possibility of other, nonparochial work following administrative leave and after care. Other recommendations included establishing a review board to assist the bishop in the evaluation of cases of abuse, a lay case manager to initiate an immediate process following an accusation, and a twenty-four-hour hotline for victims to report incidents of abuse. The 1992 Policy on Priests and Sexual Abuse of Children released by the Office of Media Relations of the United States Catholic Conference (USCC) stated: "When there is even a hint of such an incident, investigate immediately; remove the priest whenever the evidence warrants it; follow the reporting obligations of the civil law; extend pastoral care to the victim and the victim's family; and seek appropriate treatment for the offender." The USCCB (and its predecessor, the NCCB) lacked authority to direct the actions of dioceses, but the terms of the recommended actions were clear.

By 1992, with the release of the recommendations of the Ad Hoc Committee, dioceses were encouraged to comply with civil (noncanonical) law. Despite these recommendations, most bishops continued to focus on helping abusers rather than punishing them. In fact, the large majority of bishops did respond to allegations of abuse, but with a focus on rehabilitating the priest-abuser. Little response was made by the dioceses in terms of assisting the victims or holding the abusers responsible through criminal justice processes.

Criminal Justice Responses

Few cases of child sexual abuse by priests were processed through the criminal justice system. The data indicate two primary reasons for this: bishops were

Table 2 Criminal Justice System Response to Allegations of Abuse by Priests, 1950–2002 (*Nature and Scope* data)

Criminal justice response	Number of priests (N = 4,392)	Percentage of priests
Investigated	963	21.9
Charged	379	8.6
Convicted	259	5.9
Incarcerated*	149	3.4
Received jail sentence	61	1.4
Received prison sentence	100	2.2

*Twelve priests served time in both jail and prison.

more likely to take action to help the abusers (for example, through treatment) than to act to punish them, and there was a substantial delay in the reporting of most offenses. Many abuse cases were reported after the statute of limitations had expired, often decades after the abuse occurred. Traditionally, statutes of limitation in most states were approximately five to seven years after the incident occurred, or a limited amount of time after the abused child reached the age of majority. Thus, rather than being processed through the criminal justice system, most responses to abusive priests were taken in the dioceses. Additionally, in cases where abuse was reported within the statute of limitations, many parents did not support contact with civil authorities.

As shown in Table 2, data from the *Nature and Scope* study indicate that 963 cases of child sexual abuse by priests were investigated by police between 1950 and 2002. Of those cases, 379 priests were criminally charged, and 259 were convicted. A very small percent of abusers—3.4 percent of all priests with allegations of abuse—were incarcerated.

The percentage of abusive priests who were processed through the criminal justice system varied across the fourteen regions of the Catholic Church in the United States. On average, 8.6 percent of the priests in all regions who had allegations of sexual abuse were at least charged with a crime. The proportion of priests who were charged varied by region, from 4.4 percent to 17.5 percent. The reason for this variation is unknown and is not correlated with demographic characteristics of priest-abusers in those regions. In fact, demographic characteristics of the priests who abused did not have any significant effect on whether they were charged. The age of the priests when they committed their first known offense did not vary between those who were charged (38.4 years) and those who were not (38.9 years). However, those who were incarcerated were signifi-

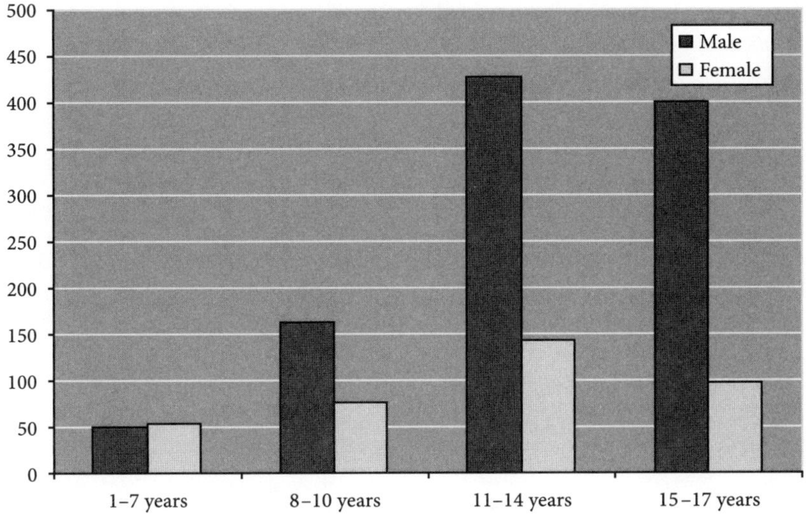

Figure 3. Distribution of age and gender of victims in cases that resulted in criminal charges against abusive priests.

cantly younger at the time of the first offense than other priest-abusers. This is consistent with the finding that the career criminal priest-abusers—those serial offenders who abused many victims over a long period of time—began abusing children early after ordination.

The three factors that did significantly differentiate those priests who were charged and those who were not were the number of total victims, the number of male victims, and the duration of the priest's abusive behavior. The priests who were at least charged with a crime had 5.3 victims on average and committed abusive behavior for an average of 7.8 years. The priests who were not charged had 2.4 victims on average and an abusive career of 4.7 years. Those priests who had many victims often had many male victims; those charged were also likely to have more male victims (4.6) than those who were not charged (1.8). This difference was even more pronounced between the priests who were convicted (5.6 male victims) and those who were not convicted (1.79 male victims). Figure 3 shows the distribution of victims by age and gender for those cases that resulted in a criminal charge against the abusive priest. Note that this distribution is nearly identical to the distribution of age and gender of victims generally, shown in Figure 2.

Despite the high number of male victims, most of the career criminal priests were generalists—that is, they victimized children and adolescents of various ages and/or genders rather than targeting a specific type of victim. They tended

Table 3 Criminal Justice System Response to Career Criminal Priest-Abusers (*Nature and Scope* data)

	Priests with ≥ 10 victims (n = 152)		*Priests with ≥ 20 victims (n = 39)*	
Criminal justice response	Number	Percentage	Number	Percentage
Investigated	79	52.0	21	53.8
Charged	45	29.6	14	35.9
Convicted	32	21.1	12	30.8
Incarcerated*	26	17.1	10	25.6
Received jail sentence	9	5.9	3	7.7
Received prison sentence	21	13.8	7	17.9

*Four priests with ten or more victims served time in both jail and prison.

to have a very long abusive career; those with 10–19 victims abused over a mean period of 18.0 years, and those with 20 or more victims abused over a mean period of 22.5 years. They began abusing within the first year after ordination, and they continued abusing children throughout much of their time in ministry. As a whole, this career criminal group was more likely to be investigated, charged, and convicted. Approximately half of the priests with ten or more victims were investigated; nearly one-third were charged, but only about one-fifth of those charged were convicted. The findings are similar for those priests with twenty or more victims. Table 3 shows the criminal career priest-abusers and the criminal justice actions taken against them.

The primary factors associated with criminal justice action seem to be number of victims (particularly male victims), duration of abusive career, and time between offense and report. Of the 379 cases where priest-abusers were charged, 221 were reported to criminal justice authorities within one year from the end of the abuse period. Most of these 221 priest-abusers (61 percent) were reported by a single victim. Thus, even the serial abusers were often charged and prosecuted for only one case of abuse, and it was usually the most recent case, not necessarily the most severe one.

Reporting trends did change noticeably over the decades. As the phenomenon of sexual abuse became better understood—mainly from the 1980s onward—reporting increased within the first year after the abuse occurred and subsequently led to a higher likelihood of a charge being filed. In fact, 87 percent of priests charged whose offenses were reported within one year of the abuse incidents were charged in the 1980s or later. But few cases of sexual abuse of minors were reported soon after they happened in the 1950s, 1960s, and 1970s. As a result, many of the priests who abused children in those decades have not been prosecuted through the criminal justice system. Considering that most cases of abuse known today occurred in those decades, it becomes clearer why so few priest-abusers have been processed through the criminal justice system.

Conclusion

Sexual victimization of children is a serious and widespread problem that can cause extensive, irreparable harm to victims. Many victims continue to be affected long after the abuse has ended; these psychological, emotional, physical, and behavioral effects can be debilitating to some survivors and permeate all aspects of their lives in both the short and long term. Many children who were sexually victimized waited years to report the abusive behavior. The timing of the reports affected whether priest-abusers were processed through the criminal justice system.

Few priests who sexually abused children were prosecuted. Those priests who were processed through the criminal justice system had significantly longer abusive careers and more victims than those who were not charged with a criminal offense. Many of the abuse cases were reported decades after the abuse occurred, however, at a time when the statute of limitations had expired. The majority of priests who were convicted were reported to police within a year of the abuse incident, and nearly all were reported within five years. In cases where priests abused multiple children, usually only one victim reported the abuse to the police. The later the decade of abuse, the more likely the victims were to report the abuse to criminal justice authorities, and the more likely the priests were to be investigated. Thus, the many abusers who were ordained in the 1940s and 1950s and abused in the 1960s and 1970s were not likely to be prosecuted.

References

Boston Globe Spotlight Team. 2004. The *Boston Globe* Spotlight investigation: Abuse in the Catholic Church. http://www.boston.com/globe/spotlight/abuse.

Gfroerer, J., and M. Brodsky. 1992. "The Incidence of Illicit Drug Use in the United States, 1962–1989." *British Journal of Addiction* 87:1345–51.

Goldstein, J. R. 1999. "The Leveling of Divorce in the United States." *Demography* 36:409–14.

Hofferth, S. L., J. R. Kahn, and W. Baldwin. 1987. "Premarital Sexual Activity among U.S. Teenage Women over the Past Three Decades." *Family Planning Perspectives* 19 (2): 46–53.

John Jay College. 2004. *The Nature and Scope of Sexual Abuse of Minors by Catholic Priests and Deacons in the United States, 1950–2002*. Washington: US Conference of Catholic Bishops.

———. 2006. *The Nature and Scope of Sexual Abuse of Minors by Catholic Priests and Deacons in the United States, 1950–2002: Supplementary Data Analysis*. Washington: US Conference of Catholic Bishops.

Mouton, F. R., and T. P.Doyle. 1985. "The Problem of Sexual Molestation by Roman Catholic Clergy: Meeting the Problem in a Comprehensive and Responsible Manner." http://www.bishop-accountability.org.

Norton, A. J., and J. E.Moorman. 1987. "Current Trends in Marriage and Divorce among American Women." *Journal of Marriage and the Family* 49:3–14.

Terry, K. J., et al. 2011. *The Causes and Context of Sexual Abuse of Minors by Catholic Priests in the United States, 1950–2010*. Washington: US Conference of Catholic Bishops.

US Conference of Catholic Bishops. 2002. *Charter for the Protection of Children and Young People*. Washington: US Conference of Catholic Bishops.

John C. Gonsiorek

3 The Interplay of Psychological and Institutional Factors in Sexual Abuse by Roman Catholic Clergy

Introduction

Sexual exploitation by clergy is typically conceptualized as psychopathological behavior by the troubled clergyperson, which is an essentially idiopathic model. Although this approach captures some important features of abuse by clergy, it is insufficient and incomplete as an explanatory mechanism. Clergy abuse, like abuse by any helping professional, is situated in a variety of organizational or institutional contexts that, to varying degrees, encourage or discourage exploitative behavior.

All helping professions have enhanced opportunity for and vulnerability to exploitative behavior, due to the power dynamics of the relationship between the helper and the person who is helped, the weaker status of those helped, and—in some cases—the countertransference involved in the work. Institutions and professions vary in their willingness to manage this problem and their effectiveness in doing so. The late 1970s and 1980s saw a considerable shift in the willingness of the healthcare professions to address exploitation by healthcare professionals. The organizational culture in healthcare shifted from denial and covert tolerance of such exploitation to generally uniform and active prohibition. Although success in reducing such behavior in healthcare has been incomplete, it has nevertheless been substantial. Comparable efforts in responding to clergy abuse have been more mixed, with a pattern of success similar to healthcare in some denominations, coupled with intransigence and resistance by other denominations. Most noteworthy among the latter is the Roman Catholic Church.

A high rate of exploitative behavior or a chronically ineffective response to such behavior on the part of a profession or institution is an indication that it is dysfunctional. Because religious institutions play dominant roles in the selection, training, formation, supervision, and management of their clergy, any such dysfunction will create climates in which exploitation is tolerated or even encouraged. Furthermore, a milieu that tolerates abuse will tend to elicit exploitative behavior in those whose individual propensity to it is marginal, as well as eliciting increasingly egregious behavior in those whose propensity is strong.

This chapter reviews sexual abuse by Catholic clergy from the perspectives of both the individual (the abusing priest) and the institution (systemic features of the Church), as well as the interactions between the two. It will also offer recommendations for change.

What Is Known—and What Isn't—about Abuse by Catholic Clergy

Basic Facts

In 1999 Lothstein introduced a discussion of sexually abusive clergy by stating: "There are no reliable actuarial studies on the prevalence, incidence and ratio of sex offenders (especially child or adolescent molesters) among the major religious denominations in the United States" (1999, 65). Similarly, Plante concluded: "We know very little about sexually abusing priests" (1999, 2). These statements remain generally accurate, yet some information is available.

The available information, although not robust due to methodological and sampling limitations, suggests some useful data and patterns. Sipe's (1990, 1995) research on self-reported sexual interests of Catholic priests estimates a 2 percent rate of true pedophilia (sexual interest in prepubescent children) and a 4 percent rate of ephebophilia (sexual interest in adolescents who are postpubescent but under the legal age of consent). This is echoed in Plante's (Plante 1999, 2006; Plante and Daniels 2004) reviews of this literature, in which it appears that the great majority (about 80 percent) of those Catholic priests who abuse minors abuse postpubescent adolescent males as opposed to children at latency or younger ages—the more typical targets of those who abuse minors. This finding is similar to the results of a study commissioned by the Anglican Church in Australia (Parkinson, Oates, and Jayakody 2009), which found that about three-quarters of the victims were male, with most between the ages of ten and fifteen. Plante and Daniels (2004) in their review note that the rate of

Catholic priests who have sexual contact with minors may be as low as 2 percent, but is no higher than 6 percent. The John Jay College report (2004), commissioned by the US Conference of Catholic Bishops (USCCB), concluded that 4 percent of male Catholic religious (of all types) had sexual contact with minors. This translates into almost 4,400 abusive clergy with over 10,000 victims.

There is nothing peculiar to the Catholic Church with regard to difficulty in getting robust prevalence data about sexual abuse by its clergy. Almost all researchers in the area of sexual abuse bemoan the fact that underestimation of prevalence seems likely, and there is well-based speculation that this underestimation may be worse for male victims, especially those abused as adolescents—precisely the group most commonly abused by Catholic clergy (see Gonsiorek, Bera, and LeTourneau 1994, especially chapter 3; see also Gonsiorek 1989).

Comparisons with other helping professions are of limited utility. In a survey of male mental health professionals, 2–17 percent reported having had sexual contact with patients at some point in their careers, but the vast majority of the victims were adult patients, not children (see Schoener 1989, 1995). Using a "credible accusations" metric comparable to the one in the John Jay College study, the number of schoolteachers estimated to have abused children is about 5 percent (Shakeshaft 2004a, 2004b).

All these estimates are riddled with imprecision. Credible accusations are carefully considered judgments, but they are nonetheless judgments, not facts. Self-reports of behaviors and sexual interests probably represent more of a floor than a ceiling and are notoriously prone to underestimation and other response biases (see Gonsiorek, Sell, and Weinrich 1995 for a discussion of the difficulty in measuring sexual orientation as just one example).

As far as the specifics of what leads abusive priests to abuse, the available information is weaker still. Lothstein (1999) notes evidence of a linkage between abnormal brain activity (specifically, fronto-temporal pathology) and paraphilias in clergy but also notes that various abnormal brain states are common in those involved in sexually deviant behavior generally. Although a number of models and typologies have been suggested as useful in understanding mental health professionals who become sexually involved with patients (Gabbard 1989, 1995; Gonsiorek 1995a; Irons 1995; Schoener and Gonsiorek 1989), these seem primarily applicable to mental health professionals and again derive almost entirely from observations of perpetrators whose victims were adults.

In short, we have very little solid information about what idiopathic factors dispose some Catholic clergy to abuse children. However, the best estimates of overall prevalence (that is, 2–6 percent) place the percentages of Roman clergy who abuse as probably comparable to rates in similar helping professions. These estimates should be viewed cautiously and as tentative, given the significant limitations of the data. It does seem clear, however, that the vast majority of Catholic priests do not sexually abuse minors. Plante and McChesney's (2011) recent volume provides more detail on these and related issues.

What More Can Be Learned

It is important to note that there are sources of information that any profession or religious denomination can use to develop some further useful, if still incomplete, data about sexual abuse by its members: claims data from carriers of malpractice insurance. For example, psychologists with malpractice insurance through the American Psychological Association Insurance Trust (APAIT) can make inquiries about the riskiest areas of professional practice nationwide and in a particular state, the most common causes of malpractice action, and typical settlements for certain malpractice actions. APAIT tracks and dispenses such information. The available information reflects the recent past, not the present, but it is helpful. APAIT also develops risk management workshops for psychologists based on the trends it has observed in malpractice actions. It provides consultations to people it insures to help manage potentially litigious situations as they emerge. These activities go beyond the scope of a traditional malpractice insurance carrier who merely defends the insured party when he or she is sued, but they are increasingly emerging as part of the risk management package provided to insured parties. Some religious denominations have taken a similar approach; for instance, the Episcopal Insurance Trust provides comparable services to its insured dioceses. Additionally, such data can be mined to identify particular kinds of professionals and professional situations that are most at risk. Since the malpractice insurance carrier has access to information about cases that have settled under terms that are not public, its composite data on cases would be more complete than data on cases in the public record alone.

This expanded role of the malpractice insurance carrier can develop only out of an objective, thoughtful, and—most important—transparent appraisal of claims data. Again, claims data are an imprecise and incomplete reflection of the complex problem of sexual abuse, but they are a start, and they have pragmatic and helpful applications. The Catholic Church has yet to avail itself of this kind of information, instead opting to summarize and analyze its internal files of "credible accusations," as in the John Jay College study (2004). Although this approach is a useful component, it is incomplete and lacking in objectivity.

Put simply, such raw data consist of judgments about "credible accusations" by Church officials whose credibility is in question. No matter how well an external entity reviews such data, the credibility problem is not overcome.

The Catholic Church has had opportunities to engage in more extensive objective research on its problem of abusive clergy. But as Lothstein (2004) describes, when confronted with the possibility of information it cannot control, the Church quashes such efforts, preferring instead to limit its data gathering to existing documents.

The Limits of Focusing on Priests Who Abuse

It would appear, then, that Catholic priests do not abuse children in greater numbers than would be expected by comparisons to similar helping professionals, although those clergy who abuse are unusual among abusers in their focus on adolescent males as victims. One would therefore anticipate that the problem of child abuse in the Church would be no better or worse than in comparable groups.

Yet the International Criminal Court at The Hague has been requested to instigate crimes against humanity proceedings against the Vatican and Pope Benedict XVI for their mishandling of cases of child abuse by Catholic clergy. Relations between Ireland, once one of the staunchest of Catholic countries, and the Vatican have been in tumult since the release of the *Cloyne Report*, which detailed a decades-long pattern of unresponsiveness, deception, subterfuge, and obstruction of justice on the part of the Church hierarchy regarding child abuse by Catholic priests in Ireland (Lyall 2011). Prosecutors in Pennsylvania and Missouri have charged members of the Catholic hierarchy of covering up child abuse. Where are the comparable governmental actions against other denominations and professions whose prevalence of child abuse by its members seems not significantly different? They do not exist.

There are two available hypotheses to explain this anomaly. The first theory, regularly if tentatively floated by Vatican officials, is that the Catholic Church is being unfairly targeted. There is no evidence for this hypothesis, which, if accurate, would require an international conspiracy of mythic proportions. The other hypothesis is that there are distinctive features about the Roman Catholic Church that enable those priests who are child abuse perpetrators to continue perpetration even after their behavior is revealed and despite their numbers seemingly being no greater than comparable professions.

The next section describes these distinctive features.

Distinctive Features of the Church Contributing to Abuse

There truly is something different about the problem of sexual exploitation in the Catholic Church—different from the problem's manifestations in health-care professions, and even different (for the most part) from its manifestations in most other Western religious denominations. The differences do not lie primarily in the usual suspects named by the left and right: celibacy; anti-Catholicism; the Church's views of women, homosexuality, or sexuality in general; the purported corruption of North American society; and greedy attorneys and litigious clients. Some of these may add to the brew, although often not in ways suggested. And as noted above, the difference is probably not in the prevalence rates of abuse.

What is distinctive about the manifestation of this problem in the Catholic Church has most to do with idiosyncrasies of church structure and organizational culture, especially the culture and structure of church leadership (for more extensive discussions, see Cozzens 2002; Oakley and Russett 2003). Simply stated, sexual exploitation in its varying forms occurs in most environments where opportunity exists. Whether such exploitation is well-managed and diminished, or whether it is tolerated and becomes institutionalized, is a function primarily of the institutional response to it. When there is a consistent clustering of exploitation, and when it remains unamenable to amelioration over time, that is a very different problem than the existence of a certain base rate of sexual exploitation in the helping professions, and of the idiopathic features of those who exploit. Instead, the core issue is a pervasive failure and dysfunction of institutional leadership.

Every helping profession or institution that has addressed the problem of sexual exploitation would like to believe that it did so voluntarily, driven by its own sense of morality and ethics. This is an illusion at best, marketing and damage control more likely. In fact, the profession or institution responded because it had to, not because it chose to. In every case, the initial responses were denial, blaming the messenger, and insensitivity. Malpractice or other civil action, adverse publicity, public outcry, and resulting pressure from policymakers necessitated the change. In most cases, change was driven by relentless attorneys, unyielding media, a few courageous victims, and even fewer courageous insiders within the profession or institution. Once change occurs, this history is conveniently forgotten and often actively distorted (see Gonsiorek 1995b; Schoener 1995).

This is not meant to indicate cynicism about the helping professions; it is merely an acknowledgment of the nature of power and human failings. The Catholic Church was no better or worse than any other institution in terms of its initial maladaptive response to exploitation. What has emerged as distinctive, however, is its ongoing intransigence in responding to the problem and its pattern of aggressively covering it up, even to the point of operating against its own self-interest. It has become an unchanging outlier, while other helping professions and religious denominations have changed. Such changes vary by profession, but they include more effective and transparent processes for handling complaints; reduced defensiveness about the reality of abuse by professionals; greater and more reliable accountability for members, especially leaders; openness to external scrutiny; more substantive roles for women; and, in religious organizations, greater and more substantive involvement of lay people in all phases of responses to complaints. As will be discussed below, there is a perverse internal logic to the Catholic Church's behavior, irrational as it initially seems, although that logic is destructive to all involved.

Boundary Challenges of the Clergy Role

One important consideration is an issue generally applicable to clergy of all denominations: the extraordinary challenges of maintaining personal and professional boundaries in the clergy role. Clergy, of all the helping professions, experience the most pointed, frequent, and intense challenges to maintaining personal and professional boundaries. Depending on the particular denomination, clerical roles may involve liturgical functions, raising funds, committee and organizational work, financial management, spiritual and personal counseling, social activities, group leadership, and other activities—all with the same people and often more or less simultaneously. Consider a comparison with healthcare professionals, who instead circumscribe their professional roles. Mental health professionals, such as psychologists, regulate such complexity because it is perceived to be so fraught with ethical and legal risk. Some state psychology boards, such as the one in Minnesota, prohibit multiple relationships outright for mental health professionals and treat them as serious ethical violations. More commonly, mental health professions limit, regulate, and caution against multiple relationships. In other words, healthcare professionals have tended to respond to the kinds of complexity of professional roles that clergy face by declaring them risky, ill advised, or even inherently unmanageable. This means that the role that clergy are expected to fill is the most complex and "boundary strained" of any helper role.

Celibacy, Denigration of Women, and Intense Homophobia

Judeo-Christian faith traditions vary considerably in their views of sexuality. The Catholic tradition is one of those least at ease with sexuality and the body; no other Judeo-Christian tradition idealizes celibacy to the same extent (Ranke-Heinemann 1990; Sipe 1990, 1995).

If one believes that the solution to the crisis of clergy sexual abuse will entail a reexamination of many aspects of sexuality, it seems likely that the Catholic Church, as it currently conceptualizes the body and sexuality, is particularly handicapped in this task. When sexual expression is perceived as illegitimate except for the purpose of procreation, and when celibacy is elevated even above procreation, it is difficult to appreciate the fundamental reality of sexual abuse. The pervasive spoiling of sexuality that typically accompanies sexual abuse cannot be appreciated if sexuality is not seen as valuable in its own right, and on its own terms, with no reference to a procreative purpose necessary. This may be one of the reasons the celibate (in aspiration, though generally not in behavior) Church hierarchy has such a difficult time coming to terms with the meaning of sexual abuse of minors, who have no legitimized procreative function. In short, to the Roman hierarchy, most sexuality has no legitimacy and is not worthy of serious concern.

Interwoven into this mix is the paradox of celibacy of Catholic clergy, a fiercely held requirement and aspiration that is typically a behavioral failure. As Sipe's work (1990, 1995) has documented, most Catholic clergy fail to maintain celibacy—some fail rarely, some occasionally, and some frequently. Yet celibacy is officially required (although actually not, as demonstrated by rarely discussed exceptions, such as the Uniate Church of Eastern Europe, which is under Vatican authority), intensely defended, and a marker of the superior clerical role (Ranke-Heinemann 1990).

The problem is not celibacy per se, but the corruption that flows from the hypocrisy surrounding its failure. After all, other denominations with married clergy contain some sexually exploitative clergy. This hypocrisy fosters a culture of deceit, lack of emotional integration, and self-delusion about personal sexuality among Catholic clergy, which then more generally impairs their attitudes, beliefs, and behaviors about sexuality. It is difficult to think of a group less well-prepared to offer emotionally integrated, morally coherent, and humane perspectives on human sexuality than Catholic clergy, who typically fake a celibacy they rarely achieve.

Another impediment exists in the Church's pervasive sexism, which unfortunately becomes framed predominantly as a question about the ordination of women. On a pragmatic level, there is a high price to pay in not having individuals socialized to take care of children (that is, women) in substantive roles in the Church's power structure. When this issue becomes predominantly focused on women as clergy, however, other options are neglected. If lay leadership were to have a substantive role, as Spohn (2004) suggests, opportunities would exist for serious (that is, independently powerful) female leadership. Even more to the point, a pool of potential female leaders whose loyalty, energy, and commitment are proven already exists: female religious. Literal priesthood need not be the only vehicle for meaningful power. Simply stated, if the leadership of the Catholic Church is serious about treating women as full and legitimate members of a faith community, it would create ways for women in the Church to have roles of power. But as Ranke-Heinemann (1990) describes, the Catholic hierarchy has a very deep investment in maintaining second-class status for women and its perverse views of human sexuality.

It is important to note the changes that have occurred in the area of sexual abuse in those denominations that have genuinely embraced women in positions of power. Once the formerly all-male leadership is integrated by gender, a focus on protecting the institution first and foremost is replaced by a focus on protecting minors and other vulnerable people; a secretive and clergy-dominated complaint process is replaced by one that is transparent and involves broader participation of the faith community; and case-by-case, capricious decision making becomes more standardized. Whether these observable changes in processes are actually effective in reducing rates of exploitation, increasing complainants' satisfaction with the complaint process, increasing confidence in church leadership, and achieving other relevant outcomes is the central question. But an array of different denominations must implement a sound and consistent research methodology regarding such questions, solving dilemmas such as those of sampling and underreporting dilemmas. The current scant, often flawed, and frequently impressionistic data of inconsistent methodologies cannot answer questions about which processes and responses produce the best outcomes.

Simply having women in power within religious hierarchies does not solve the sexual abuse problem; there is no magic bullet, and female sexual abuse perpetrators do exist (see Gonsiorek, Bera, and LeTourneau 1994, 49–52). But the shift in denominations such as Evangelical Lutheran Church in America and the Episcopal Church has been palpable, surprisingly rapid, and less contentious than members of these denominations feared. With the existence of female religious traditions in the Catholic Church as developed and venerable as those of male religious, the lack of serious efforts to engage women as substantive leaders is difficult to comprehend except as sexism, plain and simple.

The final example of the Church's distortions of sexuality discussed here is homosexuality, although other potential examples are legion. The persistent efforts of the Church hierarchy to blame pedophilia on homosexuality are without foundation from a behavioral sciences perspective (see Gonsiorek 2004 for a discussion of this issue). Similarly, the persistent efforts of the Church hierarchy to appropriate scientific credibility by couching theological arguments against homosexuality in the language and terminology of science (for example, labeling homosexuals as intrinsically disordered) are arrogant and fraudulent. This is not a useful or credible stance for an arbiter of morality.

Even in its attempts to be accepting of homosexuals, the Church has trouble with this issue. For example, Coleman (2004) describes the German bishops' criteria for possible admission of a homosexual candidate to the priesthood. They seek men who are secure in their sexual orientation, possess psychic stability, have no need to be public about their sexual orientation, deal well with intimacy, and are internally and externally accepting of the Church's teaching on homosexuality, among other factors.

Such a person is simply not likely to exist. The research that does exist on sound psychological adjustment in homosexuals consistently cites as predictive such factors as self-acceptance, a support system of other homosexuals, and comfort with reasonable disclosure (see the edited volume by Savin-Williams and Cohen [1996] for an introduction to this literature, especially chapters 5, 8, and 20). It is difficult to understand or even take seriously a position that asserts that truly accepting oneself as intrinsically disordered and avoiding disclosure can correlate with stability, security about orientation, and the ability to sustain intimacy.

In summary, the Catholic Church's teaching on human sexuality and the body has developed in such an abnegating and distorted manner that it lacks credibility, even to most people who identify themselves as Catholics. The only way it seems to make sense is as an enhancement and justification of the status of an aspirationally, but not behaviorally, celibate and aristocratic hierarchy.

Modern Corruption versus Chronic Exploitation

A predominant narrative of the Catholic hierarchy in explaining sexual abuse by clergy is that it is the modern world, not the Church, that is corrupt, and that the world's corruption is so powerful that it has permeated some clergy, who then commit abuse. This peculiarly ahistorical narrative was even featured in the recent John Jay College study (Terry et al. 2011), commissioned by the USCCB, in which the increase in supposedly deviant behavior in the broader society during the 1960s and 1970s was described as an important contributing factor to clergy abuse.

The study's authors elected not to look further back. If they had, it would have been clear that this view ignores and misrepresents documented historical reality. The Church's problems with sexually exploitative clergy go back centuries. More noteworthy, its patterns of institutional cover up and tolerance of sexual abuse are equally venerable. Liebreich's (2004) analysis of the seventeenth-century scandal of the Piarist religious order reads like a newspaper account of current clergy abuse, with pervasive child abuse by clergy, a well-developed cover up, and the protection of perpetrators at the highest levels of the Vatican, including the papacy. Plante (2006, 229–30) shows that this problem goes back to the earliest days of the Church and describes St. Basil's fourth-century recommended response to clergy abuse of minors: public flogging, followed by six months' imprisonment and then by a permanent prohibition on one-to-one interactions with minors.

Church Hierarchy as Aristocracy

At first glance, the variations in personnel practice sometimes exercised by the Catholic Church appear random and incoherent. Many institutions handling sexual abuse matters displayed variability and struggled to find workable responses before developing viable response protocols. But the Church seemed more variable than other institutions, acting at times against its own self-interest, even to being frankly self-defeating. A number of denominations allow bishops the same degree of local control that the Catholic Church does; many institutions experience episodic shifts between local and central control. Therefore, these do not seem like adequate explanations.

A more fruitful explanation is that the Catholic leadership functions as a true aristocracy in that it operates on the assumption that those outside the leadership have lesser worth and exist in large part to serve the leadership.

Clergy are above laity, high-ranking clergy count more than priests, and laity with means to support the Church have more worth than those without such means. From this perspective, the point of reference is always above: the crucial determining factors in decision making are the needs of the layer above. Different layers can have different needs, and as difficult situations reach the attention of increasingly higher layers, the operative needs change and the Church's responses seem contradictory. The immediate impression is one of chaos, but the underlying principle is that the operative needs of the next level up will govern decision making. Consistency is not especially salient; protection of the highest levels of the Church hierarchy is the central, albeit covert, governing principle.

This operating principle runs contrary to the expressed moral values of the Church, which means that the principle is unarticulated, officially denied, and often suppressed internally, even by those who use it as the basis of their actions. This hypothesis cannot be proved in any formal sense, but it can be useful in understanding the fluctuations in Church response to many of the challenges of sexual abuse. Priests who should not be reinstated nonetheless are, while those who should be languish without positions. Promotion seems driven more by loyalty than by competence. The bishops determine one course of action and the Vatican another. But the order underlying this seeming chaos is the need to maintain and, if possible, extend the power of the highest level of the Church hierarchy; all other considerations are secondary.

The drift into a sense of aristocracy may well be a risk to all holders of power. The Catholic Church seems unusual in the degree to which this sense predicts its leadership's behavior, and aristocracy is literally the political and social structure from which the leadership evolved historically. What is so distinctive about the Catholic hierarchy is that it exists without any accountability whatsoever. To even posit mechanisms of accountability is heretical, since the relatively recent (1870) manufacture of papal infallibility (see Wills 2000, especially chapter 17). Wilson's (2008) critique of clericalism raises similar issues, although his solutions focus primarily on the empowerment of laity and less on the concurrent disempowerment of hierarchy. Similar observations about Church leadership and structure can be found in Oakley and Russett's edited volume (2003), and the ideas here are akin to the points raised in Russett's concluding chapter on the tensions between democratic processes versus the monarchical structure of Church hierarchy.

This also explains the Church hierarchy's consistent inconsistency about its own policies. Much effort was expended to develop a charter to protect minors, as well as procedures and policies regarding allegations of abuse (US Conference of Catholic Bishops 2002a, 2002b). These, however, are applied inconsistently, despite much self-congratulation about progress by the Conference. For example, in a recent USCCB report, the methodology section (US Conference of Catholic Bishops 2011, 7–8) reports that on-site auditors assessing compliance with the charter did not have access to personnel files or "confidential" information (the criteria for confidentiality were not described), and that the auditors accepted the accuracy and completeness of the information provided at face value. More centrally, since "the *Charter* is silent on how records are to be kept" (7), there is no consistent protocol for records. The authors noted that there was further variation in that a single parish would sometimes keep records in varying ways from one case to another. The opportunities for faulty and so-called cooked data are considerable under these circumstances. Finally, it would appear that compliance with the charter is optional: two dioceses and seven eparchies (Eastern Rite dioceses under Vatican authority) declined to participate in the audit. It is difficult to comprehend why a staunchly hierarchical Church that purports to take its own charter so seriously does not enforce compliance. But again, there is an internal logic to this seeming irrationality. From the vantage of an aristocracy, the charter is not necessarily meant literally; it is good public relations when needed, but it is merely discarded when it limits hierarchical prerogatives.

Priesthood as Ontological Transformation

Many faith traditions conceptualize the role of priest as involving a transformation of the person. The sacramental view of priesthood in the Roman Catholic tradition involves a profound ontological transformation in the man who is made priest.

This essentially theological perspective becomes relevant in the clergy abuse crisis because it poses a significant barrier to recognizing and accepting the fact that some priests may be too flawed to actually function as priests in the real world. Rather, the implicit assumption in the Catholic tradition is that the flawed priest should be able to return to priestly functioning once he has fully reengaged his priestly role. This reengagement is spiritual and theological; behavioral and psychological considerations are secondary at best, and when they are articulated at all, they are misrepresented by being subsumed to theological considerations.

Unfortunately, none of the available literature predicting recidivism outcomes in sexual offenders suggests that such theological variables are relevant as predictors of behavioral outcomes. As a result, there is a chronic and pervasive tendency in the Catholic Church to confound forgiveness, renewal, and reconciliation in a spiritual sense with rehabilitation and fitness for duty in a psychological sense. In fact, these are apples and oranges: one does not reliably predict the other.

This phenomenon is salient for those who are already priests. The Church seems receptive to the use of mental health evaluation for screening and admission of candidates to the priesthood (see McGlone, Ortiz, and Karney 2010 for a survey of current practices in this area). When it comes to evaluating existing priests who present problems, however, Church officials often seem more oriented to obtaining the results they deem theologically and administratively desirable, rather than to obtaining an objective mental health evaluation of fitness. For example, Lothstein (2004) describes the extraordinary difficulties for centers evaluating and treating priests due to the secrecy and outright duplicity on the part of Church officials regarding such priests. The problem for the Church here is that once a man has been ontologically changed by being made priest, nontheological considerations matter little.

Catholic Church as Chameleon

Although the Catholic Church is often portrayed as a linear hierarchy, this is an incomplete characterization. Its extraordinary resiliency is due in large part to its chameleon-like structure. In fact, its structure contains a hierarchy embedded in a diverse and far-flung network of affiliated organizations. This network can advance Church interests while not being the official Church. Parts of this network can serve as scapegoats and be disavowed if their activities create too many political and public relations problems for the Church; other parts can provide institutional cover by appearing to be more theologically and intellectually diverse, and less power-oriented, components of the Church. But all the parts—including diverse religious orders and organizations; media outlets; a far-flung diocesan structure; Church-affiliated institutions in education, health care, law, and other professions; and organizations of laity—are generally and ultimately (though often indirectly) under the jurisdiction of the Church hierarchy. This is accomplished through advisors, boards, and other modes of influence ranging from direct to indirect.

Kertzer (2001) has shown how the Vatican orchestrated political campaigns against Europe's Jews in the nineteenth and early twentieth centuries, and Cornwell (1999) has discussed the culmination of these trends during the papacy of

Pius XII. Affiliated Church organizations, lay groups, and media conducted the operations. When there was too much outcry about the anti-Semitic campaign, the Church could respond that this was not the official Church speaking, but merely Catholics expressing their personal views as citizens. If there was too much political cost, the Church could even disavow or discipline such Catholic organizations. The Church could also tolerate and even promote more liberal Catholic outlets to give an appearance of balance and reasonableness and to undermine criticism. As Kertzer (2001) points out, the campaign was ultimately so effective, despite its muddy and uneven course, that it was eventually adopted in large part by the Third Reich.

A similar pattern emerges in the Church's current response to the clergy abuse crisis. Church-affiliated organizations will publicly attack victims or scapegoat others for the Church's failings. If these efforts succeed politically, their actions stand. If they generate too much public outcry, the official Church can distance itself from them or disavow them. Church-sponsored victim support organizations provide an appearance of victim sensitivity, yet they have no real effects on policy and practice. In the meantime, Church attorneys respond aggressively to abuse victims; Church lobbyists promulgate legislation undermining victims' recourse; judges, district attorneys, and legislators sympathetic to the Church protect its interests; Church organizations ostracize and undermine victims; abusing priests are protected; and Church leaders who are effective at managing such activities are rewarded with promotions. Throughout, the Church hierarchy effectively manages this shell game, at times purporting to have little to do with some of these activities—which are instead portrayed as the spontaneous actions of sympathetic, but officially not Church-affiliated, parties.

Siege Mentality as Characteristic Response to Criticism

The siege mentality can perhaps best be seen as an outcome of aristocratic leadership. The first response to criticism of Church leadership often seems to be outrage. Voicing criticism in itself makes one suspect, and unless the criticism is quickly lessened or repudiated, the Church's usual reaction is to neutralize the critic at all costs regardless of the merits of the criticism, the stature of the critic, or the cost in credibility to the institutional Church.

The operating principle seems to be that those at lower levels are always out of line if they criticize those at higher levels, because their lower status gives them no right to do so—and, in fact, it is unnatural to the order of things, and perhaps heretical, if they do so. Additionally, the Church hierarchy is proactively confused with the entire Church. The Church leadership reframes any criticism of itself as an attack on Catholicism and all Catholics. If one is a Church aristocrat, this stance is comprehensible: the leadership aristocracy *is* the Church; the laity and lower-level clergy merely function to serve the aristocracy. Since this rubric is understandably offensive to laity and lower-level clergy, as well as being amoral on its face, the rubric is never acknowledged and always repudiated at the same time that it is behaviorally consistent with the actions of the hierarchy. This characteristic may help explain the problems that the Vatican and Catholics in democratic societies have in communicating with and understanding each other. The latter have a distrust of aristocracy, while the Church aristocracy finds subversive those who do not acknowledge its prerogatives. Although developing a siege mentality is not uncommon in organizations accused of misconduct, the approach is rarely adaptive, and the extreme form it takes among the Catholic hierarchy is fueled in large part by the aristocratic structure and culture of Church leadership, and its relatively recent theological rationale.

Possibilities for Change

It has become apparent in the past decade to most unbiased observers that other helping professions and other denominations have generally instituted changes to respond more effectively to sexual exploitation than the Catholic Church. The Church is clearly unwilling to make such changes, despite its protestations to the contrary. And given its characteristics described above, it seems likely that the Church is unable to effect those changes, because they would entail other changes—such as in the Church's aristocratic structure, the role of priests, and the Church's conceptualizations about sexuality—that the Church hierarchy finds unacceptable. The hierarchy is a powerful entity in civil society, allowed to function above the law, that poses a documented, ongoing, and unmanaged risk, especially to children and other vulnerable people. The Church hierarchy will not change itself; if change is to be effected, it must be imposed from outside. Possible outside sources of change include responses to the abuse from civil society, as well as responses from Roman Catholic laity and concerned clergy outside the Church power structure.

As a behavioral scientist, it is clear to me that effective, though not perfect, changes can be made in how helping professions and religious denominations respond to exploitation by their professional members. Many such changes have been made, and professions and religious denominations have an ongoing duty to those they serve to refine and expand on these. In addition, the research base necessary to effective responses must be expanded.

As a citizen, it is clear to me that civil authorities and the judicial system have been negligent in their sworn duties to protect citizens by allowing the Catholic Church hierarchy to engage in conspiracy and obstruction of justice with minimal or no consequences to it. This can and must be remedied on both the criminal and civil law sides.

As a Catholic, it is clear to me that the current Church hierarchy is so corrupt and so focused on maintaining and expanding its own power as to be devoid of moral authority and spiritual leadership. The true Church, the community of the baptized that is the mystical body of Christ, is held hostage by that effective and ruthless organization, operating outside the law that is the Vatican and its operatives.

Recommendations

1. Greatly expand the research base on sexual exploitation by helping professionals in general, and clergy in particular. Two approaches would significantly add to our knowledge. First, a large-sample, anonymous self-report study that was conducted across different helping professions and religious denominations (using the same survey for all of them) and that assessed a broad range of problematic sexual behavior would allow cross-professional comparisons of base rates of different behaviors. Such a study would probably underestimate these problems, but it would establish a prevalence floor. Only with such a study can questions be answered about whether Catholic clergy, or any studied group, have a higher prevalence than other groups of sexually abusing minors. Such a study would also answer many other pressing questions in the area of sexual exploitation by helping professionals.

Concurrently, a second study might compare claims data on cases, both settled and adjudicated, from a broad range of malpractice insurance carriers that provide coverage for different helping professions and religious denominations. The limitations of these data are that the sample contains only those cases where claims were filed, and that they are retrospective.

These two approaches do not address limitations to the database caused by victims' reluctance to come forward, which is probably especially likely in adolescent males—the group most abused by Catholic clergy. But they are a start at addressing the limitations of current knowledge.

2. Routinely expand criminal investigations of abusive clergy as far up the leadership ladder as is warranted by the degree of cover up and conspiracy that a case presents. Patterns of transferring abusive priests, poor or deceptive record keeping, and deception about past problems are sufficiently commonplace in cases involving the Catholic Church that possible criminal conduct of those in supervisory roles of abusive priests should be regularly investigated and the supervisors should be charged if warranted. This has begun to occur in a few jurisdictions. Simply stated, until bishops, cardinals, and other members of the hierarchy are convicted and incarcerated for engaging in criminal conspiracies and coverups, the Church hierarchy will not take the issue seriously. The rule of law is undermined when powerful law breakers are insulated or exempt from the legal consequences of their actions.

3. Reduce and more tightly structure prosecutorial discretion, and investigate and remedy bias by judges, prosecutors, legislators, and other public officials who do not hold Church authorities accountable. In recent decades, the US judicial system has developed a pattern of aggressive and increasingly brutal overcriminalization. We incarcerate—in terms of both absolute numbers and percentages—more of our population than any other country in the world, and more now than at any other time in our history. With 5 percent of the world's population, we now have 25 percent of the world's incarcerated population. Accompanying this pattern are enormous costs; no increase in public safety; and an increasingly expansionist, profitable, and politically well-connected corrections industry.

Less obvious, but cut from the same cloth, is a concurrent tolerance for lawlessness among the powerful, such as the hierarchy of the Catholic Church. In a sense we have the worst of both worlds in the United States: a judicial system that aggressively victimizes the powerless, vulnerable, disabled, and disenfranchised, while it simultaneously allows lawlessness by the powerful. Garrett (2011) and Natapoff (2009) have examined such issues in their analyses of convictions of the innocent and the effects of snitching and informants, respectively.

Overcriminalization is relevant here, because it would be ineffectual to respond to clergy abuse by merely getting tough with perpetrators. That response would change nothing in the substantial institutional factors within the Catholic Church that sustain abuse. The point, rather, is that the US criminal justice system is harsh to the weak and indulgent to the powerful. Both are problems, and both must change.

Although the causes and possible remedies Garrett and Natapoff discuss are complex and beyond the scope of this chapter, one issue they both raise cuts across both aspects of the "worst of both worlds" paradox: unfettered and unaccountable prosecutorial discretion. To that issue, I would add tolerance for the expression of personal bias in the judiciary.

US public officials have sworn to uphold the law, including the Constitution. Failing to honor this oath is negligent; failing to honor it in order to protect law breaking by agents of what is, after all, a foreign entity (the Vatican) is more serious still. The First Amendment's protection of freedom of religion was not intended to protect unlawful activity, but that is how it is often currently implemented, when prosecutors shrink from warranted prosecution of members of the Church hierarchy and when judges act out of their own theological and other biases. A similar problem and lack of accountability exist with legislators and other public officials who advance legislation that benefits the Church hierarchy at the expense of the public.

4. Bar from access to children any institution with a track record of failing to protect children from abuse. When Catholic schools and other educational institutions, teaching orders, individual clergy, and members of the Church leadership demonstrate a pattern of failure to protect children, the state has an obligation to intervene and protect children from these failed institutions and individuals. This is the case with other institutions in society; even St. Basil in the fourth century appreciated the need for it. Religious liberty does not extend to permitting lawlessness and tolerating abuse.

5. Restructure civil liability statutes and procedures to pierce the veil of the chameleon-like organization of the Catholic Church and hold all components liable that have incurred liability. The deception and shell game about control, and therefore liability, engaged in by the Church hierarchy erodes mechanisms of civil justice. Arguments are made by Church lawyers for and against whether the official Church hierarchy has control over parishes, dioceses, educational and other institutions, religious orders, and

lay organizations, depending on what outcome minimizes the Church's accountability for damaging actions. This is a ruse to avoid accountability. Such tactics are not acceptable when engaged in by white-collar criminals, organized crime, or hate organizations, and they should not be acceptable in religious organizations.

6. Disempower and replace the current Church hierarchy. If Catholic laity and clergy value their Church, they can do nothing less. Financially supporting the Church hierarchy and any of the far-flung components directly or indirectly under its aegis supports and condones abuse and exploitation of minors and others. Accepting spiritual and administrative authority from the current Church hierarchy also condones and is complicit in abuse and exploitation. Rank-and-file Catholics and uncorrupted clergy can elect their own bishops, reserve their financial support solely for those institutions they create, and in so doing, free the true Church from its current corruption and mismanagement. Although this idea may seem radical, it is in fact consistent with original conceptualizations of the Church (for example, Matthew, 18:20: "where two or three gather in my name, there I am with them"). It is also similar to other criticisms from within the Church, though they are admittedly less pessimistic about the ability of the hierarchy to change itself (see Robinson 2011).

7. Refocus First Amendment protections of religious freedom to emphasize individuals' religious freedom rather than the prerogatives of religious institutions and hierarchies. First Amendment protections of religious freedom were developed to protect the freedom of individuals to pursue religious beliefs and practices of their own choosing, or to pursue none at all. Instead, what has emerged in recent decades is the use of the First Amendment by religious institutions and hierarchies to evade legal accountability for activity that, when committed by other citizens, is regarded as a crime or tort. This is especially unjust for Catholic laity, whose hierarchy is entirely self-appointed and self-chosen, and who have no mechanisms to hold the Church hierarchy accountable. Research has consistently shown (see, for example, Pew Forum on Religion and Public Life 2008a, 2008b) that many, sometimes most, Catholics disagree with Church hierarchy on a variety of social issues; yet, somehow, the religious convictions of these Catholics are treated as if they do not matter. In effect, this way of construing the First Amendment curtails the religious freedom of individuals, while it privileges that of religious institutions and hierarchies.

References

Coleman, G. D. 2004. "Clergy Sexual Abuse and Homosexuality." In *Sins against the Innocents: Multidisciplinary Perspectives on Sexual Abuse Committed by Roman Catholic Priests*, edited by T. Plante, 73–84. Westport, CT: Greenwood.

Cornwell, J. 1999. *Hitler's Pope: The Secret History of Pius XII*. New York: Viking Penguin.

Cozzens, D. 2002. *Sacred Silence: Denial and Crisis in the Church*. Collegeville, MN: Liturgical.

Gabbard, G. O., ed. 1989. *Sexual Exploitation in Professional Relationships*. Washington: American Psychiatric Association.

———. 1995. "Psychotherapists who Transgress Sexual Boundaries with Patients." In *Breach of Trust: Sexual Exploitation by Health Care Professionals and Clergy*, edited by J. C. Gonsiorek, 133–44. Newbury Park, CA: Sage.

Garrett, B. 2011. *Convicting the Innocent: Where Criminal Prosecutions Go Wrong*. Cambridge: Harvard University Press.

Gonsiorek, J. C. 1989. "Sexual Exploitation by Psychotherapists: Some Observations on Male Victims and Sexual Orientation Issues." In *Psychotherapists' Sexual Involvement with Clients: Intervention and Prevention*, edited by G. R. Schoener et al., 113–19. Minneapolis: Walk-In Counseling Center.

———. 1995a. "Assessment for Rehabilitation of Exploitative Health Care Professionals and Clergy." In *Breach of Trust: Sexual Exploitation by Health Care Professionals and Clergy*, edited by J. C. Gonsiorek, 145–62. Newbury Park, CA: Sage.

———. 1995b. "Epilogue." In *Breach of Trust: Sexual Exploitation by Health Care Professionals and Clergy*, edited by J. C. Gonsiorek, 392–96. Newbury Park, CA: Sage.

———. 2004. "Barriers to Responding to the Clergy Sexual Abuse Crisis within the Roman Catholic Church." In *Sin against the Innocents: Multidisciplinary Perspectives on Sexual Abuse Committed by Roman Catholic Priests*, edited by T. Plante, 139–53. Westport, CT: Greenwood.

Gonsiorek, J. C., W. H. Bera, and D. LeTourneau. 1994. *Male Sexual Abuse: A Trilogy of Intervention Strategies*. Newbury Park, CA: Sage.

Gonsiorek, J. C., R. L. Sell, and J. D. Weinrich. 1995. "Definition and Measurement of Sexual Orientation." *Suicide and Life Threatening Behavior* 25 (Supplement): 40–51.

Irons, R. R. 1995. "Inpatient Assessment of the Sexually Exploitative Professional." In *Breach of Trust: Sexual Exploitation by Health Care Professionals and Clergy*, edited by J. C. Gonsiorek, 163–75. Newbury Park, CA: Sage.

John Jay College. 2004. *The Nature and Scope of Sexual Abuse of Minors by Catholic Priests and Deacons in the United States, 1950–2002*. Washington: US Conference of Catholic Bishops.

Kertzer, D. 2001. *The Popes against the Jews: The Vatican's Role in the Rise of Modern Anti-Semitism*. New York: Knopf.

Liebreich, K. 2004. *Fallen Order: Intrigue, Heresy and Scandal in the Rome of Galileo and Caravaggio*. New York: Grove.

Lothstein, L. 1999. "Neuropsychological Findings in Clergy Who Sexually Abuse." In *Bless Me Father for I Have Sinned: Perspectives on Sexual Abuse Committed by Roman Catholic Clergy*, edited by T. Plante, 59–86. Westport, CT: Praeger.

———. 2004. "The Relationship between the Treatment Facilities and the Church Hierarchy: Forensic Issues and Future Considerations." In *Sin against the Innocents: Multidisciplinary Perspectives on Sexual Abuse Committed by Roman Catholic Priests*, edited by T. Plante, 123–38. Westport, CT: Greenwood.

Lyall, S. 2011. "Rupture with Vatican Reveals a Changed Ireland." *New York Times*, September 13.

McGlone, G., A. Ortiz, and R. Karney. 2010. "A Survey of Psychological Assessment Practices in the Screening and Admission Process of Candidates to the Priesthood in the U.S. Catholic Church." *Professional Psychology: Research and Practice* 41:526–32.

Natapoff, A. 2009. *Snitching: Criminal Informants and the Erosion of American Justice*. New York: New York University Press.

Oakley, F., and B. Russett, eds. 2003. *Governance, Accountability and the Future of the Catholic Church*. New York: Continuum International.

Parkinson, P., K. Oates, and A. Jayakody. 2009. *Study of Reported Child Sexual Abuse in the Anglican Church*. Sydney: Australian Synod of Bishops.

Pew Forum on Religion and Public Life. 2008a. *U.S. Religious Landscape Survey: Comparisons*. http://religions.pewforum.org/comparisons.

———. 2008b. *U.S. Religious Landscape Survey: Final Reports*. http://religions.pewforum.org/reports.

Plante, T. 1999. "Introduction: What Do We Know about Roman Catholic Priests Who Sexually Abuse Minors?" In *Bless Me Father for I Have Sinned: Perspectives on Sexual Abuse Committed by Roman Catholic Clergy*, edited by T. Plante, 1–6. Westport, CT: Praeger.

———. 2006. "Pedophile Priests: What Do We Know about Catholic Clergy Who Victimize Minors?" In *Mental Disorders of the New Millennium*, edited by T. Plante, 1:227–44. Westport, CT: Greenwood.

Plante, T., and C. Daniels. 2004. "The Sexual Abuse Crisis in the Roman Catholic Church: What Psychologists and Counselors Should Know." *Pastoral Psychology* 52:381–93.

Plante, T., and K. McChesney, eds. 2011. *Sexual Abuse in the Catholic Church: A Decade of Crisis, 2002–2012*. Santa Barbara, CA: ABC-CLIO.

Ranke-Heinemann, U. 1990. *Eunuchs for the Kingdom of Heaven: Women, Sexuality and the Catholic Church*. New York: Doubleday.

Robinson, G. J. 2011. "Changing the Culture." In *Sexual Abuse in the Catholic Church:*

A Decade of Crisis, 2002–2012, edited by T. Plante and K. McChesney, 91–102. Santa Barbara, CA: ABC-CLIO.

Savin-Williams, R. C., and K. M. Cohen, eds. 1995. *The Lives of Lesbians, Gays and Bisexuals: Children to Adults*. Fort Worth, TX: Harcourt Brace.

Schoener, G. R. 1989. "A Look at the Literature." In *Psychotherapists' Sexual Involvement with Clients: Intervention and Prevention*, edited by G. R. Schoener et al., 11–50. Minneapolis: Walk-In Counseling Center.

———. 1995. "Historical Overview." In *Breach of Trust: Sexual Exploitation by Health Care Professionals and Clergy*, edited by J. C. Gonsiorek, 3–17. Newbury Park, CA: Sage.

Schoener, G. R., and J. C. Gonsiorek. 1989. "Assessment and Development of Rehabilitation Plans for the Therapist." In *Psychotherapists' Sexual Involvement with Clients: Intervention and Prevention*, edited by G. R. Schoener et al., 401–20. Minneapolis: Walk-In Counseling Center.

Shakeshaft, C. 2004a. *Sexual Abuse of Students in Schools: What Schools Must Do to Provide a Safer Environment for Our Children*. San Francisco: Jossey-Bass.

———. 2004b. *Educator Sexual Misconduct: A Synthesis of Existing Literature*. Washington: Department of Education.

Sipe, A.W. R. 1990. *A Secret World: Sexuality and the Search for Celibacy*. New York: Brunner Mazel.

———. 1995. *Sex, Priests, and Power: Anatomy of a Crisis*. New York: Brunner Mazel.

Spohn, W. C. 2004. "Episcopal Responsibility for the Sexual Abuse Crisis." In *Sin against the Innocents: Multidisciplinary Perspectives on Sexual Abuse Committed by Roman Catholic Priests*, edited by T. Plante, 155–68. Westport, CT: Greenwood.

Terry, K. J., et al. 2011. *The Causes and Context of Sexual Abuse of Minors by Catholic Priests in the United States, 1950–2010*. Washington: US Conference of Catholic Bishops.

US Conference of Catholic Bishops. 2002a. *Charter for the Protection of Children and Young People*. Washington: US Conference of Catholic Bishops.

———. 2002b. *Essential Norms for Diocesan/Eparchial Policies Dealing with Allegations of Sexual Abuse of Minors by Priests or Deacons*. Washington: US Conference of Catholic Bishops.

———. 2011. 2010 Annual Report on the Implementation of the *Charter for the Protection of Children and Young People*. Washington: US Conference of Catholic Bishops.

Wills, G. 2000. *Papal Sin: Structures of Deceit*. London: Darton, Longman and Todd.

Wilson, G. B. 2008. *Clericalism: The Death of Priesthood*. Collegeville, MN: Liturgical.

Paul D. Steele

4 Contingent Crimes

Exploring the Sexual Abuse of Children by Clerics from a Situational Crime Perspective

Introduction

Acts of child sexual abuse (CSA) committed by members of the clergy have been described as betrayals of trust (Nason-Clark 1998), "spiritual rape" (Barton 2012, 62), organizational failures (Rosetti 1997), and even "dumb mistakes" (Dorris 2011). They are also violations of state and federal criminal laws. Therefore, theories concerning the etiology of crime can provide a useful perspective from which to plan strategies to control clergy-involved CSA. According to Sutherland (1947), theories of crime can be characterized as either dispositional or situational in nature. Dispositional theories attribute the causes of crime to the personal traits and characteristics of individuals. Popular dispositional explanations have associated crime with the offender's intelligence level, mental health, impulse control, physiological and cognitive development, socialization processes, childhood trauma, peer associations, social class origin, ethnicity, employment, educational attainment, and respect for authority. Since the emergence of positivist orientations in the nineteenth century, the primary effort of crime theoreticians has been the development and refinement of dispositional theories. It is not surprising, then, that contemporary thinking about CSA, both among scholars and the general public, places great emphasis on the distinctive pathological traits of those who engage in these acts (Wortley and Smallbone 2006). This is certainly the case in research concerning the etiology of CSA perpetrated by clerics (see, for example, Doyle 2007; Falkenhain 1997; Hanson, Pfafflin, and Lutz 2004; Haywood et al. 1996; Kennedy and Heckler 1972; Langevin, Curnoe, and Bain 2000; Plante 2007; Plante and Aldridge 2005; and Plante, Manuel, and Bryant 1996).

In contrast, situational theories focus on the participants, environmental context, and circumstances of the immediate criminal event. In a field dominated by theories that stress the trait and character differences between criminals and law-abiding citizens, situational crime theory (SCT) has nonetheless emerged since the 1980s from opportunity and environmental crime theories, symbolic interactionism, and experimental psychology (Birkbeck and LaFree 1993). The principal reason for the growing acceptance of the situational crime perspective is that there is an increasing awareness of the limitations of explanations of crime based solely on the personal traits of offenders (Birkbeck and LaFree 1993). Improvements in data collection, analysis strategies, and computer applications have facilitated the development of new methods of situational crime analysis, and the findings of situational crime research have provided the information necessary for initiating effective forms of crime prevention and intervention.

This chapter explores clergy-involved CSA through the application of SCT. Key elements of this criminal behavior are described from this perspective, and SCT is conceptually extended to link it with relevant research. I conclude with recommendations for improved control of clergy-involved CSA based on this analysis.

The Situational Crime Perspective

Effective prevention of and intervention in criminal events requires an understanding of the situations in which they occur. Although scholars vary somewhat in their definitions of a "criminal situation," they generally refer to the immediate objective and subjective setting in which the crime occurs (Furnham and Argyle 1981; Magnusson 1981; Pervin 1978; Stebbins 1972). Early opportunity theorists assume that there is a sufficient supply of motivated offenders to commit crimes, and that crimes are likely to occur when a suitable target (either a physical object in a property crime, or a person in a violent crime) is available and accessible and is not well protected by a capable guardian (Cohen and Felson 1979). Environmental criminologists have extended SCT by pointing out that all crimes occur in situations that are defined by their physical and temporal space. Situational space influences the offender's awareness of and access to crime targets, his or her chances of avoiding detection, and the effectiveness of guardians in protecting the targets (Brantingham and Brantingham 1984, 1991). Symbolic interactionists emphasize that participant behaviors are constantly formed and reshaped by their past experiences and the circumstances present in the immediate situations in which actors find themselves (Katz 1990).

An extensive body of information derived from experimental psychological research concludes that the motivation level of potential offenders is influenced by the precipitating or inhibiting elements of the situation in which they find themselves (Birkbeck and Lafree 1993). For example, frustrated individuals are more likely to commit aggressive offenses when they perceive that others are intentionally blocking the realization of their own intentions (Averill 1982), or when their strong desires are unfulfilled (Buss 1963). On the whole, situational theories consider the traits of the target victim, offender, and guardian; their emotional states, knowledge and capacities, values, and motives; the physical, temporal, historical, and ecological environments; social network, community, and institutional contexts; and situational precipitants to action. For current purposes, the components of SCT are classified into categories of actors, contexts, and precipitants.

A Situational Perspective of Clergy-Involved Child Sexual Abuse

Although evidence suggests that clergy-involved CSA exists in all religious groups, the greatest amount of contemporary public concern, media exposure, and scholarly research focuses on CSA in the Roman Catholic Church. Recently, a large study of the Church in the United States (Terry et al. 2011) reviewed the extant literature describing the actors' dispositional traits, contexts, and precipitants of clergy-involved CSA. The study also reports on research sponsored by the Church investigating the personal traits and crime patterns of offending priests, responses of the Church, and historical trends of abuse in the Church. Although SCT is not the principal focus of the report, the researchers do apply SCT to some degree in analyzing CSA events and making recommendations for the prevention of subsequent clergy-involved abuse. Rather than repeating these descriptions, the current discussion highlights how clergy-involved offending differs from nonclergy CSA events, identifies and discusses elements of situational offending, and connects SCT explanations to other research and perspectives.

Principal Actors in Clergy-Involved Child Sexual Abuse

The principal actors in incidents of clergy-involved CSA are the clergy offenders, child victims, and those who are in a position to discourage or intervene in the incident. The latter group consists of child guardians, potential offender handlers, and those who manage locations in which clergy-involved CSA occurs.

The Offending Clergy Member

An important connection between dispositional and situational explanations of clergy-involved CSA is evident in the fact that offenders bring their particular orientations and life experiences to the crime event. Their personal traits, vulnerabilities, social skills, and achievements interact with other situational factors to increase or decrease the likelihood that a sex crime will occur in that setting, at that moment.

Personal Characteristics

Like other child sexual offenders, offending clergy are predominantly male. However, their average age tends to be greater than is the case for other child abusers, since normal age at ordination precludes the likelihood of adolescents among clergy, including those clerics who offend against children. Compared to nonclergy sexual offenders, offending clerics are, as a group, better educated and less likely to come from disorganized and chaotic home environments. On the whole, they have more extensive social networks among conventional members of society and have stronger communication skills, a fact that increases their ability to access and win the trust of the child and the child's family members, successfully "grooming" the child for subsequent victimization. These skills also enable them to construct plausible rationales and alibis to evade detection and punishment. Therefore, offending clerics rarely engage in more aggressive and threatening modes of CSA than other child sex offenders (Canter, Hughes, and Kirby 1998). According to Terry and associates (2011), offending clerics are no more likely to demonstrate traits of mental illness or deviant sexual orientation than other clergy members, but they commonly have problems with inappropriate alcohol consumption, a trait they share with nonclergy sex offenders. Discussed in more detail below, alcohol and drug consumption can lessen the offender's normal restraints and inhibitions, and also provide them with a convenient post-episode rationale for their sexual misdeeds.

Terry and associates present a description of offending Catholic priests that is consistent with a situational perspective of offending when they assert that offenders are likely to suffer from personal "vulnerabilities" (2011, 54). From their description, this term is synonymous with what the literature on sex offender treatment characterizes as static risk factors that are extrasituational in nature and not amenable to change, as well as stable dynamic risk factors that require systematic treatment over an extended period of time to reduce the risk they pose for sexual victimization (Hanson and Harris, 2000).[1] Terry and associates identify several extrasituational "vulnerabilities" including prior sexual victimization, overcontrolled affect, passivity, defensiveness, "confused sexual identity" (2011, 63), psychosexual vulnerability, poor training for a celibate life, poor understanding of the harm caused by sexual victimization, loneliness and social isolation, and job-related stress. Excessive consumption of alcohol is also considered a dispositional trait of clergy offenders. Research indicates that those who become reliant on alcohol lose critical decision-making skills and impulse control. Thus, those who have a history of substance abuse could be at greater risk of offending, even when sober. However, as discussed in the section concerning situational stimuli, when offenders are inebriated, they might be more predisposed to abuse regardless of the chronicity of their alcohol consumption.

Institutionally Conferred Status

From a situational crime perspective, the special authority conferred on clerics by their religious order greatly facilitates the clergy offender's ability to access victims, engage in sex acts with them, and avoid detection and punishment for their crimes. Ironically, ordination facilitates not only the legitimate aims of the religious institution but also child sexual abuse, by imposing social role obligations on clerics and by extending the trust and respect of the denomination and religious institution to the particular clergy member. In this way, clergy-involved abuse is similar to the institutionally based sex offending that occurs in educational and child-care settings, residential facilities, and recreational environments: the offender has an institutionally bestowed authority over children and is expected to interact with them on a regular basis. Legitimate clerical role obligations require that at least some clergy members be in direct contact with children. Opportunity theorists would assert that contact with children, even in private settings, is a routine activity, in that it has been traditionally seen as normal and role-conforming behavior. The offender's legitimacy of access is also recognized by the victim's family and caregivers, and by the child victims themselves as they have conferred their respect for the religious order on the particular clergy member as well.

Frequent contact with the child can enhance the offender's opportunity to groom targeted children by carefully befriending them, desensitizing them to touch and discussion of provocative topics, and ultimately to the point of overtly sexual acts (Lyon and Ahern 2011). This progression takes time. Smallbone and Wortley (2001) found that offenders did not usually initiate sexual abuse until they knew the child for at least one year. Although there is some inconsistency in definitions of grooming, a contemporary and comprehensive one is offered by Craven, Brown, and Gilchrist (2006). They suggest that grooming is:

> A process by which a person prepares a child, significant adults and the environment for the abuse of this child. Specific goals include gaining access to the child, gaining the child's compliance and maintaining the child's secrecy to avoid disclosure. This process serves to strengthen the offender's abusive pattern as it may be used as a means of justifying or denying their actions. (297)

The careful escalation of these events and situations over time makes it difficult for criminal justice officials, family members, and the child victim to determine the intentionality of the action and the child's complicity in the ultimate criminal act. Gradual indoctrination allows offenders to deny their responsibility for the offense and define their own behavior in a more positive light. Child victims are particularly traumatized by the grooming process due to the confusion and sense of complicity in sexual activities that they know are wrong. Frequent access to the child victim's caregivers also gives the offender many opportunities to explain and rationalize repeated private contacts with the child. Given the offender's institutionally conferred authority, it is likely that the caregivers will define the contact as normal and routine.

The clergy offender is likely to avoid detection if the child feels that he or she is a willing participant in the act; such a child is less likely to report the behavior and aggressively seek punishment of the offender. Furthermore, even if discovered, the offender might neutralize the offense (Sykes and Matza 1957) and avoid serious punishment if the offender asserts that the child was the initiator of the sex act, it was an extension of legitimate sexual development training, or the child's and/or the offender's inhibitions were lowered due to the consumption of alcohol.

Motivation

Opportunity and other rational choice theories suggest that offenders are motivated to commit crimes because the perceived pleasure derived from a criminal act outweighs its perceived costs or punishments. How motivated are clergy sex offenders? It could be that some are consistently motivated to engage in CSA, suggesting that an obsessed offender would irrationally attempt to commit acts of CSA, regardless of the likelihood of success and chance of avoiding detection. However, as with most people who commit sexual offenses against children (Canter, Hughes, and Kirby 1998; Conte, Wolf, and Smith 1989), the vast majority of clergy sex offenders are not obsessively driven sex offenders (Terry et al. 2011) but rather are strategic in selecting their target victims, grooming them, and selecting the most opportune situation in which to assault them.

Framing the concept of motivation in CSA cases is complex. Using a very broad definition of motivation, one might consider attraction as a motivating force. In this sense, the offender's attraction to and fantasizing about a particular child might in fact be primarily influenced by extrasituational character traits and, therefore, be fairly consistent for an extended period of time, allowing for some situational variation when the child is present or absent, or when the offender is experiencing an emotional deficit (Ward and Siegert 2002). However, although people are likely to be attracted to a goal object before they develop a plan to achieve the goal, relatively few people are compelled by their attraction to mobilize themselves to achieve it. For example, people might be attracted to an expensive sports car and fantasize about driving it, but they are not likely to develop practical plans to own the car; instead, they decide that owning it is impractical or would detract from some other, more important goal. In the case of deviant acts such as CSA, the potential actor's motivation to commit such acts is further reduced to the degree that they have internalized social prohibitions against them. Thus, adults who are attracted to the idea of engaging in a sexual act with a child can have their motivation diminished by perceiving that the behavior is impractical, could preclude the realization of other goals, or is inconsistent with their own moral code. However, since sexual offenses do occur, obviously some individuals are not inhibited by these concerns and progress to the stage of developing detailed strategies that will maximize their chances of successfully engaging in CSA. At this stage of deliberation, situational influences become more important. Potential offenders might decide that the likelihood of detection and its negative consequences outweigh the pleasure of sexual activity with a particular child. They might then forgo for the present their plans to sexually victimize the child or seek another potential victim—who, because of less rigorous protection, greater ease of access, or other situational variables, becomes a more desirable target.

Legal definitions, as well as some clinical etiological models (see, for example, Prochaska and DiClemente 1982), of child sexual offending limit the consideration of motivation to the decision to move from the planning stage to offending behavior. From a legal perspective, thinking about and planning a crime, and even engaging in preliminary but law-abiding acts in preparation of a crime, usually does not constitute a criminal act.[2] Up to the time of the criminal act, it is possible that the potential offender can choose not to offend, at that time or even at all. The decision to actually initiate a criminal action is highly influenced by situational factors, because specific offenses occur in a particular location and at a particular time and are described as the illegal interaction between the offender and the victim. Further, the manner in which the criminal act is realized, deflected, or terminated is influenced by changes in the situational environment and the interchange between victim and offender. Thus, a cleric could be attracted to a child, develop a long-term plan to groom the child for sexual activity, and select a specific time and location to engage in the act, but he could change his mind at the last minute, or even alter or terminate the crime event when it is in progress due to changes in the environment and the behavior of the victim.

Depending on how one defines motivation, it can be seen as a fairly constant desire—in this case, to sexually victimize a child—or as an internal state that fluctuates greatly due to situational elements. As offending clerics move from personal attraction to child sexual partners and vulnerability to commit CSA to the act itself, they continue to adjust their interpretation of the situation, assessment of the likelihood of a successful outcome, and meaning of the behavior in relation to changes in the environment and the reactions of the victim, his or her guardian, and others. Thus, the likelihood of committing the crime is contingent on the dispositional traits of the offender in interaction with the nature of the situation and the negotiated reality that emerges between the actors and the contexts in which they find themselves.

The Child Victim

The majority of research studies concerning clergy-involved CSA do not report on the characteristics of the child victims. In those studies that do discuss the victim, researchers have found that children assaulted by members of the clergy are demographically distinct from the majority of CSA victims in the United States and elsewhere. CSA victims are commonly between seven and thirteen years old (Finkelhor 1994), but those abused by clergy members are more likely to be older: between eleven and fourteen (Terry et al. 2011). National and crossnational data consistently report that females are at least three times more likely than boys to be victims of sexual abuse (Sedlak et al. 2010), while children victimized by clergy are much more likely to be male (Terry et al. 2011), a finding consistent with the general overrepresentation of male victims of institution-based CSA (Parkinson, Oates, and Jayakody 2012). Because a cleric's history of same-sex activity is not predictive of CSA (Terry et al. 2011), the overrepresentation of male child victims suggests that situational issues of access and control are influential in the selection of victim targets.

The developmental issues facing boys between the ages of eleven and fourteen become important in understanding the meaning that they assign to their victimization at the hands of their clergy mentor and their subsequent reactions to it. Before adolescence and in its early stages, boys are typically moving into social associations outside of the home, but they still find themselves under the authority and influence of their parents. They are at a vulnerable developmental stage concerning their own sexual identity (Dimock 1988), have exaggerated and unrealistic notions of manhood (Bolton, Morris, and MacEachron 1989; Mills 1993), and are less likely to act on their own behalf to prevent or terminate the abuse. Given their lack of experience and perspective, they are likely to ascribe motives and meanings to the actions of religious authority figures that are skewed, and they are more likely than their older counterparts to accept the definitions supplied to them by their victimizers.

In addition, pre-adolescent and adolescent male victims of CSA are not likely to disclose their victimization to others (Collings 1995; Finkelhor, Hotaling, Lewis, and Smith 1990; Holmes, Offen, and Waller 1997; Roesler and McKenzie 1994; Spiegel 2003), even when controlling for gender (Edgarth and Ormstad 2000; Priebe and Svedin 2008) and the status of, or their relationship with, the offender (Steele 2009). Fear of negative peer reactions strongly influences male victims not to disclose their abuse (Durham 2003; Holmes, Offen, and Waller 1997). Sexually abused boys may feel that being a victim of sexual abuse is not compatible with appropriate masculinity (Browne 1991; Durham 2003; Holmes, Offen, and Waller 1997). Among adolescent boys, those least likely to disclose abuse are those who live with both parents but perceive their parents to be uncaring or nonprotective (Priebe and Svedin 2008). Boys who have been sexually abused by men report confusion about their sexual identity, fear of being regarded as homosexual by others, and concern for being a potential offender or being regarded by others as such (Durham 2003; Teram et al. 2006; Watkins and Bentovim 1992).

Children victimized by clergy differ from other CSA victims in other important ways as well. First, the relationship between the victim and offender is different. In a typical case of nonclergy CSA, the child is usually victimized by a parent, stepparent, some other family member, or paramour of the mother. In clergy-involved cases, it is extremely uncommon to find a family connection between the victim and the offender. Rather, the connection is within the context of institutional roles: the child is acting in the role of student, altar boy, member of a religious-based social or athletic group, or as a member of a family actively involved in the church, while the offender acts in a complementary role of teacher, spiritual mentor, activity leader, or coach.

Second, children who experience CSA at the hands of non–family members are usually victimized by relatively young offenders (Sedlak et al. 2010), such as peers and babysitters. In CSA cases involving clergy rather than family members, however, the offender is much more likely to be a mature adult—a difference that, coupled with the offender's institutional status, can increase his or her ability to control the behavior of the child victim.

Third, victims of CSA generally come from disrupted and disorganized home environments (Sedlak et al. 2010) and are likely to be victims of several forms of maltreatment (Finkelhor 2008). For example, among a community sample of CSA cases from state child protective services, 42.5 percent of the victims' parents or primary caregivers experienced significant personal problems, including a history of substance abuse (16.3 percent), prior criminal incarceration (11.9 percent), domestic violence victimization (10.4 percent), and/or mental illness (10.4 percent) (Steele 2004). The same study found that serious and destabilizing problems existed in 62.1 percent of victims' families, including interpersonal conflict or violence (37.0 percent), economic difficulties (26.7 percent), substance abuse (17.9 percent), and legal problems (13.3 percent).

Due to limited reporting, it is difficult to determine the degree to which victims of clergy-involved CSA also come from disorganized families: it could be that clergy offenders target vulnerable and suggestible children as potential victims, at least among those religiously involved children to whom they have institutional access. However, circumstantial evidence suggests that, relative to nonclergy cases, victims of clergy offenders come from more stable home environments. Substantial research indicates a positive relationship between religiosity and familism (Bahr and Chadwick 1985). Parents and family members are important socializing and facilitating agents of the child's religious engagement. Those who promote religious involvement to their children are likely to be involved themselves and are less likely to experience destabilizing personal and collective problems (Call and Heaton 1997; Koenig, King, and Carson 2012).

Fourth, most children engaged in deviant activities tend to have low levels of religious engagement (MacNamara 1992), but victims of clergy-involved CSA tend to have a relatively strong religious orientation, as does their family prior to the abuse episode. Because of the depth of their religious orientation, victimization by the personification of that religion can increase the typical level of trauma experienced by CSA victims by depriving them of their religious ethos (Barton 2012; Bland 2001; Fater and Mullaney 2000). This is especially the case if the religious order does little to sanction the offender (Nason-Clark 1998).

Guardians, Handlers, and Managers

As Felson suggests, "a case can be made that the offender is not the most important actor for explaining crime. . . . Those who interfere with offenders, however inadvertently, play an even more central role in crime and its prevention" (1995, 53). Those who are in a position to prevent or intervene in clergy-involved abuse include guardians, who directly supervise potential victims; handlers, who supervise potential offenders; and managers, who supervise the locations in which crime events are likely to occur (Brunet 2002; Felson 1995).

Guardians

The most obvious guardians of minor children are their immediate family members or legally recognized guardians. The families of child victims of clergy-involved CSA differ from those of most CSA victims in that they tend to be more stable, intact, and not suffering from social problems such as poverty, substance abuse, or a criminal history (Steele 2008). They are more religiously active than the families of nonclergy victims and are likely to have introduced the child into the religious orientation and community in which he or she is victimized. As such, they are part of what emerges as the deviant sexual culture (Gagnon and Simon 1967): while not being offenders themselves, their routine religious activities unintentionally facilitate the abuse of the victim. In fact, from a routine activities perspective, the greater the guardian's involvement in the church, the greater the access that offending clergy will have to the victim.

Family members and other guardians are very likely to trust the offender in his or her role as a clergy member. This is another way in which clergy-involved CSA cases are distinct: in these cases, family guardians are respectful of authority, especially the spiritual authority of the church. If the child reports abuse to his or her parents or guardians, the family members' level of trust in the clergy member as a representative of their religion makes it difficult for them to fully accept the allegations, and they may suggest that the child might be angry at the clergy member for some reason or might have misinterpreted the event. In nonclergy cases, families are typically skeptical of officially reporting CSA due to an overriding mistrust of civil authority (Steele 2009). The literature concerning child abuse disclosure shows that the reactions of parents and caregivers strongly influence the child's likelihood to make and sustain formal complaints against the offender to the criminal justice system, child protective services, or other authorities (Hershkowitz, Horowitz, and Lamb, 2007; Lyon and Ahern 2011). In fact, the contingent notion of offender decisions to abuse a child has its parallel in the decision making of the child. Child victims are likely to make small, nonincriminating, and partial disclosures to parents and other authorities and judge their reaction, before deciding to make full and explicit disclosure (Petronio, Reeder, Hecht, and Ros-Mendoza 1996; Staller and Nelson-Gardell 2005). Therefore, the immediate reaction of guardians to the child's partial report of abuse largely influences the child's full disclosure and thus the guardians' likelihood to intervene on the child's behalf.

When the child is beyond the direct supervision of the parents, the guardian role is transferred to other adult authorities. Ironically, in the case of clergy-involved CSA, the clergy offender is cast in the guardian role, responsible for the child's welfare during an overnight camp out, a school field trip, or even during the school day. A protective strategy in such instances is to broaden the surveillance of children by including other parents, members of the clergy, or coteachers as temporary guardians until the child is once again under the care of a parent. However, peer clerics and others, even if not engaged in deviant sexual activities themselves, might be reluctant to report offenders without clear and compelling evidence and/or if they are fearful of the negative consequences that such a report might have for the offender, their religious order, or themselves.

Handlers

Handlers are people in positions of authority over the potential offender. Because of their supervisory role, they are able to monitor the behavior of subordinates and sanction them when they act inappropriately. Clergy assigned to duties within a religious community are more likely to be subject to direct oversight than those assigned to a parish. In the former case, potential offenders have limited access to victims, and they are more closely observed by superiors as well as peers. Those serving in a parish and/or as counselors, teachers, or coaches are less likely to be under the immediate supervision of handlers. This pattern was observed in the John Jay College (2004) study of CSA in the Catholic Church: diocesan priests were less likely to be immediately supervised and more than twice as likely to be identified as sex offenders than religious priests. Furthermore, as members of formal organizations progress to more advanced positions, they enjoy greater autonomy and less direct oversight (Trice and Sonnenstuhl 1988). More senior clergy are in a position to avoid detection, since their superiors might be located at great distance from their location and have little face-to-face interaction with them.

Managers

Managers supervise the environments that are potential locations for clergy offenders to commit acts of CSA. Managers can prevent a location for which they are responsible from becoming a crime scene by being physically present, conducting indirect surveillance through electronic monitoring, or by modifying the location to reduce its attractiveness as an environment conducive to crime. Each of these strategies reduces the privacy of actors in that location. SCT suggests that offenders avoid detection and reaction by seeking private locations for their criminal activities. One way that clergy offenders neutralize place managers is to assault the child in a location that they manage themselves on a relatively permanent basis. For this reason, a popular location for clergy-involved CSA is in the offender's home (Terry et al. 2011). Diocesan priests were the most likely offenders among Catholic clergy, and the offenders were primarily domiciled in the parish rectory, which could have been a shared living space with other priests. In these instances, the offender might pick a time for the abuse episode when the other resident clergy were absent, making the offender the exclusive manager of the crime location, at least on a temporary basis. Terry and associates (2011) note, however, that other parish priests were likely to observe, be indirectly aware of, or suspect that a colleague was engaged in CSA, but they were unlikely to report it to authorities for fear of reprisal. In this sense, they were ineffective as place managers.

The offense could also occur in a location that is only temporarily under the offender's management, such as a campground or office where the permanent location superintendent has temporarily granted manager status to the offender. Even in the victim's home, guardians might allow the offender to have private time with the victim, thus temporarily granting the offender manager status in the child's bedroom, for example (see Terry et al. 2011).

The Context of Clergy-Involved Child Sexual Abuse

For Miethe and Meier (1994), the context of criminal events consists of its physical location, the interpersonal relationship between the victim and offender, and the behavioral setting. For the purpose of this discussion, I will make finer distinctions within each category.

Physical Location

The physical location can be described as a type of location or as a geographical locale of a particular size. As noted above, the type of location favored by clergy offenders is a private one that they control, because this improves their chance of completing their sex crime without interruption and avoiding detection (or, if detected, it gives them an apparently legitimate excuse for spending time with the child in private). Research on CSA episodes that do not involve clerics indicates that the home of the child victim is the most common location of such crimes, because that is where the child spends most of his or her time, and the offender is typically a family member or friend of the family who has access to the child's home. As discussed earlier, since clerics are seldom family members of the victim, the cleric's residence is a favored location for CSA. Routine activities theory also suggests that locations where offenders interact with victims for legitimate reasons—such as school offices, camp locations, sports venues, or church properties—are common locations for these crimes, because they place the victim and offender in proximity for conventional and justifiable reasons.

Criminal events can also be situated by their geographical locale. Although social scientists have long asserted that crime is more prevalent in socially disadvantaged urban areas (R. Sampson and Groves 1989), the recent use of spatial analytical techniques has allowed criminologists to identify locations of high risk for criminal behavior (Eck et al. 2005). Criminologists have identified when and how often offenders, targets, and guardians interact in a particular geographical space. Sex offenses are most likely to occur in socially disorganized environments, where there has been a breakdown of community surveillance and willingness to protect victims. However, I have been unable to identify any research studies that determine the location of geographical "hot spots" for clergy-involved sex offenses. Rather, the type of location, as noted above, seems to be the best descriptor of the locations of these types of crimes.

However, there are other ways in which aspects of the geographical locale can be helpful in understanding the situational nature of clergy-involved sex crimes. Neighborhoods influence life outcomes for children and families in both direct and indirect ways. It is well understood that children and families are affected by their interaction with the other residents of their neighborhood. Social learning theories of crime suggest that children are more likely to become juvenile delinquents if they live in a neighborhood that is disproportionately populated with gang members, drug dealers, and other criminal mentors. These theories illustrate an important neighborhood compositional effect: that the residential makeup of the neighborhood explains why those who live there experience particular life outcomes (Kirby 2008). For example, one would expect that the reaction of neighborhood residents to the plight of a child who has been victimized by a member of the clergy, or their reaction to the victim's family, would vary depending on what proportion of the residents were members of the same religious group, or on the level of personal religiosity and public display of religious symbolism present there. Specifically, a child victim and his or her family who were members of the Catholic Church would be treated differently in a neighborhood with strong Catholic tradition and public activities and a large proportion of Catholics than they would be in a more Protestant, or secular, neighborhood. In some religious groups, members are practically encapsulated in the social networks made up of other church members, and they might be largely ostracized for questioning the ordained leaders of the church.

Furthermore, there is something about living in a particular neighborhood that affects behaviors and life outcomes regardless of the individual characteristics of its residents: the influence of the neighborhood on children and families can be contextual in nature. For example, Anderson and colleagues have found that, even after controlling for several individual-level factors, residents of neighborhoods with high rates of poverty and unemployment were less likely to have seen a doctor in the previous year (Anderson and Davidson 2001; Anderson et al. 2002). Also, Kirby (2008) has demonstrated that being poor while residing in a poor neighborhood poses fewer barriers to healthcare access than being poor and residing in a middle-class or mixed-class neighborhood. He concludes that poor people living among others with similar circumstances are able to tap into the collective knowledge of how to access the services that exist in poor neighborhoods, while poor people living in mixed-class neighborhoods are isolated from the knowledge network of their more affluent neighbors. Similarly, neighborhoods with a strong and active religious participation might unwittingly facilitate the activities of motivated clergy offenders by promoting events and activities that make potential child victims accessible to the offenders. Also, if an alleged clergy offender, the church, the faith, and authority figures in general are supported in a neighborhood, there is a greater risk of a collective negative response to the child and family for disclosing the abuse. In this way, offenders are structurally facilitated through the suppressing contextual effect of the neighborhood's values and beliefs. It should be noted that Terry et al. (2011) show that some dioceses with low concentrations of Catholics sometimes have rates of abuse similar to or even higher than those with high rates of Catholic residents in the area. Given the statistically exceptional nature of clergy-related CSA, such a finding does not necessarily prove that there is no neighborhood effect in these cases, because rare events are seldom normally distributed. It does suggest, however, that further research is needed to specify the effect of ecological context on these crimes.

Victim-Offender Relationships

As noted earlier, most CSA victims are assaulted by members or friends of the child's family. Although clergy members might become friends, possibly as a grooming strategy, they are rarely members of the family. Rather, they are accorded the prestige associated with their role in the church. In general, social distance between the victim and offender influences the willingness of the child to report abuse to authorities: children are less likely to disclose when they have been victimized by members of their immediate family (Steele 2009). However, the authority of the clergy offender reduces the likelihood that the child would disclose his or her victimization, as compared to reporting other friends of the family.

Behavioral Setting

Miethe and Meier (1994) assert that the frequency, modus operandi, motivations, and predisposing and precipitating factors of criminal events are influenced by the functional properties of the microenvironments in which they occur. The most common settings for crime are the home, school, workplace, and leisure environments (Lynch 1987).

Although less common, the religious environment is another behavioral setting that shapes the reason why the victim and offender are there (Davidson 1989), the roles they occupy, and how they interact. The relationship between the child victim, his or her family, and the clergy offender is defined by their normal and routine roles within their religious group. In particular, persons in positions of social responsibility are seen to be trustworthy and can easily manipulate the situation in a way that leaves victims and guardians more vulnerable to manipulation, too.

Religious and other legitimate social institutions can exert social control to produce conformity to institutional and societal conduct norms. Complaints concerning violations of institutional norms can be lodged with those in leadership roles within the organization, and they can engage in appropriate institutionally defined responses to those who violate norms. Social control within institutions is complicated by the leaders' desire to maintain organizational boundaries, authority, and autonomy. Religious authorities have reserved the right to sanction members and ordained clerics who violate religious tenets within the purview of their own rules concerning appropriate institutional penalties. They assert their authority over the conduct of their members and feel little responsibility to notify those outside of the institution of their efforts to produce compliance with institutional norms of conduct.

When behaviors violate norms that are exclusive to the religious institution, church authorities reserve the exclusive right to intervene with the offender.[3] However, CSA is a behavior that also violates the norms of other social institutions, including the criminal justice system's prohibition against such behavior. It is possible that both the religious and justice institutions might punish the clergy offender by, respectively, laicizing and imprisoning him or her. In other situations, institutions might compete for precedence in punishing the norm violator. The criminal justice system, backed by the authority of secular government, asserts its precedence over the religious organization to punish clergy sex offenders, even if authorities within the religious group disagree with the decision to punish and choose to use other forms of social control, such as psychiatric treatment or spiritual mentoring. The government's assertion of precedence, then, constitutes an intrusion into the religious organization's sovereign authority to control the behaviors of its members. If required by law to report incidents of clergy-involved CSA to justice officials, the religious organization is essentially implicating one of its own members who holds a position of trust. Ceding authority beyond institutional boundaries makes public the organization's failure to control this disgraceful behavior and can result in undermining public perceptions of the religious order. For reasons of boundary and image maintenance, it is not surprising that the Catholic Church and other religious organizations have been reluctant to actively and publicly engage in the sanctioning of sex-offending clerics. Thus, from the perspective of SCT, the institutional context in which the CSA occurs can limit the effectiveness of guardians, managers, and handlers to the degree that they attempt to protect the religious order against threats to its authority and legitimacy.

Temporal Context

SCT suggests the time of the offense is influenced by characteristics of the offender, victim, guardian, and environment. For example, during the school year, young people are most likely to commit crimes on weekday afternoons, after school is over and before their parents come home. Residential burglaries in suburban neighborhoods are more likely to be committed in the late morning and early afternoon, when guardians are out of the home. The time at which shoplifting offenses occur is influenced by the hours of operation of retail businesses, and crimes committed around bars are influenced by their closing time. Generally, most types of crimes occur more frequently during evening hours. Under the cover of darkness, offenders can approach their targets or lie in wait for victims; run less risk of discovery by guardians, handlers, or passersby; avoid detection; and be able to successfully escape from the crime scene. Some forms of sexual assault are more likely late at night, particularly date rapes and the sexual assault of adult victims by strangers. Children are more likely to be assaulted at times when guardians are absent: school-age children are not often assaulted during school hours, but their risk increases dramatically in the afternoon and early evening when school guardians and handlers relinquish control of the child. Crimes tend to be less frequent on weekdays and in the winter, when people spend more time at home—where they are better protected and able to guard their possessions. Exceptions to this pattern, of course, are crimes committed between family members.

Few data indicate that clergy-involved CSA occurs more commonly at a particular time of the day or day of the week, or during a particular season. However, due to the child's age, clergy-involved offenses are probably less common in the late-evening hours. Clergy assaults occur when clergy temporarily become guardians: for boys between the ages of eleven and fourteen, this is most common in the afternoon and early evening. The exception to this rule is when the clergy member has supervision of the child overnight. It could also be that social activities such as camping trips or overnight travel to athletic and social events supervised by clergy could increase the likelihood for late-night, summer, and weekend assaults.

SCT views longer time periods and historical epochs as contributing to the background context in which crime events occur. The prevalence of CSA changes very gradually over time (Sedlak and Broadhurst 1996), and the characteristics of offenders, victims, contexts, and modus operandi change even more slowly. Although some research suggests that when interpersonal crimes become commonplace, they are processed in a more informal, routinized, or administrative manner in the justice system (Spohn, Beichner, and Davis-Frenzel, 2001; Wooldredge and Thistlewaite 2004), CSA is a relatively rare offense and is not subject to these patterns. It is possible that crimes that are rare in a broad sense might become commonplace in particular deviant subcultures, changing the perception of their commonality and normalcy among members of that subculture. However, subcultural explanations do not fit well with the situation of clergy-involved CSA. The public does not consider CSA to be anything other than an extremely rare occurrence (Olafson, Corwin, and Summit 1993). Terry and associates (2011) report that in the Catholic Church, victims, offenders, church authorities, parishioners, and members of the community at large were unaware of the prevalence and consequences of CSA until at least the 1980s, quite some time after acts of CSA committed by priests had reached their highest rate in the United States. When these events were most common, the principal actors in the Church considered the crime to be exceptional: each victim believed that his or her suffering was an experience that no one else had had; guardians made no effort to protect children from representatives of the church; and authorities considered the rare detected offender to be driven by some individual pathology, rather than some larger institutional or societal influence. The Church apparently did not believe that the offense warranted a Church-wide reaction and preventative response until 1985.

In discussing CSA among Catholic priests, Terry and associates (2011) assert that the abuse of children by Catholic priests in the United States was temporally influenced, becoming most prevalent during the 1960s and 1970s, a distinctive period of questioning, conflict, and rapid social change in America and other Western industrialized nations. According to their data, CSA was uncommon in the Church prior to this period, and there were few institutional controls in place. Once Church authorities became aware of CSA among their priests, efforts were made to control the problem, albeit with some early denial and delay in action. As the result of better training, Church declarations, changes in policy about the oversight of children in church activities, and increased socialization of church members and the general public, the prevalence of priestly CSA has diminished greatly. Interestingly, many of the vulnerabilities (Terry et al. 2011, 54) noted earlier that distinguish offending priests existed among priests prior to the 1960s and 1970s. Nevertheless, the researchers conclude that these at-risk clergy members were catapulted into deviant sex acts because of the questioning of social values and higher rates of crime and substance abuse in the world in which the offenders found themselves. One problem with this argument is that, even among the most politically active groups of the time, there was no serious social movement intended to promote the sexual abuse of children. There is little doubt that traditional roles and authority structures were under assault during this time, but this general questioning of social values did not extend to the sexual violation of children.

Terry and associates could be correct in their interpretation that the historical and temporal combination of societal risk and weak institutional controls caused the dramatic increase in CSA within the Catholic Church. Another possible explanation is that clergy-involved sex offenses were quite prevalent at earlier times, but that the victims did not enter adulthood at a time of growing awareness and sensitivity about victimization. The growing social conscience of those who were children and adolescents in the 1960s and 1970s, coupled with the emergence of media reports in the early 2000s concerning extreme cases of CSA in the Church, could have motivated victims from the 1960s and 1970s to report abuse, albeit decades after it had ended. Those abused prior to this time might not have reported that fact because they had died or were not motivated to publicly disclose their victimization.

Precipitants of Clergy-Involved Child Sexual Abuse

It is important to distinguish between contextual risk factors, predisposing traits, and situational precipitants to crime. Contextual risk factors are characteristics of the environment that influence the likelihood of criminal events at that location, while the actor's predisposing traits transcend particular environments. These can change or be changed over time, but they do not influence the occurrence of a criminal event independent of the interaction between the principal actors within that environment. A precipitant provides the stimulus to the criminal event at a particular point in time (Pervin 1978). Potential offenders and victims may find themselves in an environment conducive to crime, but no criminal event occurs if they lack a stimulus to motivate them to initiate the crime. Most discussions of criminal stimuli assume that they are spontaneous and unintentional in nature, and that they quickly change the offender's motivation and his or her assessment of the situation.

Precipitants vary in nature from the slightest and most unintentional contextual change or action on the part of the victim or guardian to intentional and overt manipulations of the environment by offenders. Routine activities theory suggests that offenders are rational in their decision making, and that most people who engage in interpersonal violence do so when they are triggered by what they see as an unjustified or overwhelming provocation to act (Katz 1990).[4] However, precipitants influence the emotional state of the criminal event's actors. Researchers have characterized the thought processes of those who are emotionally agitated as a state of "hot cognition," in which their ability to weigh other stimuli, preexisting values, and the consequences of their action in a rational manner are diminished by the emotions they are experiencing (Roisier et al. 2009; Thagard 2006). For example, some rape episodes result from what the rapist defines as unfair treatment, ridicule, or lascivious conduct on the part of the victim (Scully and Marolla 1984). Clerics who sexually offend against children might believe that the victim has acted in a provocative way or at least has indicated a willingness to participate in sexual activities. What amounts to an unmanageable level of provocation or enticement varies between people, but some behaviors violate consensus values and are beyond the range of acceptable deviation from societal norms (Edwards 2006).

Extreme acts of deviance such as CSA are not excused by the law. While the court makes some provision for provocation, it does not fully exonerate offenders unless provocation can be successfully used as a legal justification or defense. Sexual contact with a child is a crime, regardless of any claims of provocation or complicity in the act, since the criminal law views children as incapable of understanding the consequences of engaging in sexual activities with an adult. Since most child victims of clergy offenders have been groomed over a long period of time, any indication of complicity is likely the result of the cleric's manipulative behavior.

Crimes are also precipitated when conditions develop that otherwise diminish the offender's judgment and self-control (Gottfredson and Hirschi 1990) or the victim's ability to defend him- or herself. Being under the influence of alcohol or psychoactive drugs is the most widely recognized acute dynamic risk factor influencing the sex offender's inhibitions and appreciation for the consequences of his or her actions beyond the immediate situation (Johnson 2007). Furthermore, alcohol consumption may lead the offender to misinterpret the behaviors of others (Lang 1993) and overreact in situations where the offender feels provoked (Pliner and Cappell 1974). Excessive alcohol consumption is mentioned by Terry and associates (2011) as a vulnerability of Catholic priests who offended against children during the 1960s and 1970s.

Terry and associates (2011) also regard alcohol consumption as a situational precipitant: in many instances the priest offender and child victim consumed alcohol immediately before commencing sexual activity. In this sense, the precipitant has been intentionally introduced into the situation by the offender. Interestingly, research has shown that drinking is related to interpersonal aggression only among people who anticipate that consumption will lead to aggression (Derman and George 1988; Leonard and Senchak 1993). This suggests that one way situational alcohol consumption precipitates CSA is as a form of self-fulfilling prophecy: clergy who are motivated to sexually abuse a child will introduce alcohol into the situation with the expectation that they will act on their intentions. Johnson (2007) asserts that offenders consume alcohol because they know they will lose self-control in the situation and allow themselves to do what they wanted to do—in this instance, sexually abuse a child. Another way in which drinking precipitates interpersonal violence is that it allows offenders to disavow their deviant actions (Abbey 1991; Collins 1981; Fagan 1990). Deviance disavowal can manifest in a number of ways. Offenders might say that they blacked out during the sex crime episode, and thus they cannot be fully to blame for their behavior (Johnson 2007). Terry and associates (2011) indicate that Catholic priest offenders assert that they are not truly evil persons; they just have a problem with alcohol, which they consider to be a disease outside of their personal control.

Conclusion

Miethe and Meier explain the importance of the situational crime perspective when they assert that:

> Any adequate theory of crime must account for the convergence in time and space of motivated offenders and potential crime targets. The value of theories of victimization is in their recognition of how the routine activities of everyday life create the supply of opportunities, whereas traditional theories of criminality identify the factors that trigger offender motivation. The particular situational context is where the union of motivated offenders and criminal opportunities takes place. (1994, 179)

This chapter briefly described clergy-involved CSA as the result of the complex interaction between actors and their environment. From a situational crime perspective, clergy offenders use their institutionally conferred status and authority and the performance of the routine activities associated with their clerical role to access child victims, gain their confidence and that of the children's family members and other guardians, and thus become able to groom the child over a relatively long period of time. Clerics who are vulnerable to committing acts of CSA scheme to place themselves in a private environment that they control, at least on a temporary basis, but they are not likely to implement their abuse strategy until precipitated to do so. Those who are inclined to do so initiate their sexual abuse plan when they are stimulated to do so in a protected environment, and when their inhibitions have been suppressed by psychoactive substances or a constructed rationale sufficient to enable them to disavow their deviant behavior. Once initiated, the clergy offender's CSA plan is subject to his or her interpretation of the situation. Offenders' judgment of the environment and their interactions with the child are likely to become increasingly distorted as their emotions are heightened. Still, an element of rational self-preservation and control might remain to alert even the most motivated offender to suspend his or her plan at a point of plausible deniability if confronted with resistance from the child or unexpected changes in the environment. Thus, episodes of CSA involving clerics are contingent on the unfolding interaction between the offender and the child victim.

Traditional efforts to control clergy-involved CSA have been based on dispositional theories of crime that attempt to identify and normalize psychological traits and behavioral differences that identify those at risk for committing sexual offenses. Some proactive efforts to reduce clerical stress and social isolation have resembled job training and restructuring. For example, as a form of primary prevention, the US Conference of Catholic Bishops (2001) disseminated *The Basic Plan for the Formation of Priests*, intended to ease men's transition into clerical roles and reduce the stresses related to them. Reactive dispositional tactics have included various forms of psychological, spiritual, and substance abuse therapy. Changing offender traits and vulnerabilities through cognitive-behavioral and substance abuse treatments has proved effective in reducing the likelihood of sexual reoffending (Hanson and Morton-Bourgon 2004). Historically, reactive therapies have been pursued in private, which may serve the religious order's specific intention of rehabilitating the offender and general aim of maintaining institutional legitimacy and boundary control, but which has left the organization vulnerable to the condemnation of its members and the general public. In a practical sense, dispositional approaches alone are likely to fail in controlling clergy-involved CSA because the offenders are difficult to identify and deter from their criminal behavior.

A number of approaches to prevent clergy-involved CSA can be derived from the situational crime perspective (Wortley and Smallbone 2006). Among these are efforts to sensitize potential child victims to inappropriate grooming activities and to encourage them to tell their guardians when they experience these acts. One example of this strategy is the adaptation of the well-known Good Touch–Bad Touch curriculum by the Catholic archdiocese of Evansville, Indiana (M. Sampson 2011). Another approach is to eliminate private encounters in places where CSA might occur by requiring that at least one other adult observe or participate in any child-clergy interactions at that location. Improving safety in schools, places of worship, and other institutional environments through increased surveillance is another prevention approach suggested by SCT. Environmental redesign, the use of electronic surveillance technologies, and training of place managers can improve the safety of children in locations where clerics might engage in sexual abuse or inappropriate pre-abuse behaviors. As a final example, policies that ban alcoholic beverages in locations where clergy and children interact with each other could limit the precipitation of CSA episodes.

In conclusion, dispositional approaches have little primary preventive value with a population of clergy sex offenders, because most of them engage in CSA with only one child victim and are only identified after the crime has occurred (Terry et al. 2011). Although effective treatment approaches for all sex offenders should be supported and encouraged, a balanced plan of situational risk reduction offers our best hope for preventing clergy-involved CSA. Improving the awareness of the possibility of the abuse, teaching children to understand the meaning and risk associated with interactions intended to groom them for victimization, improving environmental safety, and restricting situational precipitants should form the foundation of our efforts to control clergy-involved CSA in the United States.

Notes

1. In contrast, acute dynamic risk factors are those of a more immediate, situational nature (Witt and Schnieder 2005).

2. Exceptions include crimes of conspiracy, which are not usually related to sexual offenses.

3. This is the case as long as the means of intervention does not violate a conduct norm of some other institution. For example, punishing a sinner by permanent physical injury or death is not allowed in the United States, as it would constitute a violation of the government's exclusive right to punish.

4. Nonrational criminal offenders present a different situation: for these rare individuals, the mere possibility of engaging in the criminal act is a sufficient precipitant to

result in a criminal outcome. For example, the only motivation to act that an obsessed sex offender needs is to be aware of and have access to a potential victim.

References

Abbey, A. 1991. "Acquaintance Rape and Alcohol Consumption on College Campuses: How Are They Linked?" *Journal of American College Health* 39:165–69.

Anderson, R., and P. Davidson. 2001. "Improving Access to Health Care in America: Individual and Contextual Indicators." In *Changing the U.S. Health Care System: Key Issues in Health Services, Policy and Management*, edited by R. Anderson, T. Rice, and J. Kominski, 3–30. San Francisco: Jossey-Bass.

———, et al. 2002. "Access to Medical Care for Low-Income Persons: How Do Communities Make a Difference?" *Medical Care Research and Review* 59 (4): 384–411.

Averill, J. 1982. *Anger and Aggression: An Essay on Emotion*. New York: Springer-Verlag.

Bahr, H., and B. Chadwick. 1985. "Religion and Family in Middletown, USA." *Journal of Marriage and Family* 47 (2): 407–14.

Barton, B. 2012. *Pray the Gay Away: The Extraordinary Lives of Bible-belt Gays*. New York: New York University Press.

Birkbeck, C., and G. LaFree. 1993. "The Situational Analysis of Crime and Deviance." *Annual Review of Sociology* 19: 113–37.

Bland, M. 2001. "The Psychological and Spiritual Effects of Child Sexual Abuse When the Perpetrator Is a Catholic Priest." PhD diss., Chicago School of Professional Psychology.

Bolton, F., L. Morris, and A. MacEachron. 1989. *Males at Risk: The Other Side of Child Sexual Abuse*. Beverly Hills, CA: Sage.

Brantingham, P., and P. Brantingham. 1984. *Patterns in Crime*. New York: Macmillan.

———. 1991. *Environmental Criminology*. Prospect Heights, IL: Waveland.

Browne, A. 1991. "The Victim's Experience: Pathways to Disclosure." *Psychotherapy: Theory, Research, Practice, Training* 28 (5): 150–56.

Brunet, J. 2002. "Discouragement of Crime through Civil Remedies: An Application of a Reformulated Routine Activities Theory." *Western Criminology Review* 4 (1): 68–79.

Buss, A. 1963. "Physical Aggression in Relation to Different Frustrations." *Journal of Abnormal Psychology* 67 (1): 1–7.

Call, V., and T. Heaton. 1997. "Religious Influence on Marital Stability." *Journal for the Scientific Study of Religion* 36 (3): 382–92.

Canter, D., D. Hughes, and S. Kirby. 1998. "Paedophilia: Pathology, Criminality, or Both? The Development of a Multivariate Model of Offence Behaviour in Child Sexual Abuse." *Journal of Forensic Psychiatry* 9 (3): 532–55.

Cohen, L., and M. Felson. 1979. "Social Change and Crime Rate Trends: A Routine Activity Approach." *American Sociological Review* 44 (5): 588–608.

Collings, S. 1995. "The Long-Term Effects of Contact and Noncontact Forms of Child Sexual Abuse in a Sample of College Men." *Child Abuse and Neglect* 19 (1): 1–6.

Collins, J. 1981. "Alcohol Use and Criminal Behavior: An Empirical, Theoretical, and Methodological Overview. In *Drinking and Crime: Perspectives on the Relationship between Alcohol Consumption and Criminal Behavior*, edited by J. Collins and M. Wolfgang, 288–338. New York: Guilford.

Conte, J., S. Wolf, and T. Smith. 1989. "What Sexual Offenders Tell Us about Prevention Strategies." *Child Abuse and Neglect* 13 (2): 293–301.

Craven, S., A. Brown, and E. Gilchrist. 2006. "Sexual Grooming of Children: Review of Literature and Theoretical Considerations." *Journal of Sexual Aggression* 12 (3): 287–99.

Davidson, R. 1989. "Micro-Environments of Violence." In *The Geography of Crime*, edited by D. Evans and D. Herbert, 59–85. New York: Routledge.

Derman, K., and W. George. 1988. "Alcohol Expectancy and the Relationship between Drinking and Physical Aggression." *Journal of Psychology* 123 (2): 153–61.

Dimock, P. 1988. "Adult Males Sexually Abused as Children." *Journal of Interpersonal Violence* 3 (2): 203–21.

Dorris, B. 2011. "Clergy Sex Victims Want Dallas Episcopal Shake-Up." SNAP: Survivors Network of those Abused by Priests. http://www.snapnetwork.org.

Doyle, T. 2007. "Clericalism and Catholic Clergy Sexual Abuse." In *Silenced Victims: The Sexual Abuse Crisis and the Catholic Church*, edited by M. Frawley-O'Dea and V. Goldner, 147–62. Mahwah, NJ: Analytic.

Durham, A. 2003. *Young Men Surviving Child Sexual Abuse: Research Stories and Lessons for Therapeutic Practice*. Somerset, NJ: Wiley.

Eck, J., et al. 2005. *Mapping Crime: Understanding Hotspots*. Washington: Department of Justice, National Institute of Justice.

Edgarth, K., and K. Ormstad. 2000. "Prevalence and Characteristics of Sexual Abuse in a National Sample of Swedish Seventeen-Year-Old Boys and Girls." *Acta Paediatrica* 88 (3): 310–19.

Edwards, M. 2006. "Law and the Parameters of Acceptable Deviance." *Journal of Criminal Law and Criminology* 97 (1): 49–100.

Fagan, J. 1990. "Intoxication and Aggression." In *Drugs and Crime*, edited by M. Tonry and J. Wilson, 241–320. Chicago: University of Chicago Press.

Falkenhain, M. 1997. "Child Sexual Abusers among Roman Catholic Priests and Brothers: A Cluster Analytic Study." PhD diss., St. Louis University.

Fater, K., and J. Mullaney. 2000. "The Lived Experience of Adult Male Survivors Who Allege Childhood Sexual Abuse by Clergy." *Issues in Mental Health Nursing* 21 (2): 281–95.

Felson, M. 1995. "Those Who Discourage Crime." In *Crime and Place*, edited by J. Eck and D. Weisburd, 53–66. Monsey, NY: Criminal Justice.

Finkelhor, D. 1994. "Current Information on the Scope and Nature of Child Sexual Abuse." *Future of Children* 4 (2): 31, 46–48.

———. 2008. *Childhood Victimization: Violence, Crime, and Abuse in the Lives of Young People*. New York: Oxford University Press.

Finkelhor, D., G. Hotaling, I. Lewis, and C. Smith. 1990. "Sexual Abuse in a National Survey of Adult Men and Women: Prevalence, Characteristics and Risk Factors." *Child Abuse and Neglect* 14 (1): 19–28.

Furnham, A., and M. Argyle. 1981. Introduction to *The Psychology of Social Situations*, edited by A. Furnham and M. Argyle, xiii–lvi. Oxford: Pergamon.

Gagnon, J., and W. Simon. 1967. *Sexual Deviance*. New York: Harper and Row.

Gottfredson, M., and T. Hirschi. 1990. *A General Theory of Crime*. Palo Alto, CA: Stanford University Press.

Hanson, R., and A. J. R. Harris. 2000. "Where Should We Intervene? Dynamic Predictors of Sexual Offense Recidivism." *Criminal Justice and Behavior* 27 (1): 6–35.

Hanson, R., and K. Morton-Bourgon. 2004. *Predictors of Sexual Recidivism: An Updated Meta-Analysis*. Ottawa: Public Works and Government Services Canada.

Hanson, R., E. Pfafflin, and M. Lutz, eds. 2004. *Sexual Abuse in the Catholic Church: Scientific and Legal Perspectives*. Rome: Liberia Editrice Vaticana.

Hershkowitz, I., D. Horowitz, and M. Lamb. 2007. "Individual and Family Variables Associated with Disclosure and Nondisclosure of Child Abuse in Israel." In *Child Sexual Abuse: Disclosure, Delay, and Denial*, edited by M. Pipe, M. Lamb, Y. Orbach, and A. Cederborg, 63–76. Mahwah, NJ: Lawrence Erlbaum Associates.

Haywood, T.W., et al. 1996. "Cycle of Abuse and Psychopathology in Cleric and Non-Cleric Molesters of Children and Adolescents." *Child Abuse and Neglect* 20:1233–43.

Holmes, G., L. Offen, and G. Waller. 1997. "See No Evil, Hear No Evil, Speak No Evil: Why Do Relatively Few Male Victims of Childhood Sexual Abuse Receive Help for Abuse-Related Issues in Adulthood?" *Clinical Psychological Review* 12 (1): 69–88.

John Jay College. 2004. *The Nature and Scope of Sexual Abuse of Minors by Catholic Priests and Deacons in the United States, 1950–2002*. Washington: US Conference of Catholic Bishops.

Johnson, S. 2007. *Physical Abusers and Sexual Offenders: Forensic and Clinical Strategies*. New York: Taylor and Francis.

Katz, J. 1990. *Seductions of Crime: Moral and Sensual Attractions in Doing Evil*. New York: Basic.

Kennedy, E., and V. Heckler. 1972. *The Catholic Priest in the United States: Psychological Investigations*. Washington: US Catholic Conference.

Kirby, J. B. 2008. "Poor People, Poor Places and Access to Health Care in the United States." *Social Forces* 87 (1): 325–55.

Koenig, H., D. King, and V. Carson. 2012. *Handbook of Religion and Health*. 2nd ed. New York: Oxford University Press.

Lang, A. 1993. "Alcohol-Related Violence: Psychological Perspectives." In *Alcohol and Interpersonal Violence: Fostering Multidisciplinary Perspectives*, edited by S. Martin, 121–48. Rockville, MD: National Institutes of Health.

Langevin, R., S. Curnoe, and J. Bain. 2000. "A Study of Clerics Who Commit Sexual Offenses: Are They Different from Other Sex Offenders?" *Child Abuse and Neglect* 24 (4): 535–45.

Leonard, K., and M. Senchak. 1993. "Alcohol and Premarital Aggression among Newlywed Couples." *Journal of Studies on Alcohol* (Supplement 11):96–108.

Lynch, J. 1987. "Routine Activity and Victimization at Work." *Journal of Quantitative Criminology* 3 (4): 283–300.

Lyon, T., and E. Ahern. 2011. "Disclosure of Child Sexual Abuse: Implications for Interviewing." In *The APSAC Handbook on Child Maltreatment*, 3rd ed., edited by J. Myers, 233–52. Thousand Oaks, CA: Sage.

MacNamara, P. 1992. *Conscience First, Tradition Second: A Study of Young American Catholics*. Albany: State University of New York Press.

Magnusson, D. 1981. "Wanted: A Psychology of Situations." In *Toward a Psychology of Situations: An Interactionist Perspective*, edited by D. Magnusson, 9–32. Hillsdale, NJ: Lawrence Erlbaum Associates.

Miethe, T., and R. Meier. 1994. *Crime and Its Social Context: Toward an Integrated Theory of Offenders, Victims, and Situations*. Albany: State University of New York Press.

Mills, A. 1993. "Helping Male Victims of Sexual Abuse." *Nursing Standard* 7 (1): 36–39.

Nason-Clark, N. 1998. "The Impact of Abuses of Clergy Trust on Female Congregants' Faith and Practice." In *Wolves within the Fold: Religious Leadership and Abuses of Power*, edited by A. Shupe, 85–100. New Brunswick, NJ: Rutgers University Press.

Olafson, E., D. Corwin, and R. Summit. 1993. "Modern History of Child Sexual Abuse Awareness: Cycles of Discovery and Suppression." *Child Abuse and Neglect* 17 (1): 7–24.

Parkinson, P., K. Oates, and A. Jayakody. 2012. " Child Sexual Abuse in the Anglican Church of Australia." *Journal of Child Sexual Abuse* 21 (5): 553–70.

Pervin, L. 1978. "Definitions, Measurements, and Classifications of Stimuli, Situations, and Environments." *Human Ecology* 6 (1): 71–105.

Petronio, S., H. Reeder, M. Hecht, and T. Ros-Mendoza. 1996. "Disclosure of Sexual Abuse by Children and Adolescents." *Journal of Applied Communications Research* 24 (3): 191–99.

Plante, T. 2007. "Homosexual Applicants to the Priesthood: How Many and Are They Psychologically Healthy?" *Pastoral Psychology* 55 (4): 495–98.

Plante, T., and A. Aldridge. 2005 "Psychological Patterns among Roman Catholic Clergy Accused of Sexual Misconduct." *Pastoral Psychology* 54 (1): 73–80.

Plante, T., G. Manuel, and C. Bryant. 1996. "Personality and Cognitive Functioning among Hospitalized Sexual Offending Roman Catholic Priests." *Pastoral Psychology* 45 (1): 129–39.

Pliner, P., and H. Cappell. 1974. "Modification of Affective Consequences of Alcohol: A Comparison of Social and Solitary Drinking." *Journal of Abnormal Psychology* 83 (4): 418–25.

Priebe, G., and C. Svedin. 2008. "Child Sexual Abuse Is Largely Hidden from the Adult Society: An Epidemiological Study of Adolescents' Disclosures." *Child Abuse and Neglect* 32 (12): 1095–108.

Prochaska, J., and C. DiClemente. 1982. "Transtheoretical Therapy: Toward a More Integrative Model of Change." *Psychotherapy: Theory, Research, and Practice* 19 (3): 276–88.

Roesler, T., and N. MacKenzie. 1994. "Effects of Childhood Trauma on Psychological Functioning in Adults Sexually Abused as Children." *Journal of Nervous and Mental Disease* 182 (2): 145–50.

Roiser, J., et al. 2009. "Hot and Cold Cognition in Unmedicated Depressed Subjects with Bipolar Disorder. *Bipolar Disorder* 11 (2): 178–89.

Rosetti, S. J. 1997. "The Effects of Priest-Perpetration of Child Sexual Abuse on the Trust of Catholics in Priesthood, Church, and God." *Journal of Psychology and Christianity* 16 (2): 197–209.

Sampson, M. 2011. *Good Touch/Bad Touch: How to Tell the Difference, Pre-K through Third Grade.* http://www.evansville-diocese.org.

Sampson, R. J., and W. B. Groves. 1989. "Community Structure and Crime: Testing Social Disorganization Theory." *American Journal of Sociology* 94 (4): 774–802.

Scully, D., and M. Marolla. 1984. "Convicted Rapists' Vocabulary of Motive: Excuses and Justifications." *Social Problems* 31 (5): 530–44.

Sedlak, A., and D. Broadhurst. 1996. *Third National Incidence Study of Child Abuse and Neglect (NIS-3).* Washington: Department of Health and Human Services, National Center on Child Abuse and Neglect.

Sedlak, A., et al. 2010. *Fourth National Incidence Study of Child Abuse and Neglect (NIS–4): Report to Congress.* Washington: Department of Health and Human Services, Administration for Children and Families.

Smallbone, S., and R. Wortley. 2001. *Child Sexual Abuse: Offender Characteristics and Modus Operandi.* Canberra: Australian Institute of Criminology.

Spiegel, J. 2003. *Sexual Abuse of Males: The SAM Model of Theory and Practice.* New York: Brunner-Routledge.

Spohn, C., D. Beichner, and E. Davis-Frenzel. 2001. "Prosecutorial Justifications for Sexual Assault Case Rejection: Guarding the 'Gateway to Justice.'" *Social Problems* 48 (2): 206–35.

Staller, K., and D. Nelson-Gardell. 2005. "A Burden in Your Heart: Lessons of Disclosure from Female Preadolescent and Adolescent Survivors of Sexual Abuse." *Child Abuse and Neglect* 29 (12): 1415–32.

Stebbins, R. 1972. "Studying the Definition of the Situation: Theory and Field Research Strategies." In *Symbolic Interaction: A Reader*, edited by J. Manis and N. Meltzer, 337–55. Boston: Allyn and Bacon.

Steele, P. 2004. *Assessment of One-by-One: A Safe Kids/Safe Streets Initiative in*

Huntsville, Alabama. Washington: Department of Justice, Office of Juvenile Justice and Delinquency Prevention.

———. 2008. "Responding to Child Sexual Abuse in the United States: Facing Challenges in the Civil and Criminal Justice Systems." *Forum on Public Policy* 4 (3): 41–57.

———. 2009. "Child Abuse among Marginalized Groups: Cultural and Governmental Influences on the Perpetration of Sexual Maltreatment in American Indian Country." *Forum on Public Policy* 5 (1): 1–33.

Sutherland, E. 1947. *Principles of Criminology*. Philadelphia: J. B. Lippincott.

Teram, E., et al. 2006. "Towards Malecentric Communication: Sensitizing Health Professionals to the Realities of Male Childhood Sexual Abuse Survivors." *Issues in Mental Health Nursing* 27 (5): 499–517.

Sykes, G., and D. Matza. 1957. "Techniques of Neutralization: A Theory of Delinquency." *American Sociological Review* 22 (5): 664–70.

Terry, K. J., et al. 2011. *The Causes and Context of Sexual Abuse of Minors by Catholic Priests in the United States, 1950–2010*. Washington: US Conference of Catholic Bishops.

Thagard, P. 2006. *Hot Thought: Mechanisms and Applications of Emotional Cognition*. Cambridge: MIT Press.

Trice, H. M., and W. J. Sonnenstuhl. 1988. "Drinking Behavior and Risk Factors Related to the Work Place: Implications for Research and Prevention." *Journal of Applied Behavioral Science* 24 (4): 327–46.

US Conference of Catholic Bishops. 2001. *The Basic Plan for the Formation of Priests*. Washington: US Conference of Catholic Bishops.

Ward, T., and R. Siegert. 2002. "Toward a Comprehensive Theory of Child Sexual Abuse: A Theory Knitting Perspective." *Psychology, Crime, and Law* 8 (4): 319–51.

Watkins, B., and A. Bentovim. 1992. "The Sexual Abuse of Male Children and Adolescents: A Review of Current Research." *Journal of Child Psychology and Psychiatry* 33 (2): 197–248.

Witt, P., and J. Schnieder. 2005. "Managing Sex Offenders by Assessing Dynamic Risk Factors." *Sex Offender Law Report* 6:49, 54–57.

Wooldredge, J., and A. Thistlewaite. 2004. "Bilevel Disparities in Court Dispositions for Intimate Assault." *Criminology* 42 (2): 417–56.

Wortley, R., and S. Smallbone. 2006. "Applying Situational Principles to Sexual Offenses against Children." In *Situational Prevention of Child Sexual Abuse*, edited by R. Wortley and S. Smallbone, 7–35. Monsey, NY: Criminal Justice.

Sandra Yocum

5 The Priest and Catholic Culture as Symbolic System of Purity

The priest remains an anomalous figure of spiritual authority even in a culture as religiously pluralist as US society and, perhaps surprising to some, even in his own Roman Catholic world. His lack of attachment to any particular household makes him available to every person and to the broader community. What separates him from other males in the social order is his sacred vow to remain celibate, and his celibacy is tightly intertwined with his unique spiritual powers: changing bread and wine into the body and blood of Christ and forgiving an individual's sins through the rite of confession—or, in contemporary Catholic parlance, the rite of reconciliation. Because of these particular spiritual powers, the priest's designated role is as mediator of the divine, which makes him an object of fascination and suspicion, of devotion and danger. One begins to understand how the priest may be viewed simultaneously with deep fear and deep trust because of his access to a power that ostensibly brings God's life into one's very body and soul. What follows in this chapter offers little in the way of an explanation of why some of these men sexually abuse children. Nor is the particular focus on the priest's distinctive vow to be construed as identifying celibacy as the principal cause of sexual abuse. Rather, the focus here is on the priest's close identification with access to the divine within the complex social and cultural systems that Catholics inhabit and how that identification affects responses to clerical sexual abuse.

The chapter will examine the priest's symbolic role within the Catholic cultural system using Mary Douglas's classic analysis of cultural systems of purity and danger. The analysis begins with a brief overview of Douglas's description of culture in terms of systems of purity. The next section presents common descriptions of the priest as divine representative found in the widely used Catholic textbook, the *Baltimore Catechism*, descriptions that are reinforced in religious ritual and the Catholic subculture. In the third section, the discussion turns to the continuities and changes in the descriptions and ritual roles of the priest after major changes in Catholic culture around 1965. Using the framework of "purity and danger" may seem out of place in discussing the religious beliefs of people whose lives began in the mid-twentieth century or later. Rarely would Catholics think about their religious traditions or the priest in the stark terms of purity and danger. Yet the Catholic enactment of faith through sacramental practices directly involves human bodies touching, washing, eating, drinking, and speaking and hearing intimate secrets. The contact is highly controlled through the ritual form, with participants either seeking or claiming worthiness to participate. Taken together, the Catholic ritual life bears many characteristics of the symbolic systems of purity that Douglas examines.

Let me be very clear from the beginning. What follows is neither a defense of the symbolic system or of the priest's role as depicted here, nor is it a reductive claim about the mere functionality of sacred ritual or contemporary Catholics' collapse of the identity of the priest with that of the divine—that is, God. Effective symbolic systems of purity mediate meanings in far more subtle and complex ways. They point indirectly through signs and symbols to the deeper values and beliefs that escape articulation in plain terms. The power of these signs and symbols and of the one who enacts them through rituals lies in their subtleties, their indirectness. In what follows, I want to bring into focus the truly unique conception of the priest within Catholic culture. My hope in doing so is to shed some light on the absolute depth of the destabilizing impact that sexual abuse perpetrated by Catholic priests has on their victims, the victims' immediate community of believers, and the wider community of both believers and skeptics.

Mary Douglas's Analysis of Systems of Purity

To aid in analyzing the symbolic force of the priest in US culture, this chapter borrows analytical insights from Douglas's *Purity and Danger: An Analysis of Concepts of Pollution and Taboo* (1966). Approaching its fiftieth anniversary of publication, her structural analysis admittedly shows its age and is not free from controversy. Still, the usefulness of that analysis persists, at least in examining the cultural context that shapes perceptions of and responses to Catholic clergy as perpetrators of sexual abuse. Douglas provides a lens through which one can more easily see the contours of Catholicism as a culture. Her own Catholic upbringing may help explain her attentiveness to factors particularly relevant here: the enduring force of rituals and spiritual authority in establishing or at least reinforcing a culture's "basic categories, a positive pattern in which ideas and values are tidily ordered" (1966, 52). "Symbolic systems of purity" play critical roles in maintaining that tidy order (48).

Douglas identifies undercurrents that she must navigate to avoid the pull toward reducing purity laws to mere magic or superstition or to a primitive person's confusion of good hygiene with authentic spirituality. These undercurrents are relevant to this chapter's focus on the symbolic system in which the Catholic priest plays a significant role. Douglas asserts that "an emotional and prejudiced approach to ritual has led anthropology down one of its barrenest perspectives—a narrow preoccupation with belief" (1966, 30). This point is critical in this context in two ways. First, those who share the "emotional and prejudiced approach to ritual" may simply ignore the powerful symbolic significance of the priest as the carrier of ritual meaning within a thoroughly modern Catholic's experience of religious faith. Second, those who identify Catholicism with disembodied belief may lack the understanding necessary to attend to the depth of the internal conflict that a priest's sexual misconduct precipitates in those who have found their life's meaning through Catholic ritual.

Douglas provides additional insights into the ways in which the contemporary situation masks the ongoing force of ritual. People who live in modern societies negotiate multiple cultural systems. The multiplicity alone obscures the profound influences that "symbolic systems of purity" continue to have, and a person's engagement in any particular symbolic system is usually more fragmentary than in a less diversified social order, such as those more geographically bounded tribal communities that were the traditional object of anthropologists' study. Fragmentation also reinforces the assumption that the true essence of religion resides in the interior, as a private matter associated with an individual's discrete system of personal beliefs. The contemporary emphasis on religious experience as primarily individual and interior draws attention away from the ongoing power of communal and external dimensions in a Catholic's faith expressed through rituals.

The Catholic Church possesses many elements of a self-sufficient social system that makes possible its endurance as a culture. It has its own highly bureaucratized, governing body known as "the hierarchy": the pope, archbishops, and bishops, who operate within their own system of law, called canon law. This social system can be mapped geographically onto every nation in the world by virtue of its political structure. Its head, the pope, oversees an independent territory, Vatican City; he also serves as the bishop of Rome, a city of enormous symbolic significance in the West. The pope, as the first among the bishops, appoints other bishops to oversee the church in dioceses throughout the world. Dioceses are specific geographical areas whose boundaries are determined under the Vatican bureaucracy's guidance, though they usually reflect the territorial contours of a particular region's social and political order. Each diocese is divided into parishes, and parishes in turn are usually defined as geographical areas with clear territorial boundaries. Priests bring the church's symbolic system, its life of faith, into the parish in the name of the bishop. "The Church" in its fullness exists in each of these locales through the physical presence of these ordained men.

In the United States, where religious movements are free to organize themselves within the wide boundaries of civil law, the Catholic Church remains distinctive precisely because of its elaborate and quite visible transnational social and political structure. Returning to Douglas's discourse on "purity and danger," her description of culture includes elements particularly helpful for recognizing how this highly organized social structure generates and sustains its culture through ritual. She explains: "Any culture is a series of related structures which comprise social forms, values, cosmology, the whole of knowledge and through which all experience is mediated. . . . The rituals enact the form of social relations and in giving these relations visible expression they enable people to know their society. The rituals work upon the body politic through the symbolic medium of the physical body" (1966, 153). Catholicism exemplifies all the elements of culture as described here.

Catholics understand themselves as bound to all other Catholics in a community that mediates the divine through rituals—that is, sacraments, particularly baptism, communion, and reconciliation. Priests are the principal enactors of those rituals, which visibly express the nature of the Catholic community. The sacramental enactment of Catholic culture draws its powerful formative influence through "the symbolic medium of the physical body." The priest's symbolic force is deeply embedded in the association of his consecrated body with the body of Christ that is made manifest in the consecration of bread and wine and in the body of Christ, a frequently used image to describe the visible Church's hierarchically structured community. The priest's vow of celibacy serves as the sign of his dedication to God through his self-sacrifice, and his physical purity testifies to his worthiness to consecrate bread and wine so that it can become the sacrament—a visible sign—of the body and blood of Jesus Christ. The priest's parishioners have access to the sacred meal through his power to absolve their sins, and that absolution in the sacrament of confession purifies them and makes them worthy to consume the bread and wine that the priest alone has the power to transform.

This intertwining of the priest's commitment to purity and his mediation of God's relationship to the Catholic faithful brings into focus how the Catholic world functions as a symbolic system in which purity plays a major role. Those who lack a sacramental relationship with the priest remain outside the community's boundary and, in effect, are cut off from the intimate access to the communal participation with the divine that the priest offers through the rituals of baptism, communion, and confession. Catholics are for the most part not particularly conscious of this "series of structured relationships" (Douglas 1966, 153) unless something threatens the structure of their religious world. Sexual abuse perpetrated by those who are supposed to be the carriers of purity threatens the very foundation of this structure. The depth of the threat helps to explain the vitriol generated in response to the current spate of Catholic clerical abuse. Reactions concerning the guilt of Catholic priests seem to exceed the reaction to other functionaries accused of sexual abuse, such as coaches, leaders of scout groups, and even other Christian ministers. On the one hand are those who vehemently deny the seriousness of the situation, either by accusing the media of persecution or reducing the problem to one of a few bad apples. On the other hand are those who suspect all priests as potential perpetrators, regardless of the evidence. Both of these reactions assume the priest's singular importance in the mediation of the divine within Catholicism's symbolic system of purity. His fall from purity seems to implicate the whole system.

The Priest as Representative of Christ

Understanding the priest as the mediator of the divine, the representative of Christ, was commonplace in the religious instruction of Catholics who grew up in the closely knit US Catholic subculture in the 1940s and 1950s. Catholics in that subculture, whether they were children or adults, drew their understanding of the Catholic faith from some version of the *Baltimore Catechism*. They witnessed its enactment in their frequent participation in the rituals of mass and confession and had its teachings reinforced at home, in school, and among their Catholic neighbors.

The catechism as a teaching tool has a long history in Christianity. In 1789 the first diocese in the United States was established in Baltimore—hence, its designation as the primal see—that is, the first formal establishment of a Catholic bishop in the new US republic. To ensure uniform teaching of the Catholic faith, particularly in the religiously pluralist United States, an English-language catechism was written and distributed under the auspices of the US bishops and so became known as the *Baltimore Catechism.* In the mid-twentieth century, Catholic students from grade school through high school, just like their parents and teachers, learned their faith from this single source. Though presented in varying degrees of sophistication appropriate for different age groups, the basic content varied little.

Students usually learned about their Catholic faith through memorizing the questions and answers in their catechism. In some cases, teachers, many of them religious sisters, expected students to recite the questions as well as the answers exactly as they appeared in the text. A misplaced or wrong word, even one synonymous with the original, rendered the response completely wrong. Given its near-exclusive use, the catechism conveyed to both child and adult, religious and lay, the reality of a clearly defined, well-ordered existence for those who dwelled within the boundary of the Catholic world. Participation in the daily rituals of parish life within a well-defined Catholic subculture, especially for those who attended parish schools, reinforced the Catholic order described in the catechism. As will be evident in what follows, Catholic culture of the 1940s and 1950s easily fits the standard category of overdetermined, which made the 1960s seem even more chaotic as Catholic practices were transformed.

It is instructive to review relevant portions of the *Baltimore Catechism* because it explains the role of the priest to children as well as adults. Again, it is important to remember that within the Christian religious world, the divine is made manifest in human form—that is, in Jesus Christ. A consistent message in the catechisms is the close identification between the priest and Jesus. The message in the catechism offered few of the theological nuances one might find in other sources from the period. What follows draws on a variety of versions of the catechism, and the extensive quoting throughout the chapter from catechisms written for different audiences is an attempt to convey the ubiquitous message that associates the priest with Jesus, and even with God. For most Catholics, however, these connections between the priest and Jesus remain to a large extent oblique, roundabout, and part of a complex symbolic system, rather than a simple one-to-one association.

In *A Catechism of Christian Doctrine: Revised Edition of the Baltimore Catechism, No. 2* (1941), a junior high student learned the following responses to questions that explain how the holy is made accessible. One question asks: "Who is the principal priest in every Mass?" The response states as a matter of fact: "The principal priest in every Mass is Jesus Christ." It goes on to say that Jesus "offers to His heavenly Father, through the ministry of His ordained priest, His body and blood which were sacrificed on the cross" (1941, 70). The bodily identification between "Jesus Christ" and "His ordained priest" has many layers within this ritual context. First, the priest acts as Jesus Christ every time he consecrates bread and wine. Second, the celebrant is identified as belonging to Christ as "His ordained priest." Finally, the priest has power to make Christ's body and blood present. The exclusivity of this power was heightened through the actual ritual practice insofar as the priest was, up to the late 1960s, the only one who could touch the consecrated hosts and drink the consecrated wine. Catholic children often heard stories that highlighted the sacred nature of the priest's hands. The liturgical rubric prior to the liturgical reforms of the mid-1960s demanded that, once he touched the consecrated host with his index finger and thumb, he was to keep the finger and thumb touching lest a crumb from the host fall unattended on the altar. The priest, for children who imbibed these images, served as a figure of danger and fascination, holding divine power in his very hands. One can easily imagine the confusion generated in a child inappropriately touched by a priest.

The other power of the priest frequently cited is the power to forgive sins. In the same catechism, under "Lesson 29. 'Penance,'" the following question is posed: "Whence has the priest the power to forgive sins?" The response once again identifies the priest with Jesus Christ: "The priest has the power to forgive sins from Jesus Christ, who said to the apostles and to their successors in the priesthood: 'Receive the Holy Spirit; whose sins you shall forgive, they are forgiven them, and whose sins you shall retain, they are retained'" (1941, 75). The key word in this answer is "power." The priest has power from Christ to forgive an individual's sins. In her chapter "Powers and Dangers," Douglas suggests "a correlation: where the social system explicitly recognizes positions of authority, those holding such positions are endowed with explicit spiritual power, controlled, conscious, external, and approved—powers to bless or curse" (1966, 120). Catholic children learned that the priest has power "to forgive sins" or to restore one's relationship to God, to ensure eternal happiness rather than eternal damnation. The ritual of confession highlighted the priest's seeming "powers to bless or curse."

The ritual in which the power to forgive sins is enacted had definite parameters. Through the late 1960s, the power was limited to a prescribed ritual. A child and the priest learned very specific parts for the ritual, and it took place in a very particular space, small, dark, and intimate as the child or adult spoke through a screen or veil to a priest whose ear was bent to hear. Just as important, if not more so, the priest was not face to face with the person who was confessing sins. The symbolic power of this intimate exchange, which remains forever a secret conversation between the confessor and the sinner, is evident even in popular culture. Many a fine movie and television episode has been based upon the never-to-be-broken seal of the confessional.

The proscriptions of the confession ritual do not necessarily prevent a child or adult from identifying the power to forgive with the person of the priest rather than with the symbolic actions. In Douglas's discussion of a correlation between spiritual powers and social systems, she continues: "Where the social system requires people to hold dangerously ambiguous roles, these persons are credited with uncontrolled, unconscious, dangerous, disapproved powers—such as witchcraft and evil eye" (1966, 120). The priest's power to forgive sins remains ambiguous. The ambiguity is apparent in the very existence of the confessional box, which was created to mitigate threats to purity posed by such a deeply personal exchange, particularly for women confessing sins of an intimate nature. The protection was viewed as mutual, as much protecting the chaste priest from the seductive wiles of women as protecting innocent women from the sexual proclivities of priests.

Most Catholics born prior to 1965 can recall with a mixture of amusement and discomfort their childhood experience of stepping across the threshold into the liminal space of the confessional box. In the 1950s and well into the 1960s, Catholic children crossed that threshold to make their weekly confession. Few assumed the priest's power regarding matters of sin ended when he stepped over the threshold of the confessional box. It was "ambiguous" because the power was identified not with the space but with the actions of the priest. The rapid decline in the practice of confession has generated much speculation among scholars, from theologians to historians and social scientists, and a great deal of concern among church officials. The sheer rapidity of the decline may indicate that a fissure already existed in the Catholic symbolic system of purity even among Catholic children who studied the 1941 version of the *Baltimore Catechism*. Still, one can easily imagine the grave distress of those victims of sexual abuse who understood the priest to be the means to restoring their good relationship with God and, at the same time, experienced him as the cause of their estrangement from God.

The conflict for a devout child victimized by a priest is further reinforced in the *Baltimore Catechism*'s explanation of how a man becomes a priest through the sacrament of holy orders. The catechism describes "Holy Orders" as "the sacrament through which men receive power and grace to perform the sacred duties of bishops, priests, and other ministers of the Church" (1941, 90). The response to the next question outlines four basic "requirements [so] that a man may receive Holy Orders worthily" (90). The key lies in the adverb "worthily," which is repeated in the question and response. The first requirement is that "he be in the state of grace and be of excellent character; *second,* that he have the prescribed age and learning; *third,* that he have the intention of devoting his life to the sacred ministry; *fourth,* that he be called to Holy Orders by his bishop" (90). The second and fourth are relatively straightforward, reflect the role's public nature, and define the structured relationship between priest and bishop. The first and third, though more difficult to discern, are clearly more critical as the very next answer makes clear: "The effects of ordination to the priesthood are: *first,* an increase in sanctifying grace; *second,* sacramental grace, through which the priest has God's constant help in his sacred ministry; *third,* a character, lasting forever, which is a special sharing in the priesthood of Christ and which gives the priest special supernatural powers" (90–91). The third effect receives further explanation in the next question concerning "the chief supernatural powers," which "are: to change bread and wine into the body and blood of Christ in the Holy Sacrifice of the Mass, and to forgive sins in the sacrament of Penance" (91). The section continues by posing the question: "Why should Catholics show reverence and honor to the priest?" The catechism follows the logic of the previous answers in clear, unambiguous terms: "Catholics should show reverence and honor to the priest because he is the representative of Christ Himself and the dispenser of His mysteries" (91). In less than two pages of text, the responses convey clearly that the man ordained to the priesthood has been enveloped in a special relationship with God and given "supernatural powers" that seem to coincide with the permanent change in his internal state of being, his "character."

Admittedly few Catholics consciously think in terms of a simple correspondence between the priest and God. Yet many have some sense of the priest as "the representative of Christ himself," a man granted a special "character, lasting forever." In recognizing this association, one might more easily imagine the depth of confusion, pain, and anger for a child, parents, and other believers who are confronted with a priest who is a sexual abuser. A child who has memorized the correct answers concerning the special character of the priest is ill equipped to understand this man as his or her abuser.

This image of the priest as Christ pervades all versions of the *Baltimore Catechism*, though with some minor variations. *Father McGuire's The New Baltimore*

Catechism and Mass, No. 1, Official Revised Edition (McGuire 1942), includes elaborate black-and-white illustrations. Its "No. 1" designation indicates that it is for elementary students, for whom illustrations would reinforce what appears in the questions and answers. The section explaining the mass, for example, includes an ink drawing of the Last Supper with the chapter title "What the Mass Means to Me." A commentary provides an unambiguous explanation of what it means. The quotes that follow attempt to capture the emphases found in the written text. The voice is that of a child who exclaims, "When I look at the beautiful picture of **the Last Supper** I say to myself: 'Our Lord certainly loved His Apostles. How I wish I were there! They were the only ones present.'" The child explains the true identity of the "Last Supper" as "the *first time* Mass was offered. . . . The *first time* that Christ commanded His priests to do exactly what He had just done—offer the Sacrifice of the Mass." The child's lament over his absence turns into an exclamation of joy. "But **I am there!** Yes, that is true every time I am at Mass. Because in every Mass our Lord *again* offers Himself to Almighty God **for me,** through the actions of His priest at the altar. At Mass, I too can receive Holy Communion" (1942, 134). The priest plays the key role in bringing the child into contact with Christ—with "Almighty God"—so that the child can enter into this "holy communion."

Catechism, No. 1 includes other illustrations, though they appear without first-person commentaries. Another one relevant to this discussion features visual images of the mass ritual, enhanced with imaginative renderings of what is present but invisible. In this case, the picture depicts a very familiar Catholic sight, at least prior to 1964: the priest with his back to the viewer and two altar boys kneeling on either side of the priest, with their backs also to the viewer. These human figures are dwarfed by the image of a very large crucifix behind the altar. Hovering above the distorted corpus appears a line drawing of a dove (the Holy Spirit) plus a bearded father figure. Rays of light extend out from the God image, here the Holy Trinity—Father, Son, and Spirit—with little cherubs serving as the picture's border. The accompanying text, the questions and answers, emphasizes that the mass is "the same sacrifice as the sacrifice of the cross." So in addition to attending Jesus's last supper, the child also witnesses the crucifixion every time he or she attends mass. The priest, as mediator, makes this access possible: "Christ, through the priest, offers Himself to God in an unbloody manner under the appearances of bread and wine" (1942 95). Even though the version for younger children includes very little written text about the supernatural powers inherent in holy orders, the striking images, perhaps even more effectively than the written text, encourage children to use their imaginations to fill in what remains invisible when they attend mass. The priest, flanked by altar boys on either side, stands at the center between the visible sacred elements and the invisible supernatural world. Perhaps such images came to the minds of some children in their encounters with priest-perpetrators as they groomed their victims.

Full participation in the mass—that is, receiving holy communion—required weekly confessions, also mediated through the priest. The instructions for confession in *Father McGuire's The New Baltimore Catechism and Mass* explain even to the elementary student that "Penance is the sacrament by which sins committed after Baptism are forgiven" (102). The primary means for "worthily" receiving the sacrament include "confessing our sins to the priest" and "being willing to do the penance the priest gives us" (102). Of course, not every child paid attention to the catechism lesson or took the teaching to heart, but for those who did, the priest held enormous power over the child's access to God.

Adult instruction varied little from that found in the children's catechism. In *A Manual for Teachers of Religion: A Guide Prepared for Use with a Catechism of Christian Doctrine, No. 2 Revised Edition of the Baltimore Catechism*, Rev. William J. Cavanagh elaborates on answers found in the second-level catechism concerning the priest's role. In "Lesson 3: The Keepers of the Eucharist," the text identifies the Last Supper as "the first Mass" (1947, 365) and offers reassurance that at daily mass "until the end of time, this change of bread and wine into the body and blood of Christ will continue to be made in the Church by Jesus Christ, through the ministry of His priests" (353). In a subsequent commentary, Cavanagh describes the ritual actions in detail: "At the Consecration of the Mass the priest takes bread in his hands and says, 'This is My body.' Then he takes the chalice of wine and says, 'This is My blood.' The priest does exactly the same thing our Lord did at the Last Supper" (355). The description is suggestive of a bodily identification between the priest and Jesus. Earlier in the *Manual* the teacher of religion receives an invitation, or perhaps a command: "RESOLVE: To say a prayer today for the priesthood that enables this sacrifice to continue" (205). The prayer request reinforces the critical role of the priest in making Christ's sacrifice present and contains a covert threat of divine absence that would inevitably follow if the priesthood disappeared.

Direct connections to Jesus are further reinforced in the teacher's instructions concerning holy orders. An explanation of the sacrament of extreme unction is also included in this lesson. So at this juncture, a brief explanation of the priest's role in administering the sacrament of "Extreme Unction," or the last anointing, is appropriate. In the tidy order of the Catholic world well into the 1960s, Catholics hoped that one of the last contacts they would have on this earth would be with a priest. Devout Catholics often carried a card stating: "In case of emergency, please contact a priest." A priest oversaw a Catholic's transition into this world at baptism and transition into adult life at marriage, unless the individual chose the life of a priest or religious sister, or nun. If God's providence or luck cooperated, the priest also oversaw the final transition into the world to come. A man was granted this mediational power through the rite of holy orders, which made him a priest.

The explanations of holy orders offered to the catechism teacher make clear the source of the priest's power. Like the first mass, "The first ordination of men to the holy priesthood took place in the upper room on Holy Thursday night" (Cavanagh 1947, 257). The text includes specific citations from scripture that identify the apostles who followed Jesus as the first priests. The section reinforces the distinctive identity of the priest not only in terms of his mediational role in performing the sacraments but also in terms of his bringing other boys into this special relationship with God: "From time to time in every parish, certain boys, like the Apostles, receive a call from our Lord to follow Him and become priests. This is a divine call because it comes from God. . . . The boy usually talks over his vocation with a priest who guides him during his early years, for he must learn to love for Christ and God" (257). Here, the priest becomes the articulator of God's call to "the boy" who is considering the priesthood, as "our Lord" did with the apostles. One might imagine a priest using this mentoring role as an opportunity to groom a victim.

The *Manual* depicts priestly preparation as a long and demanding commitment but encourages the catechist to deliver a message of assurance that "they are pleasant years because he [the boy] knows that one day he will be another Christ." That day comes with "Holy Orders," when ordination "imprints on the soul of the priest a lasting character that marks him a priest forever and which gives the priest special supernatural powers" (Cavanagh 1947, 258). Cavanagh had placed the Catholic priest's symbolic role within a believer's cultural anthropology when he explained that the role of "priest" as "the one who offered sacrifice to God" arose at "the beginning of the world" (258). The difference comes in the origins of the Catholic priest's power to offer sacrifice, which—as explained later in the text—comes through the bishop, who received his powers from a succession of bishops reaching back to Jesus's ordination of the apostles: "In the ordination ceremony, the newly ordained priests kneel before the bishop, who places both hands on the head of each, saying at the same time: 'Receive the Holy Ghost, whose sins you shall forgive, they are forgiven them; and whose sins you shall retain, they are retained.' In truth, the priest is 'another Christ,' for he possesses the supernatural powers to change bread and wine into the body and blood of Jesus Christ and to forgive sins" (259). The bishop passes on the "supernatural powers" through his hands on the head of each man being ordained, reinforcing the hierarchical character of this power that distinguished the ordained from all other Catholics.

Douglas's use of the image of "Chinese boxes" (1966, 165) to illustrate the complexity of a culture's "series of structured relationships" seems an apt choice to describe the intricacies of Catholic culture's "symbolic system of purity" outlined in these excerpts from various catechisms. Douglas admits that the relationship between pollution and the moral order "is far from straightforward," but that admission does not deter her from "returning to the idea of society as a complex set of Chinese boxes, each sub-system having little sub-systems of its own, and so on indefinitely for as far as we care to apply the analysis." She continues: "It is my belief that people really do think of their own social environment as consisting of other people joined or separated by lines which must be respected" (165). The intricate patterns of interactions among God, Holy Ghost, Jesus Christ, priest, bishop, catechist, student, boy aspiring to become a priest, parent, woman religious, and parishioner produce a moral order whose stability depends on each person's abiding in his or her assigned place and interacting with others in their proscribed roles.

Father Connell's *New Confraternity Edition, Revised Baltimore Catechism, No. 3* (1949) explains in more detail to its intended audience—young adults—the lines that join and separate and "must be respected" in the relationship between the nonordained—that is, the laity—and the ordained. *Catechism, No. 3*, is meant to instruct those ready to assume their role as adults in the Catholic "sub-systems." In these subsystems, priest, bishop, and lay person are the key components: "The priests, especially parish priests, assist the bishops in the care of souls" (1949, 83) and "the laity can help the Church in her care of souls by leading lives that reflect credit on the Church, and by co-operating with their bishops and priests, especially through Catholic Action" (84). The *Catechism, No. 3*, further instructs its young adult audience about the intricacies of the Church's subsystems: "If the Church were a merely human organization, it could not have survived for nineteen hundred years. But the Church is a divine organization, found by the Son of God, receiving life from the Holy Ghost, who on Pentecost came down upon the apostles, the first bishops, to give them light and strength, and to dwell in the Church, as its soul, until the end of time. As members of the Church we all share in this divine life" (85). The text provides its reader with the only logical conclusion: "These thoughts should urge us to be faithful to our obligations as Catholics" (85). The obligations appear as yet another "complex set of Chinese boxes," another "sub-system": "We should unhesitatingly accept the teachings of the Church, make use of the means of holiness the Church provides, and obey all the Church's laws, with the conviction that Christ Himself is teaching, sanctifying and ruling us through His representatives, the superiors of the Church. Above all, we should always be loyal to the Pope, the Vicar, or earthly representative, of Jesus Christ" (85). The pope is not the only representative of Christ that a young adult Catholic might encounter. In the subsequent section on holy orders, the *Catechism, No. 3*, provides an etiquette lesson: "In showing reverence and honor to the priest one shows reverence and honor to Christ Himself, for the priest in a very true sense is 'another Christ.' In this country it is the custom to honor priests by addressing them with the title 'Father.' The custom of tipping the hat to the priest is praiseworthy" (260). The lesson continues with further instructions about interacting with those of greater authority: "The proper way to address a bishop and archbishop is 'Your Excellency'; a cardinal, 'Your Eminence.' The Pope is addressed as 'Your Holiness'" (260). The intricate relationships among Son of God, Holy Ghost, apostles, Church, teachings, laws, pope, bishops, priests, and laity are laid out in a series with "each sub-system having little sub-systems of its own, and so on indefinitely for as far as we care to apply the analysis" (Douglas 1966, 165). One can easily imagine how hard it would be for someone thus instructed to come to terms with a priest as sexual predator.

Another version of the catechism, titled *The Parish Catechism* (Farrell 1954), states its purpose on the title page as the instruction of "Non-Catholic People in the Basic Teachings of Religion," adding that adult Catholics might find it "useful for study clubs, parish missions, lenten reading and so forth" (title page). This text highlights additional layers of commonly employed symbolic meanings besides those already mentioned that enfold the priest. In addition to identifying the priest with the twelve apostles, the text explains: "Your parish priest shares in the priesthood of Jesus Christ that has been passed down for 1900 years through the bishops of the Catholic Church" (84). The subsequent question, number 381, asks: "What are the chief powers of Christ that your parish priest shares with Jesus Christ?" The answer makes clear the personal connection between each parishioner and Christ that is made possible by the presence of "your parish priest," and once again the operative word is "power"—"powers to bless and curse": "Your parish priest has the power to teach and preach in the name of Christ, the power to offer Christ in sacrifice (Mass), the power to forgive sins (confession), the power to give other Sacraments, and the power to bless and sanctify" (84). Every priest "must give his whole life to the service of God and His Church and by prayer, word and example help people to save their souls" (85). "Your parish priest" possesses manifold powers that transverse the distance between heaven and earth and eradicates a time gap of almost two millennia, all within your parish.

Immediately following the description of the priest as one dedicated completely to God is an explanation of why priests are unmarried. The response states simply: "Priests do not marry because for them the single state is a holier state counseled by Christ and by Scriptures" (85). The key phrase is "for them," which separates them "from us"—that is, the laity. The separation includes dwelling in "a holier state," which fits very well with Douglas's "belief that people really do think of their own social environment as consisting of other people joined or separated by lines which must be respected" (1966, 165).

Perhaps to explain the matter to this catechism's explicitly designated audience of "non-Catholic people," another question is posed concerning why the priest is addressed as "Father." The answer suggests yet another anomalous aspect of the priest's symbolic role, and the way in which he is "joined" rather than "separated by lines which must be respected": "The priest is called 'Father' because he gives spiritual life to his children (his parishioners) when he baptizes them and gives them other Sacraments. He also teaches his children, as a loving father, the way to happiness in this world and in the world to come" (Farrell 1954, 85). In an additional note to the question, Farrell describes the appellation as "a term of respect and love given by the Catholic people to their priest" (85). He addresses the biblical prohibition of calling any man father in the way we call God "Father" by observing that we are not forbidden to call our biological father by that term. So the term "father" provides one more powerful image to characterize this celibate male's symbolic force. The priest gives "spiritual life to his children," whether those children are chronologically adults or children. The instruction goes on to respond to the question, "387. What should be your attitude toward priests?" The answer leaves little room for doubt: "You should always speak with reverence about priests, because they are the representatives of God and possess the powers of Jesus Christ. You should show outward signs of respect like tipping your hat or bowing to priests. You should work with your parish priests in your parish organizations. You should pray for priests" (85). Not even the slightest hint of the possibility of priestly misconduct appears in this response. Such a caution would have been unthinkable, completely out of place. The parishioner is instructed not only to act respectfully in face-to-face interactions with a priest but also to speak respectfully even when talking to someone else about a priest. For those taught the "proper attitude," it might prove difficult to speak against a priest even for a minor infraction, let alone to accuse him of sexual misconduct.

This particular catechism, intended for adults, explicitly proclaims the priest to be the "representative of God" and possessor of "the powers of Jesus Christ" as well as a "spiritual father" to his parishioners. As has already been noted, these claims are constantly reinforced in the symbolically powerful rituals that a priest performs. Douglas pinpoints some of the characteristics of particularly effective rituals that help explain here how Catholic rituals produce such profound effects on their participants: "The more personal and intimate the source of ritual symbolism, the more telling its message. The more the symbol is drawn from the common fund of human experience, the more wide and certain its reception" (1966, 137). The sources of the Catholic priests' symbolic power draw deeply from the "common fund of human experience," including the priest's identity as a "father"; his ability to offer nourishment—a sacred meal, reenacting Jesus's last supper, transforming bread and wine into the very body and blood of Christ; and his power to undo a person's alienation from God in confession, where a person reveals intimate sources of shame. The priest's abstention from the most basic of human relationships, those of sexual intimacy, also draws from "the common fund of human experience." His lack of personal intimacy signals to those who know the exclusive demands of sexual intimacy that the priest is unattached and therefore available to enter into an intimate relationship with each and every one of his parishioners.

The priest's location at the boundary between the sacred and the profane; between God and ordinary elements of bread and wine; and between God and ordinary people—the laity—places him in a precarious position. In her discussion of "social pollution," Douglas focuses on boundaries as the areas in which pollution threatens. She considers threats relative to "external boundaries" and transgressions from "the internal lines of the system." She also considers "the margins of the lines," as well as the "danger from internal contradictions, when some of the basic postulates are denied by other basic postulates, so that at certain points the system seems to be at war with itself" (1966, 146). The priest seems to be teetering on "the margins of the lines" between ordinary human life and the divine. The priest must remain close to yet separate from the laity to enact his ritual role as "representative of God" and possessor of the "powers of Jesus Christ" (Farrell 1954, 85). Critical to that closeness and separation is the priest's commitment to celibacy. His enactment of holiness illustrates, in Douglas's words, "how the symbolism of the body's boundaries is used in this kind of unfunny wit to express the danger to community boundaries" (1966, 147). If one attaches central significance to the priest in the community's ability to maintain its boundaries between the sacred and profane, then his failure to maintain his purity, in turn, poses a threat to the whole symbolic system.

The boundaries within the symbolic system—that is, the proscribed relationships among those within the Catholic community—prove far more complex. For those seeking concrete evidence of this complexity, Marie Keenan's extensive analysis of clergy sexual abuse in Ireland provides an interesting case study. In her *Child Sexual Abuse and the Catholic Church: Gender, Power, and Organizational Culture* (2011), she provides extensive data, including interviews with clergy perpetrators, that illustrate the systemic aspects of the problem.

Rationalization of the sexual violation takes many forms. The priest who engages in sexual activity with a child may convince himself that sexual relations with a child or adolescent male does not violate his vow of celibacy. The innocence that children represent, the priest's identification with a boy attracted to the priesthood, may create the illusion that no line has been crossed. The blame placed on the victim, the child, as tempter may, in a twisted way, be seen by many Catholics—including the victim's parents, other priests, bishops, and even the victim him- or herself—as the child's, rather than the priest's, violation of certain physical boundaries. The altar boy, as suggested by the illustration described earlier, dwells in the same liminal space as the priest at the altar. He kneels or stands right next to the priest. He comes close, perhaps too close, to the sacred: "Physical crossing of the social barrier is treated as dangerous pollution. . . . The polluter becomes a doubly wicked object of reprobation, first because he crossed the line and second because he endangered others" (Douglas 1966, 165). Giving more credence to the powerful impact of this symbolic system may help us appreciate the depth of a child's fear that he or she is the polluter, the one who has crossed a boundary into very dangerous territory—the place in which one comes into contact with the divine. Again, Douglas's observations prove instructive: "A polluting person is always in the wrong. He has developed some wrong condition or simply crossed some line which should not have been crossed and this displacement unleashes danger for someone" (136). The child may be viewed (wrongly, of course!) as the "polluting person" and thus the one who "unleashes danger for someone." The perceived danger usually extends beyond the child to the priest, the child's family and friends, and other parishioners—to the whole symbolic system of purity that the child and everyone else perceives as a medium for a relationship to Jesus, or God. In other words, the displacement extends into the realm of the unknown, the mysterious realm of the transcendent, in deeply destabilizing ways.

Catholicism from 1964 to the Present

Admittedly, even among those Catholics thoroughly ensconced in the world depicted in the *Baltimore Catechism*, many recognized priests to be limited, ordinary human beings. Then came the 1960s, a time when most Americans in varying degrees experienced an unraveling of familiar social and cultural structures. American Catholics' experiences of that unraveling often included the dissolution of a bounded Catholic world and its power as a singular religious authority. The mid-twentieth-century suburban eclipse of the urban, neighborhood-based Catholic subculture accelerated the effects of the changes wrought by the reforms implemented after the Second Vatican Council (1963–65), a worldwide council of Roman Catholic bishops. Some changes initiated by the council disrupted the central rituals that gave form and expression to Catholic symbolic structures; among the most disruptive were changes to the mass.

The altering of the mass also disrupted the ritual enactment of spiritual authority mediated through the priest. One example will have to suffice here. In the overdetermined Catholic culture in which every ritual gesture possessed transcendent meaning of eternal import, the seemingly simple change in the priest's position while celebrating mass communicated a shift in Catholicism's symbolic world. Prior to 1964, the priest had his back to the congregation; he faced a usually elaborately decorated altar that held a tabernacle containing consecrated bread. In other words, the priest faced the divine, Christ's dwelling, the locale of the real presence of Jesus in communion. Since the implementation of liturgical reforms, the priest now stands behind an altar placed in the middle of the sanctuary and faces his congregation, a very different orientation that undid a set of "Chinese boxes" within Catholic symbolic substructures. The lines that created the relationship between the priest and his congregation were in a sense redrawn, displaying a change in the priest's symbolic mediation of the transcendent.

To include this particular liturgical change in a discussion of clerical sexual abuse of minors in late-twentieth-century American Catholicism should not be interpreted as viewing Catholic clerical abuse of minors as primarily a historical anomaly caused by the rapid changes of the late 1960s and early 1970s. No doubt, particular instances of clerical sexual abuse in those decades reflect the historical period in which the abuse occurred, but such abuse is sadly not limited to a particular period. The inclusion of the liturgical change here is to make another point. Reactions to the priest's reorientation during the celebration of the mass included both extremes. Some understood this and a host of other liturgical changes as the tragic destruction of Catholics' experience of the sacred order. Others believed the changes to be a harbinger of still more welcome changes, including the end of celibacy—a key marker of separation between priest and laity. The reactions at both ends of the spectrum and the many in between demonstrate the deeply felt sensibilities concerning the priest's role in those rituals that enacted a Catholic symbolic system of purity.

The dramatic reactions to a seemingly simple shift in liturgical rubric place in sharp relief the far more serious disruptive potential of clerical sexual abuse on victims and others in the believing community. Douglas again helps us understand the powerful effects on those who seek to maintain the lines of structured relationships that join and separate people in creating a tidy ordering of the world: "Uncomfortable facts, which refuse to be fitted in, we find ourselves ignoring or distorting so that they do not disturb these established assumptions" (1966, 48–49). Within the Catholic world, the priest as sexual abuser, especially of innocent children, simply does not fit with what Catholics assume to be true about priests: they are " another Christ," and ordination "imprints on the soul of the priest a lasting character that marks him a priest forever and which gives the priest special supernatural powers" (Cavanagh 1947, 258). The attempt to fit a sexual abuser into the Catholic set of Chinese boxes proves impossible, the complex substructures come undone, and the patterns shatter. The varied reactions at both extremes to the "uncomfortable facts" begin to make sense, at least in terms of the threat to a symbolic system that holds so much meaning to a significant number of believing Catholics. Some responded with denial, others by placing abusers outside the substructures. Still others threw away or smashed the Chinese boxes, dismissing the whole system as corrupt. The tight structures of identification between priest and Jesus Christ for those still recalling their lessons from the *Baltimore Catechism* provided little room for a margin of error.

Exclusive reliance on the *Baltimore Catechism* waned after the Second Vatican Council, and the text has virtually disappeared in today's Catholic Church. One may rightly challenge its continuing influence. Yet the overdetermined Catholicism articulated in the *Catechism* and reinforced in rituals still has effects, not only as nostalgia but as living memory expressed in so much of the testimony of victims. Again, Keenan's study in Ireland (2011), where the teaching was similar to that in the United States makes these ongoing effects very clear. Consider the many victims, even as adults, who describe their sense of shame and confusion over their own spiritual welfare and their struggle to understand their own transcendent worth and to recover a faith in the existence of a loving God.

Despite the disappearance of the ubiquitous *Baltimore Catechism*, many elements of its teachings concerning the priesthood remain in new renditions that replaced the old standby. *A Catholic Catechism* (1959), still in use in its fifth printing in 1964, provided a familiar description of holy orders, though this was now placed in a section that also treated the sacrament of marriage. The emphasis here is on the permanence of the sacrament's effect, like that of the sacrament of marriage. Placing the two sacraments together also somewhat ironically highlights the distinctive role of celibacy in the priesthood in ways that pairing it with extreme unction did not: "The sacrament of Orders brings to the soul an impress that can never be lost. It is called the 'character' of the sacrament" (*A Catholic Catechism* 1959, 230). A priest "is united in a very special way to Christ, the heavenly High Priest, and is made like to him." The answer reiterates the permanency of his Christ-given "priestly authority . . . power to celebrate the Eucharist, to administer the sacraments of Baptism, Penance, and Anointing of the Sick, and also to consecrate and bless." The answer also emphasizes that the priest may use his powers only if he is "appointed to do so by the rightful authorities in the Church" (230). The final arbiter of a priestly vocation is the bishop. The section ends with a resolution, written in the reader's voice, that has a familiar ring. "For my life: I will honor priests because of their holy office; I will pay attention to their teaching and will pray for them. If I am a boy, I will give some serious thought and prayer all through school to the idea of becoming a priest; and if I think God wants me as a priest I will talk it over with my parents and with some priest who knows me well" (231). Little had changed for adults or children in this fifth printing's account of the priesthood. The upheavals associated with the 1960s had yet to arrive.

Another catechism, first published in 1958 and revised in 1970, bearing the title *A Catechism for Adults*, invoked familiar descriptions of the priest. The author, Rev. William J. Cogan, assured his readers that Jesus ensured the continuation of his work on earth by establishing "the Priesthood, through the Sacrament of Holy Orders" (Cogan 1970, 87). The chief powers are "1) to change bread and wine into the Body and Blood of Jesus, and 2) to forgive sins." Priestly authority comes "from Jesus Christ, the Second Person of the Holy Trinity." And priests remained unmarried "because—1) the single life is a holier life, recommended by Christ; 2) being single, they can give themselves entirely to God and the care of the people" (89). The text, like the one still printed in 1964, gives little evidence of changes in teachings concerning the priesthood.

A few contemporary texts give some credence to those who attribute the rise in cases of clergy sexual abuse in the 1970s to identity confusion among priests. The Fall 1973 issue of *Chicago Studies: An Archdiocesan Review* was titled "An American Catechism." The "priest" is notable for his absence in "Church," an article in that issue whose author, Richard P. McBrien, is a priest. In a question concerning how to "preserve the distinctive authority of our bishops and pastors" while encouraging the laity's active involvement, McBrien acknowledges the fear that some may have "that our primary concern today is to strip bishops and pastors of their power" (1973, 250). His response invokes the Second Vatican Council, whose teaching he describes as working "to incorporate the whole People of God into the decision-making process of Church life and mission for which every member of the Church—laity, religious, and clergy alike—are responsible (*Dogmatic Constitution on the Church,* n. 30 and 33)" (250). The symbolic system based on clear boundaries between priest and laity enacted in sacramental ritual is simply dissolved in this account. In another article in the issue, "Sacraments," Jared Wicks, a Jesuit priest, describes how Christ's presence is found in communion. Wicks identifies Christ's presence "through Scripture and preaching" (1973, 361). He also mentions "the presiding priest," whose role is "to gather us, lead us in prayer, and bring our homage to God." Christ is also present in "the whole community." Noticeably absent is the standard reference to the priest's central symbolic function as Christ's representative; the bodily presence of Christ is identified with "the food offered us" (361). This explanation aligns very well with the previously discussed physical reorientation of the priest and assembly, with the altar between them, rather than the priest being between the assembly and the altar. It certainly suggests a very different role for the priest as mediator.

A 1979 catechism, *In His Light: A Path into Catholic Belief* suggests a similar diminishment of the priest's role as God's distinctive representative. Rev. William A. Anderson ends his response to "What Is the Ordained Ministry?" with this simple comment: "Since we are all priests through our baptism, a more exact term for the ordained priest would be presbyter" (Anderson 1979, 165). He then highlights the "ordained ministers" as those who "share Christ's message with all people" and who therefore "should become familiar with the Word of God and be able to communicate that Word in as clear and understandable a way as possible." He also acknowledges "a special call to the service of worship and celebration." Here the priest acts not in the person of Christ but "in the name of the Church" (165). The sacrament of holy orders is described as "a special commitment and consecration by which the ordained minister is set aside to serve the people of God" (166). Anderson mentions nothing about a permanent change in character. Rather, he says: "Certain charisms and gifts are shared with the ordained minister, both for personal sanctification and for building up the kingdom of God here on earth" (166). Such alternative perspectives have been overtaken by more familiar descriptions of the priesthood in subsequent versions of the catechism.

Pope John Paul II promulgated a new version of the official catechism for the entire Church in 1992. The *Catechism of the Catholic Church* (1994) is an English translation of that catechism. With nearly 800 pages of questions and answers, it does not serve as a classroom text in the way that the *Baltimore Catechism* did. In an effort to make the content more accessible to catechists, the US bishops translated and published the *Compendium: Catechism of the Catholic Church* (US Conference of Catholic Bishops 2006), a 200-page distillation of the *Catechism of the Catholic Church*. Those who teach catechism are expected to use this official summation of church teachings to guide their lessons' content.

The *Compendium* is the final catechism to be reviewed in this chapter. Much of what was found in the *Baltimore Catechism* appears in the *Compendium*. The church's hierarchical structures appear as critical as ever in establishing the "series of structured relationships" that provide the tidy ordering of the Catholic's world. The ordained receive attention in "Part One: The Profession of Faith," an explanatory commentary on the creed, which is the basic statement of Catholic faith. In the commentary on the statement "I believe in the Holy Catholic Church," priesthood is included under the heading "The Faithful: Hierarchy, Laity, Consecrated Life." The *Compendium* carefully explains the unique role of the hierarchy among "the Faithful" in the "Holy Catholic Church." Question 179 leaves little doubt concerning the hierarchy's divine origins: "Why did Christ institute an ecclesiastical hierarchy?" The answer communicates the benefits of the Catholic Church's ordained ministry: "Thanks to the sacrament of Orders, bishops and priests act in the exercise of their ministry in the name and person of Christ the Head" (2006, 51). A key image here is "Christ the Head," Christ as authoritative leader, rather than, say, shepherd, servant, or other images used elsewhere. The discussion does acknowledge the participation of the lay faithful as well as bishops in the "priestly office of Christ" (53). The parish priest receives no singular treatment in any question in this section. A description of the "personal character" of "ecclesial ministry" includes bishops and deacons as well as priests. The text clearly states that "each minister, in virtue of the sacrament of Holy Orders, is responsible before Christ who called him personally and conferred on him his mission" (52). The phrase "representative of Christ" is not used to describe the priest.

The symbolic force of the priest appears more clearly in "Part Two: The Celebration of the Eucharist." The *Compendium* echoes earlier catechisms in identifying the divine and historical origins of the mass—"Jesus instituted the Eucharist on Holy Thursday" (2006, 81). The Eucharist's power follows from its origins: "Communion with divine life and the unity of the People of God are both expressed and effected by the Eucharist" (82). As in the past catechisms, here the priest remains at the boundary between the sacred and profane, on "the margins of the lines" between ordinary human life and the divine: "The celebrant of the Eucharist is a validly ordained priest (bishop or priest) who acts in the Person of Christ the Head and in the name of the Church" (83). A noteworthy addition here is "validly ordained," which clearly demarcates the lines between those who might wrongly claim the right to exercise such sacramental power and those who receive that power through orders from a bishop in full communion with the Roman Catholic Church. Contemporary threats to the boundaries of the priesthood abound, particularly from those who claim the right to ordination, including women and married men.

As in other recent catechisms, specific treatment of the sacrament of holy orders appears in the same section as the sacrament of marriage, in a chapter titled "The Sacraments at the Service of Communion and Mission." As discussed above, this pairing is different from the *Baltimore Catechism*'s pairing of holy orders with extreme unction. The *Compendium* explains that the two sacraments, "Holy Orders and Matrimony, confer a special grace for a particular mission in the Church to serve and build up the People of God" (2006, 92). The mission identified with holy orders is that given "by Christ to his apostles . . . to be exercised in the Church until the end of time." So what has not changed is the close identification of the ordained with Christ. As the *Compendium* explains, "through a special gift of the Holy Spirit, this sacrament enables the ordained to exercise a *sacred power* in the name and with the authority of Christ for the service of the People of God" (92–93). To highlight the transcendent nature of priestly power, the text proclaims that the "the sacrament of Holy Orders" is manifest in "the divine plan of salvation" even before the coming of Jesus. Contemporary priesthood is "prefigured in the Old Covenant" where priests served in the Jewish temple. "These prefigurations find their fulfillment in Christ Jesus who by the sacrifice of the cross is the 'one mediator between God and men' (1 Timothy 2:5)" (93). The description continues with a subtle distinction between Christ as priest and the ordained: "The one priesthood of Christ is made present in the ministerial priesthood." This point is reinforced with a quote from Saint Thomas Aquinas: "Only Christ is the true priest, the others being only his ministers" (93). Despite the distinction, the priest's close identification with Christ in his role as the necessary mediator between Christ and the nonordained remains clear in these explanations.

The *Compendium* places more explicit emphasis on the distinctive powers of the bishop in contrast to the priest than did the *Baltimore Catechism*. What occurs to every ordained man is an "'anointing of the Spirit' who seals the priest with an indelible, spiritual character that configures him to Christ the priest and enables him to act in the name of Christ the Head" (2006, 94). However, only "Episcopal ordination confers the fullness of the sacrament of Holy Orders . . . teaching, sanctifying, and ruling" (93). The priest's relationship to the bishop receives a fuller explanation: "As a co-worker of the order of bishops he [the priest] is consecrated to preach the Gospel, to celebrate divine worship, especially the Eucharist from which his ministry draws its strength, and to be a shepherd of the faithful" (94). The emphasis on the distinctive effects of a bishop's ordination (in a text published by the US Conference of Catholic Bishops) invites readers to raise questions concerning the bishops' effectiveness in "teaching, sanctifying, and ruling" in response to clerical sexual misconduct, particularly those who allowed the reassignment of priests known to be serial abusers.

The *Compendium* does address the celibacy requirement and even includes certain exceptions among the ordained. According to this text, bishops are the only members of the hierarchy who must be celibate. The explanation then notes that in the "Latin Church," men who seek ordination for the priesthood must remain celibate. The "Latin" distinction allows for exceptions such as the Uniate Church of Eastern Europe, which has a tradition of married priests. The section also explains the special status of deacons in the Roman Catholic Church: "Married men can be ordained to the permanent diaconate" (95). Despite these exceptions, celibacy continues to remain symbolically significant in distinguishing Catholic clergy from the laity.

The continued insistence on a celibate priesthood has certainly been at the center of the debates concerning the sexual abuse crisis. Douglas observed that "no other social pressures are potentially so explosive as those which constrain sexual relations," and she mentions, almost as an aside, that her discussion of various African tribes' regulation of sexual relations "may throw some light on the exaggerated importance attached to virginity in the early centuries of Christianity" (1966, 187). Her relatively sympathetic rendering of the early Christian constraint on sexual relations attributes the "high value" placed on virginity to the Christian effort "to create a new society, unbounded and without coercion or contradiction." Virginity enacts the desired bodily perfection of impermeability and serves "the project of changing the role of the sexes in marriage and in society at large" (187). Douglas's account, in turn, "may throw some light" on contemporary US bishops' staunch defense of celibacy. In 1995 Pope John Paul II outlined in his encyclical letter *The Gospel of Life* the idea of two cultures: the "culture of life" and the "culture of death." Sexual activity divorced from its procreative end figures prominently in John Paul's description of the "culture of death." Many US bishops see as a critical part of their role continuing to protect the Catholic community from the polluting forces of the "culture of death" operative in contemporary secular society. The bishops proclaim that the Church offers a "culture of life"—what Douglas would call "a new society" (1966, 187)—as exhibited in its enactment of proper sexual relations. In this context of two sharply divided cultures, celibacy remains a distinctive sign of the Church's ritual purity in its expression of itself as a social body, distinct from the corrupt world it inhabits.

The final point to be considered from the *Compendium* concerns the clear reaffirmation of the distinctive effects that ordination has on those who receive the sacrament. Every man undergoes a transformation through "a special outpouring of the Holy Spirit which configures the recipient to Christ in his triple office as Priest, Prophet, and King, according to the respective degrees of the sacrament" (2006, 95). This transformation is what in other sources is called an "ontological change"—that is, a change in the priest's very being: "Ordination confers an indelible spiritual character and therefore cannot be repeated or conferred for a limited time." The change sets the ordained man apart from the rest of the baptized community and establishes his role as acting in the person of Christ. Priests exercise their "sacred ministry . . . not on their own authority, nor even by mandate or delegation of the community, but rather in the Person of Christ the Head and in the name of the Church. Therefore, the ministerial priesthood differs essentially and not just in degree from the priesthood common to all the faithful for whose service Christ instituted it" (95). The challenges in reconciling this understanding of a man ordained to the priesthood with a man accused of sexual abuse of a minor are manifold. Citing this teaching here is intended to provide cultural context, not to defend a bishop's reluctance to remove a priest from his ministry despite evidence of sexual misconduct. Within contemporary Catholicism's symbolic system, the "priest" remains a man who "differs essentially and not just in degree" from all other Catholics in his relationship to "the Person of Christ."

Conclusion

An understanding of Catholicism as a complex cultural system of purity helps to make sense of certain distinctive aspects of Catholic clergy sexual abuse. Appropriate care for victims requires some understanding of the Catholic world they inhabited and may still inhabit, including an understanding of the priest's central role in that symbolic system where priestly purity signifies his special access to the sacred. Dealing with priests who perpetrate sexual abuse and those who seek to protect them, especially other priests and bishops, requires an understanding of who they understand themselves to be in their roles as men whose ordination permanently transforms them. In this symbolic system, priests are "ontologically changed," from which transformation comes their power to act as mediators between the divine and the human. Criticism of clerical culture as well as the hierarchy as aristocracy call attention to problems deeply embedded within today's Catholic culture, but these descriptors fail to capture the breadth and depth of the symbolic force that the ordained continue to carry within Catholic culture.

The sacraments and the priests who enact the sacramental rituals are part of a powerful symbolic system that evades easy explanations, especially for those who assume that such systems have disappeared in modern cultures. In concluding her chapter on "External Boundaries," Douglas acknowledges that there exists a "relation between individual preoccupations and primitive ritual. But the relation is not the simple one which some psychoanalysts have assumed" (1966, 152). In other words, the attraction of rituals cannot be reduced to individuals "trying to cure or prevent personal neuroses by their public rituals." To reduce Catholic rituals to neurotic impulses obscures their powerful attraction for many who experience Catholicism's sacramental world in deeply positive ways.

Many Catholics assume that the world exists because a deeply mysterious existence or reality—that is, God—creates and sustains everything that exists, and they also assume that God cares deeply about each one of them and seeks a unity with them expressed through certain rituals, the sacraments. The divine seeks a personal intimacy made possible in God's constant love and mercy manifest in Jesus Christ, who agrees to be present in the simple elements like water at baptism and consecrated bread and wine at a mass. For many Catholics, priests they know effectively mediate these caring actions—one of many factors that make responding to clergy sexual abuse so painful.

Rituals mediate the symbolic power of realities experienced simultaneously as threat and creative potential. Douglas (1966) explains this dual character very well. Children and adults seduced by priests often feel themselves caught up in this paradox. Lured into relationships because of a sense of being specially chosen, given their understanding of the priest's proximity to the divine, they then fear that God has betrayed them or, even worse, judged them as evil and then abandoned them to some kind of just punishment. Given the review of the literature here, there is no doubt that Catholics learn at an early age about the close identification of the priest with Christ. This identification is reinforced with the account of ordination as creating a permanent change in the man who becomes a priest. Celibacy in a sense enacts this distinctive identity. The priest is set apart; he remains pure to serve more fully as Christ in the sacred rituals. Entering into this world even imaginatively helps to make clear the utter confusion of a child, or even an adult, who is the subject of the inappropriate sexual advances of a priest. Attempts to clarify what exactly it means to identify the priest with the person of Christ, its relation to celibacy, or even to give an account of what it means to claim that ordination produces a permanent change in a man remain scarce in texts like those reviewed here.

For those outside of the Catholic community, helping victims and preventing future incidents of sexual abuse require fuller appreciation of the Catholic culture as an intricate symbolic system in which the priest mediates the divine. For those who remain Catholic, in addition to caring for victims and attending to prevention, a more difficult question remains: How can the Catholic Church provide an account of the priesthood that acknowledges the fact that those ordained remain mere human beings, with all the frailties of their fellow travelers in faith, without undercutting the power of its symbolic system, its sacramental world, as mediating the divine? The centrality of the priest as configured in the Church's symbolic system of purity creates severe psychological and social constraints on those who deal most directly with the abusers. Yet the system is already under great pressure for not addressing the failings of those men whose ordination has not transformed them into the self-sacrificing person of Christ, but rather has provided them with opportunities to take advantage of those taught to respect them as if they were another Christ. The threat goes beyond those directly involved in the scandal of sexual abuse. It threatens the whole symbolic system that remains a powerful expression of faith for many who are still part of the Catholic community. The threat to that system puts an enormous burden on victims of abuse (unfairly, of course!) and undermines the resolve of those directly responsible for redressing the wrongs caused by past cases of abuse and implementing fully the changes necessary to prevent new incidents of clerical sexual abuse. The crisis of clergy sexual abuse brings into sharp relief the desire to preserve those deeper values and beliefs that the sacraments attempt to enact through the ritual actions of priests and the Catholic faithful.

References

Anderson, W. A. 1979. *In His Light: A Path into Catholic Belief.* Dubuque, IA: William C. Brown.

A Catechism of Christian Doctrine: Revised Edition of the Baltimore Catechism, No. 2. 1941. Paterson, NJ: St. Anthony Guild.

A Catholic Catechism. 1959. Herder and Herder.

Catechism of the Catholic Church. 1994. Washington: US Catholic Conference.

Cavanagh, W. J. 1947. *Manual for Teachers of Religion: A Guide Prepared for Use with a Catechism of Christian Doctrine, No. 2 Revised Edition of the Baltimore Catechism.* Milwaukee, WI: Bruce.

Cogan, W. J. 1970. *A Catechism for Adults.* Rev. ed. Chicago: Adult Catechetical Teaching Aids.

Connell, F. J. 1949. *The New Confraternity Edition, Revised Baltimore Catechism, No. 3.* New York: Benziger Brothers.

Douglas, M. 1966. *Purity and Danger: An Analysis of Concepts of Pollution and Taboo.* London: Routledge.

Farrell, M. W. 1954. *The Parish Catechism.* Chicago: United Book Service.

John Paul II. 1995. *The Gospel of Life.* New York: Random House.

Keenan, M. 2011. *Child Sexual Abuse and the Catholic Church: Gender, Power, and Organizational Culture.* New York: Oxford University Press.

McBrien, R. P. 1973. "Church." In "An American Catechism." Special issue, *Chicago Studies: An Archdiocesan Review* 12 (3): 241–53.

McGuire, M. A. (1942). *Father McGuire's The New Baltimore Catechism and Mass, No. 1, Official Revised Edition.* New York: Benziger Brothers.

US Conference of Catholic Bishops. 2006. *Compendium: Catechism of the Catholic Church.* Washington: US Conference of Catholic Bishops.

Wicks, Jared, S.J. 1973. "Sacraments." In "An American Catechism." Special issue, *Chicago Studies: An Archdiocesan Review* 12 (3): 312–64.

Diana Garland

6 Don't Call It an Affair

Understanding and Preventing Clergy Sexual Misconduct with Adults

A social worker who is known and trusted in the community welcomes into her office Susan, a thirty-five-year-old first-time client and a member of the social worker's church.[1] Susan is obviously distraught.[2] No, she tells the social worker, she has never been in counseling before. "I'm not quite sure where to begin," Susan says. But then she plunges into her story, as though fearful that otherwise she might lose her nerve. In a low voice, trembling with emotion, Susan blurts out that she has had an "affair" with their pastor. She is quiet for a few moments. Then, as she rocks back and forth, tears streaming down her face, the words come quickly, in between sobs. She says she had gone to her pastor because her husband was depressed and uncommunicative, and she was worried about him. The pastor had listened compassionately and expressed his concern for her loneliness as a result of what he called her husband's "emotional abandonment." He encouraged Susan to come to see him regularly for counseling during this difficult time, and soon she was meeting him several times a week. She was grateful to spend time with this man who was so gentle and kind to her. She began to meet him in his office as well as at a state park, where they could take long walks together and talk and pray in the beauty of God's creation.

After several weeks, he began saying she was an answer to his prayers for someone who could help him in his ministry. In his office, he prayed with her, holding her hand in both of his. He confessed to her that his marriage was not satisfying and that he was deeply attracted to her. He would hold her close and then kiss her gently. When she became upset by his advances, he apologized profusely, saying she was just so beautiful, and he loved her. How could such a love be wrong? He bought her books, often books on prayers or spirituality, as a way to apologize, and for a time he would not touch her at all. But then he would embrace her again. Before she realized what was happening one afternoon, they had sexual relations in his office.

Susan felt guilty and horrible at having "tempted" the pastor into this relationship, yet she felt incapable of ending it; she thought she loved him. She felt trapped by her own feelings and desperate because there was no one with whom she could talk except the pastor himself, and he simply said he couldn't imagine that God would want to deny them the love they had found together. He often called her at work or at other times when they could have private conversations. She felt her life was spinning out of control, and she was haunted by her feelings of sinfulness and fear that her husband would discover what she was doing.

A week before she came to see the social worker, she decided to drop by the pastor's office unannounced, to seek some comfort and direction. As she pulled her car in front of the church, however, she saw another woman leaving his office. Something about the look on the other woman's face told Susan in a flash that she was not the only one with whom the pastor was involved. In that moment, it was as though a spell was broken. Susan left before the pastor knew she had been there. Susan realized she needed help, and that help had to come from somewhere besides the pastor or the church. She had come to the social worker because she needed to talk to someone who would understand how desperate and horrible she feels. The words stop, but the tears and rocking continue. Then Susan says, "I just can't stop crying; I just want to die."

Susan described herself as a seductress, but in fact she was the victim of clergy sexual abuse. She sought out her pastor for counsel, and he used her vulnerability as an opportunity to exploit her. The fact that her pastor allowed her to carry the blame for their sexual involvement was an additional abuse of his power as a spiritual leader. The reality of clergy sexual abuse of adults, usually women, is a more difficult issue to understand than the abuse of children because there is the assumption that if both parties are adults and there is no physical coercion, then the relationship is consensual. In fact, however, when persons with power—including social workers, counselors, pastors, seminary professors and administrators, and religious employers—attempt to seduce into sexual relationships those over whom they have power, the relationship cannot be defined as consensual.

The Old Testament reports that the sons of the priest Eli misused their position to engage in sexual misconduct with women serving at the Tent of Meeting (1 Samuel 2:12). Historians trace sexual abuses between clerics and laity, senior clerics and novitiates in orders, and priests and nuns back through the medieval church (Shupe 1998). One twelfth-century bishop fathered sixty-five children; another church leader, Pope Innocent VIII (d. 1492) bragged publicly about his brood of "bastards" (Jackowski 2004). Nathaniel Hawthorne's classic novel *The Scarlet Letter* tells the story of social ostracism suffered by a young woman who engages in "adultery" with the popular parish pastor.

In recent history, journalists have reported high-profile cases of clergy sexual misconduct (CSM) of adults when it has resulted in legal action.[3] For example, in 2006 the archbishop of the International Communion of Charismatic Churches (ICCC) in Atlanta was forced to resign as a consequence of a lawsuit charging him with using his position and spiritual role to manipulate women into having sex with him, members of his family, and others, including visiting pastors, for many years. There were allegations that he had fathered a number of children by women in the congregation he led (Jewell 2006). Numerous case studies of clergy sexual misconduct have also been published (see, for example, Anonymous 1995; Clarion 2007; Cooper 2002; Fortune 1989; Miller 1993; Poling 1999; Religion News Service 2002). These accounts include cases from diverse faith traditions, including Protestant, Catholic, Church of Jesus Christ of Latter Day Saints (Gerdes, Beck, and Miller 2002), Buddhism, and nontraditional religious movements (Adam 1998; Jacobs 1984; Oxenhandler 2008).

In my own community in Texas, Matt Baker, a Baptist pastor who was married with young children, was convicted of murdering his wife in 2006 in order to marry a woman in her early twenties, Vanessa Bulls. Bulls had been despondent over her divorce when Baker spotted her in the church sanctuary, asked her about her divorce, and offered her counseling. Six months later, their relationship became overtly sexual. When Baker's wife, Kari, was found dead, Bulls did not report the four-month relationship to police, ashamed and fearful she would be held responsible for Kari Baker's death, which was ruled a suicide. But Bulls realized that it may have been murder, and Baker led her to believe that she was equally culpable. Three years later, Bulls's testimony against Baker led to his conviction. At the trial, a dozen women claimed that Baker had made sexual advances toward them. The local newspaper called it an "unholy affair" and identified Bulls as Baker's "mistress" (Witherspoon 2010).

High-profile cases that end up in the courts have the effect of communicating that CSM takes place rarely, because these cases are about a few sociopathic, charismatic leaders who are caught as their behavior becomes more and more outrageous. As a consequence, average congregations with average leaders are perceived not to be at risk. That perception is false.

Prevalence of Clergy Sexual Misconduct

My colleagues and I conducted the first study of CSM based on a random survey of the US adult population (Chaves and Garland 2009). We found that 3.1 percent of women who attend religious services at least monthly reported that at some time during their adult life, they had been subjected to a sexual advance by a clergyperson or religious leader in their own congregation; 67 percent of those clergy or leaders were married to someone else at the time of the advance. Thus, one in thirty-three women in congregations has been subjected to a sexual advance by a religious leader in her congregation during her adult life. The average American attends a congregation of 400 adults, and 60 percent of congregations' members are female, suggesting that there are, on average, seven women per congregation who have been the target of CSM. Of the entire sample, 8 percent of congregants reported having known about CSM occurring in a congregation they had attended. All of the offenders were male, and 96 percent of the victims were female. Of course, CSM does not occur evenly across congregations, but these statistics demonstrate the widespread nature of CSM and refute the commonly held belief that it is a matter of a few charismatic and powerful leaders who prey on vulnerable followers.

I also conducted a qualitative study based on interviews lasting one to two hours with forty-six individual targets of CSM, each from a different congregation, and with fifteen persons who reported CSM in the life of someone close to them: seven husbands of offended women, a mother of an offended adult daughter, a friend of an offended woman, four fellow congregants of the offended, and two congregational staff members serving with an offender.[4] I also interviewed two offenders. The sample compares roughly to our national study, in which 96 percent of the offended were female and all offenders were male (Chaves and Garland 2009). Of the forty-six targets in this sample, 4 (8.7 percent) were male, and all four of their offenders were male—three Catholic and one Mormon. Forty (95 percent) of those who offended the forty-two women we interviewed were male. I therefore continue to use male pronouns for offenders and female pronouns for offended, with the disclaimers that my findings document that both men and women offend, and that the offense can be either heterosexual or homosexual in nature.

Of those I interviewed, the religious groups of the offended at the time of the CSM include the following in descending order of representation: Roman Catholic, Baptist, Methodist, Lutheran, Seventh Day Adventist, Disciples of Christ, Mormon, Apostolic, Calvary Chapel, Christian Science, Church of

Christ, Episcopal, Friends, Mennonite, evangelical nondenominational, and Reformed Judaism. The order should not be construed to suggest that CSM is more common in some denominations than others, given the nonrandom nature of our sampling and the widely varying size of these denominational groups. Rather, it suggests the widespread nature of CSM. Most offenders held the position of priest or pastor, but they also included religious leaders in the categories of chaplain (in the armed services and at a college), superior in a religious order, rabbi, and leader (in religious groups without pastors or priests).

Since the time of the CSM, some of the offended had changed their religious identity or eschewed religion entirely as a result of their experience, but a number have continued to be active congregants, although virtually all have moved to a different congregation, if they are still active. The states where the offended lived ranged from Maine to California and from Washington to Florida. Five of the interviewees (11 percent) were African American, which suggests that members of this group were underrepresented in our sample; the national survey found that 50 percent of those experiencing CSM at some time in their adult life were African American.

Those Who Offend

It is difficult to study religious leaders who have committed CSM because participating in research puts offenders at what they perceive to be risk for lawsuits or loss of employment if their identity is discovered. Similarly, nonoffending leaders in congregations where CSM has occurred are usually unwilling to discuss their congregation's experience for fear of exposing the congregation to the risk of litigation. Friberg and Laaser (1998) studied twenty-five religious leaders who had been reported for sexual misconduct and concluded that the most common offender is a man who is reasonably successful and has a combination of narcissism, sexual compulsion, and need for affirmation. Others have reached similar conclusions (Francis and Baldo 1998; Steinke 1989).

The effects of CSM on the lives of offenders whose offense becomes known to superiors or to the congregation vary widely. In several cases known to me, the pastor simply started a new congregation in the same town or city, splitting the old congregation as loyal congregants followed him to the new one. Other offenders move and are hired by existing congregations, some unaware of and some with knowledge about the offenders' past behavior. In still other situations, the congregation forgives the offender for the misconduct, and he continues to lead in the same congregation. In congregations with central denominational governments and in other religious organizations, superiors may choose quietly to relocate an offender, suspend him for a period of time or permanently, and/or require him to receive psychological treatment as a condition of continuing or returning to leadership.

Care for the Offended

The offended whom I interviewed told me that the clinicians—social workers and psychologists—from whom they sought help in the aftermath of CSM did not address the abuse of power or the spiritual nature of the abuse they had experienced. The helping professionals identified the experiences of these congregants as affairs. Obviously, helping professionals need to understand the dynamics and consequences of CSM in the lives of the offenders, the offended, their families, and their congregations as communities. According to the literature on CSM, patterns that characterize clergy sexual abuse may not be evident in every case of the abuse, but they are common enough to provide guides for helping professionals and the women they seek to help, so that both parties can understand the dynamics of the experience (Garland 2006).

The Offender "Grooms" the Victim

"Grooming" is a process whereby the religious leader breaks down a woman's defenses, making her feel special—perhaps by pointing out her spiritual gifts—or in other ways using his position as a religious leader to develop a close relationship with her and isolate her from others. He uses personal warmth to obscure his true intention. According to Patrick Carnes (1997), some of the ways the offender demonstrates this warmth include expressing admiration, caring, and concern; indicating that he looks forward to a long-term relationship with her; making affectionate gestures and touches; talking about a shared project; and complimenting her and sharing personal confidences with her in ways that are inappropriate for a relationship between a religious leader and parishioner.

He co-opts religious and spiritual language into an agenda designed to meet his own needs. It is a gradual and subtle process, and one that has extraordinary power, desensitizing the victim to increasingly inappropriate behavior, while rewarding her for tolerance of that behavior. He speaks for God, saying things like, "You are an answer to my prayer. I asked God for someone who can share my deepest thoughts, prayers, and needs and He sent me you." Later, she may find this trite and feel humiliated that she believed him, but at the time, it is a powerful way to exploit her and silence her doubts, throwing off her inner moral compass (Liberty 2001). After all, spiritual leaders are expected to act in one's best interests, and he is capitalizing on vulnerabilities he has found in her to exploit. Grooming is essentially seduction in a relationship in which he holds spiritual power over her.

Clergy have organizationally sanctioned and easy access to intimate settings under profoundly intimate circumstances. They are permitted an instant intimacy not normally granted to other people in society. We tend to follow a spiritual leader's lead and trust him. If a minister invites someone seeking counseling into his office and closes the door, she will most likely assume that counseling is always done this way. If the minister is leading toward a sexual relationship, the congregant would have a hard time figuring that out and stopping him. With that kind of trust, he can easily minimize her concerns and doubts about the appropriateness of their relationship, first slowly nudging against and then crossing her sexual boundaries (Fortune 1999). The first boundary crossings may be covered on his part by claiming a lack of intention. For example, if he hugs her or touches her in a way that is just slightly over the edge of appropriateness, she may question her own ability to discern what happened. If she does question or confront him, he may say things like "I was just trying to comfort you" or "I was just communicating how dear our friendship is" (Carnes 1997). As a consequence, she may berate herself and actually feel embarrassed for having questioned his intentions. Because of the unusual level of trust that women place in religious leaders, offenders are able to deprive their victims of their usual resources for discernment, good judgment, and action. The first actions seem small; for example, how could Susan tell someone about the pastor holding her hand in both of his in prayer without sounding like she was sexualizing a small act that he intended as comfort?

The Victim Is Trapped

As one interviewee said, "Compared to him, who was I?" Women are often justifiably convinced that no one will believe them. The church deacons may believe the woman "asked for it," or that she tempted the offender. Others may well believe that she was dressed inappropriately or somehow was sending him sexual signals. Indeed, she may even on some level have wanted the offender to be attracted to her. She may have been lonely and found him attractive. But that does not excuse his behavior or condemn her feelings. She trusted him to be a safe spiritual leader.

When his behavior becomes overtly sexual, it is very likely that she has no one to whom she can turn but the offender himself to sort out her confusion. If she confronts him, he may apologize profusely, minimize what happened, back up in the grooming process, and wait until she has once again placed her trust in him. Victims often question their own stories, wondering if they remember events correctly, or if they are making too much out of the leader's first overtures. What the victim does not realize is that she is already caught by the secrecy. If she tells anyone at this point, she might not be believed, or she might be labeled a seductress. If she does not tell anyone, he will continue to cross her personal boundaries, and others will later question why she did not do something sooner. There is no way out at this point that does not shame her, even if she wants out. Whatever else she is feeling, she is confused. Sometimes on one level she enjoys the attention and affection she is receiving from him, making it harder for her to escape, even though she is alarmed and frightened. These emotions deepen the attachment—he is the only one with whom she can discuss her feelings.

Carnes defines "betrayal bonds" (1997) as the strong attachment of a victim to someone who is destructive to him or her. And Mary De Young and Judith Lowry write: "The nature of this bond is distinguished by feelings of intense attachment, cognitive distortions, and behavioral strategies of both individuals that paradoxically strengthen and maintain the bond" (1992, 165).

The Victim Blames Herself

Women blame themselves for their sexual relationships with religious leaders. Everyone wants to believe that they have the power to make decisions and act on them: "What we must remember is that a person's moral agency, that is, her sense of what is right for her and her ability to act on it, is severely compromised when someone she trusts is manipulating her" (Fortune 1999, xii). Given her heightened vulnerability (which he has accentuated), her trust of her religious leader, his willingness to be unethical, and the mandate of secrecy, the setup for her abuse is complete. She may accede or comply because she does not want to lose what is important and valued in the relationship, which may include affirmation, support, and caring (Kennedy 2003).

Because the offender is controlling the definition of reality at least to some extent, he can define the situation as mutual consent, thus leaving the victim feeling responsible. She feels safer if she believes she is to blame than if she believes she was not in control of what happened, even though that blame leaves her with a deep sense of shame. A question that often helps her later to realize what was happening is, "Would this have happened if he was your neighbor and not your pastor?" Overwhelmingly, the answer is "no." And as she says "no," she begins to face the truth that he had power and authority that made meaningful consent impossible for her (Liberty 2001).

Sexual abuse is inherently shaming. Whenever one person treats another as an object to be used to gratify needs rather than as an individual worthy of respect, the user shames the one used (Horst 1998). This shaming is accentuated when the user is a spiritual leader. The victim feels deeply ashamed of what has happened—of what she perceives she has done, of what she has caused. And "if the minister in question is a skillful emotional manipulator rather than an emotional thug, he is likely to try to convince the woman, and himself, that she really does want his sexual advances" (Horst 1998, 25), deepening her sense of shame and her feelings of responsibility.

The Victim's Physiological and Psychological Symptoms

Clergy sexual abuse creates overwhelming stress in victims, who may develop post-traumatic stress disorder as a result of the relationship itself. The disorder may be exacerbated when the relationship ends, whether or not that ending comes with public disclosure. The trauma that women experience in clergy sexual abuse is even more profound than in catastrophic events because of the breach of trust involved (Flynn 2003). The victim may develop any number of physical or emotional symptoms related to the stress caused by the relationship, bringing her to the attention of a physician, to whom she may reveal the source of her stress.

The Victim May Try to End the Relationship

The victim may feel caught, unable and perhaps even unwilling to extricate herself from the relationship. She may pray for deliverance, but no help seems to come. She cannot reach out to anyone for help, realistically fearing community condemnation and marital destruction, if she is married. She may also feel attached to the offender, in the same way that many victims of domestic abuse are attached to their abusers. One survivor of clergy sexual abuse wrote: "Only God knew the whole story. And God didn't seem to care. . . . No one would understand the web in which he had entrapped me. . . . I was an expert at deceiving. It was my only way to survive" (quoted in Poling 1999, 66–67).

The Religious Institution Responds

Margaret Kennedy records one woman's experience: "I do not want to hurt the man in question, though I know I am far from being the only woman he has damaged. I know he goes on as ever—and with the Bishop's knowledge and therefore acceptance I presume. The Bishop merely shrugs his shoulders and says: 'I know, but what can I do if the man denies it and I have no direct proof?'" (quoted in 2003, 228).

The Anglican priest who abused this woman was later defrocked, not for professional misconduct but for adultery. Kennedy (2003) reports that the woman had to go into hiding because of threats to her life. The victim often is rightfully frightened of what the offender might do if she reports his behavior.

Congregational and denominational bodies have been slow to respond to reports of clergy sexual abuse, often blaming the victims and being more concerned about taking self-protective stances to avoid legal or moral responsibility for the behavior of their leaders than they are about the well-being of those who have been harmed. Whether the relationship is accidentally discovered or the woman reports it, congregations often discredit and blame the offended. Women victimized in religious organizations where they are employed may be forced to resign, losing their careers. Church leaders often close ranks around the offender and seek to silence those reporting the CSM (Poling 1999, 19). Thus, the crisis is compounded, with women losing their community, their vocation, and their connection to the church. The multiplying losses are overwhelming.

The Community Urges Forgiveness

The community often urges the offended and her family to forgive the abuser out of a desire to put the ugliness behind them, allowing the religious leader to escape the consequences of his behavior. Moreover, clergy sexual abuse traumatizes the soul in the same way that injury traumatizes the body: "Asking a victim to forgive the offender early in the process is like asking someone to play basketball with a broken leg" (Horst 2000, 32). Forgiveness cannot be forced or willed. It will come only with healing of the wounded soul and eventually of the community itself. Because of the urging to forgive and the shunning they experience, and because the offender has used and abused his role as God's representative as a way to get to them, some women leave the church and never come back. They rightly experience the urging of others to forgive as a minimizing of the damage that the offender has done and is capable of doing in the lives of others. The victim recognizes the public apology he may proffer as a means of maintaining his leadership role: she has heard it before. It is part of his pattern of grooming, now used with the larger community. Nothing has changed except that she has been publicly disgraced.

A few of the victims I interviewed found support. Somewhere they found people who could hear their stories with understanding and who dealt justly with the offender, removing him from the position of power where he could have continued to offend. They provided the victim with support and relationships that helped her begin healing. They provided consultation and support to her family and the community who were also victims of the abuse of power that had taken place.

There needs to be an acknowledgement of what happened and who was responsible, with genuine remorse and repentance by those who have done harm. Encouraging the victim to be silent or to forget or minimize what has happened to her is not encouraging forgiveness; in fact, it is quite the opposite. Forgiveness may include speaking out about what happened, remembering the abuse and being an advocate for others who have been silenced, using anger to work against violence and abuse. It brings the private process into public view, and in that way it is a powerful force for change.

The Victim Begins to See Herself as a Survivor

Surviving clergy sexual abuse is a life-changing experience. One woman writes: "The damage has been done, and I continually have to fight with myself not to be defined by the damage" (quoted in Poling 1999, 79). Many women have to live with the damage in secret because our culture does not have a framework for understanding their experiences. The impact on survivors of sexual abuse by spiritual leaders is greater than on survivors of other forms of power abuse. Because part of coping with trauma is spiritual, sexual abuse by a spiritual leader further complicates the recovery process.

Professional Responses and Intervention

Often, these women's shame and overwhelming fear that their secret will come out into the open kept them from seeking help until after the relationship began to unravel, if they sought help at all. Nevertheless, some did seek help prior to the end of the abuse.

A woman may look for help for other matters, or because she wants to find a way to end the abuse but finds herself unable to do so. She may be so depressed or anxious that she refers herself for help, or others may refer her, perhaps without knowing about the fundamental cause of her anxiety and depression. She needs to hear that the very act of seeking help, even if she has not been able to end the relationship, took tremendous strength. She will continue to regain power that has been taken from her when she decides that the offender's behavior is wrong and must be stopped. But that point may not come without hard work and strong support (Hopkins 1998).

Even if the victim learns the words "clergy sexual abuse," she may still feel overwhelmed with guilt, wondering how she could have ever let such a thing happen, particularly when confronted over and over with the judgment of others during a time when she is struggling with depression and anxiety. Language is critical. It makes all the difference in the world to call her experience "abuse" instead of "an affair," and to call her "a victim" rather than "an adulteress" or "mistress." Otherwise seemingly innocent conversations by friends who do not know her role in the congregational crisis and who use the language of "affair" and "that woman" create repeated shame and trauma.

Working with a clinician who understands the process of clergy sexual abuse can be the beginning of survival. The victim also needs to be connected to other survivors; she is not the only one, and others' stories that parallel hers, whether in writing or in support groups, can give her great insight and solace. Research indicates that reading, studying, and other self-education efforts can be critical tools in helping victims understand their abuse and come to terms with it. Flynn (2003) found that self-education promoted autonomy, provoked the righteous anger necessary for trauma integration and healing, and stimulated creative problem solving. Helpful resources include Nancy Poling's *Victim to Survivor: Women Recovering from Clergy Sexual Abuse* (1999), Elisabeth Horst's *Recovering the Lost Self: Shame-Healing for Victims of Clergy Sexual Abuse* (1998), and the early but still excellent resource by Marie Fortune, *Is Nothing Sacred? When Sex Invades the Pastoral Relationship* (1989). Patrick Carnes's *The Betrayal Bond: Breaking Free of Exploitative Relationships* (1997), although not only about clergy sexual abuse, provides another framework that helps victims become survivors.

Janice Goldfein (2004) suggests that the first therapeutic stage following a traumatic event includes offering compassion, hope, and an understanding of what has happened to the victim. She needs reassurance that the range of emotions and physiological responses she is experiencing are to be expected and are not pathological. A clinician can explain the neurochemistry of trauma and assess whether the victim needs a medical evaluation, especially if she is not sleeping or she is depressed or suicidal. She may also be concerned about sexually transmitted diseases, particularly if she learns that the offender had multiple victims. Her anxiety may not have allowed her to face that topic; she should be encouraged to seek a medical evaluation.

Exploring the spiritual dimension of her trauma will come as she struggles with her feelings about God, her church, and how her spiritual life may have been severely attacked. However she recovers, she will need help in finding the meaning in what she has experienced and, in time, the positive changes she has experienced—developing new skills, new understanding of herself and of God, and greater confidence in herself (Goldfein 2004). This process may take months or years, depending on the breadth and depth of devastation she has experienced, the support available to her, and her own coping resources. As noted above, some victims never return to formalized religion or participation in a faith community.

The victim may discover that one of the ways she can find meaning in this experience is to do whatever she can to ensure that the offender does not hurt others. She has a number of options that she may need help in exploring. Depending on the context, they may include filing a criminal complaint, filing a civil suit for damages, reporting the abuse to church authorities, filing a complaint with an ethical standards or licensing board, filing a complaint with the local Equal Opportunity Employment Commission, asking the church for reimbursement for therapy and other costs, and, of course, doing nothing (Maris 1995). If she does report the offender, she risks being revictimized. At a time when she may be struggling to stop blaming herself, the message she may hear, either subtly or blatantly, from those entrusted with the responsibility to adjudicate complaints and hold religious leaders accountable, may reinforce her sense of responsibility, shame, and failure (Liberty 2001). As she talks with an investigating committee or board of elders or trustees, her language may fall short of naming her experience in a way that reflects the deep damage done by her predator. As a consequence, they may hear her call the relationship an affair, and they may label it a consensual one. The victim needs to be prepared before giving testimony, therefore, and she may well want to have legal counsel advise her or be present. She will be speaking to people who probably do not understand the issues of power, grooming, and victimization involved. An advocate can accompany and support her through this process of giving testimony and pursuing a response from the congregation.

Some congregations and denominational bodies have responded to the problem of clergy sexual abuse by developing justice-seeking policies. Many more have not. It is important to find the policies that are currently relevant to the congregation, denomination, and/or institution in which the abuse occurred. Some organizations and congregations will carefully protect the victim's identity; others will not. She may need a professional's help in ferreting out the policies relevant to her situation and determining the risks she will face and protections afforded to her. Few people know the definitions of sexual harassment, the behavioral flags that signal potential abuse, or the scope of what is considered sexual misconduct, harassment, or abuse. They do not know what redress is possible in their church or institution, or whom they should contact.

Depending on the laws of a given state, the abuse of power the victim has experienced may be considered a crime—for example, if she was in a counseling relationship with a pastor, a student in a religious college or seminary, or an employee in a religious organization. Sexual harassment is prohibited in the workplace and in educational institutions by federal and state laws. Sexual malfeasance is a broader category and includes any sexualized conduct occurring between a person in a position of trust with an adult entrusted to his or her professional care, regardless of that adult's receptivity or even invitation. Faith communities can be held liable for sexual malfeasance of their clergy under several legal theories (Underwood 2003).

Although the secrecy of these arrangements makes it impossible to know with any certainty, it appears that many congregations are quietly settling with women out of court and providing them with financial resources for counseling, needed medical care, and/or settlement packages if they have lost their employment or careers. One of the conditions of these agreements is often guarantees of silence by all parties. Although the financial help may be important, the practice of silencing often drives victims and their families away from those who could be supportive to them in a time of great anguish.

Women need help with their family relationships as they begin to move on with their lives. Some women decide not to tell their husbands at all, fearing the husbands' reactions (violence or abandonment). Consequently, they deal with the trauma and struggle on their own, creating silence and distance in their marriages. If a victim does tell her husband, marital counseling is almost always needed. Nevertheless, she also needs time alone in counseling to process what happened to her without having to guard what she says in front of her husband. The victim's husband and perhaps other family members will also need help in grasping what has happened and in dealing with his (and their) rage; they are secondary victims (Hopkins and Laaser 1995). Although at some point the husband and wife will have to deal together with her guilt over the pain experienced by her family, they also need some individual therapeutic space and time.

Most of the resources available for victims recognize that partners and other family members are likely to feel rage at what has happened, cautioning them to take care not to direct their rage at the victim. Although that may be good advice, it often comes far too late. The victim herself often does not understand in the beginning what has happened to her. If she initially understands what she has experienced as an affair, her husband's anger and sense of betrayal will be aimed directly at her. As she begins to come to terms with her experience as abuse and nonconsensual, and if her husband has struggled to stay with her despite her having an "affair" with the pastor, it may now sound like she is making excuses for her behavior. She, in turn, may find him a ready target for the anger that is growing within her over what has happened to her; he does not seem to support her fragile, newly constructed understanding of clergy sexual abuse and her emerging understanding that she did not cause the abuse. Only the most committed marriages can survive this kind of anger and the rending of mutual trust.

Both spouses are probably also dealing with the spiritual crisis of the loss of their church community and close friends and spiritual leader, as well as the swirl of multiplying crises and possible public shame they each have experienced. Every aspect of their relationship may be affected, including their ability to be intimate with one another if she is having flashbacks to the abuse (anonymous 1995).

Conditions Contributing to the Prevalence of CSM

As important as understanding the psychological dynamics of CSM is for those professionals faced with intervention on behalf of and treatment of those affected, CSM is so widespread that there must be characteristics of congregations that allow CSM to occur and continue with such frequency. Shupe has called CSM "normal" in the sense that it is ubiquitous in religious community life, noting that "bad pastors" are no less surprising than "fleecing accountants, seducing professors, crooked cops, pilfering bankers, money-laundering corporate executive officers, and philandering therapists" (2007, 7). To describe CSM, Shupe uses the term "elite deviance," which refers to illegal and/or unethical acts committed by persons in the highest corporate and political strata of society, who run little risk of exposure or serious punishment even though their deviance poses danger to the well-being of many others (Simon and Eitzen 1982). Therefore, I have sought to identify the social conditions common to the communities in which CSM occurs that allow or encourage CSM. Identifying these conditions may point us to possible strategies for preventing or reducing the incidence of CSM.

The Qualitative Research Project

I published an article reviewing the literature on CSM with adults that started with the same case study that introduced this chapter (Garland 2006). Then several articles about my research on CSM were published in various newspapers and other venues. As a consequence, a number of offended persons voluntarily contacted me, seeking to know more about this work. Support groups also willingly disseminated news of the project via their websites. These contacts formed my initial nonrandom sample of interviewees; others were added as information about the project traveled to and through clinicians and support networks for survivors of CSM.

I initially planned to travel to congregation sites and conduct interviews there. Some of the offended were still living with the secret of the offense, however, and I faced the difficult task of finding a venue for an interview that they deemed protected from community or family awareness. Additionally, given the offense they had experienced, meeting with a researcher in a secluded space had the potential of creating undue anxiety. After struggling with these issues in attempts to arrange sites for the first two interviews, I proposed to subjects that we conduct the interview by phone. I found that subjects actually preferred the private nature of a phone call, which is how the remaining interviews were conducted. The use of phone interviews also allowed me to expand the reach of this project geographically, enabling me to obtain a much larger and more diverse sample. The phone venue had limitations, however, such as eliminating my ability to observe nonverbal behavior.

A single statement focused the interview: "I understand that you experienced a sexual encounter with a religious leader; I want to learn what leads to religious leaders engaging in sexual behavior with people in their congregations, so tell me about how it began." Such an unstructured interview protocol is justified when looking at phenomena that have not been previously studied. I probed for specific behavioral details of how the relationship between the offended and the offender developed and became sexualized, as well as descriptions of the environmental (social and physical) context for the relationship.

I coded transcripts of the interviews for themes that would suggest the interpersonal and organizational contexts in which CSM developed and, in many cases, continued over extended periods of time. In naming the themes, I intentionally avoided using terms in the extant literature and instead used the actual language of the participants in order to avoid attributing meanings that they did not intend. So instead of using terms such as "grooming," I used behaviorally specific codes, such as the following: "saying he admired me," "gave gifts," and "asking for or giving hugs or kisses." When an interviewee said "he gave me special attention," I probed further: "If I were making a movie, what would that scene look like; what did he do or say that felt like special attention?" For more information about the research and sampling methods, see Garland and Argueta (2010).

Most of the offended identified the experience they had with their religious leaders as romantic affairs. Nevertheless, eleven experienced verbal abuse; six were physically threatened as a way to keep them silent or sexually compliant. Six women described violence and rape. I identified five common themes concerning the contexts and situations in which CSM takes place.

No Response to Situations That "Normally" Prompt Action

Most of the offended said that they had felt uncertain of what was happening in their relationships with their religious leaders. Spouses, friends, and other congregational leaders also were uncertain about the meaning of what they observed, and so they did nothing. Their trust in the leader was stronger than their trust in their own perceptions of the situation. In fact, their view of the leader altered how they interpreted what they were experiencing.

For example, when Darla's pastor asked her out to a restaurant for coffee, where he used sexual expletives in casual conversation, she was shocked and "thrown off balance" that a religious leader would use such sexually graphic language. She remembered telling herself "that it was more evidence that he was an authentic leader and further reason to trust him." The pastor's language broke social norms, and instead of confronting him with his inappropriateness as she might have done with another man, she allowed him to redefine the social norm. Graphic sexual language became a sign of authenticity.

The offended was confused about the meaning of behavior when she would otherwise have been confident in her understanding—for example, if it had been the behavior of a peer and not of a spiritual leader. Significant others also experienced this confusion and inaction, suggesting that it is the aura of leadership that is operating in the social system and not just a lack of perception on the part of the offended. In fact, significant others often encouraged their partners to trust the religious leader despite what otherwise would have been serious warning signs. For example, Wendy's husband found e-mail messages from their pastor professing romantic feelings for Wendy. Wendy was "spiraling into depression," however, and her husband believed they had nowhere else to turn for help, so he encouraged Wendy to continue counseling with the pastor.

In retrospect, the interviewees and those close to them realized that they had ignored obvious signs. They had no cognitive categories for understanding a religious leader who was acting sexually toward them or a loved one, so they labeled the behavior as something they did have a category for—their own overactive imaginations or sensitivities. They had no frame of reference for seeing and recognizing a trusted religious leader's sexual misbehavior, but they had cognitive frameworks for mistaken meaning in social situations. All of us have misread the behavior of others at one time or another, and we learn to give people the benefit of the doubt so as to read the best possible meaning into the behavior of someone we trust. For example, in an interview Samantha described a dinner with her priest: "In the car on the way home, I wondered what on earth had happened. Because I wasn't able to face that he had made advances, I convinced myself that it was just a mistake after all, that my imagination was running wild, and that a priest wouldn't attempt something sexual with me or anyone—and especially not this priest, who was such a good friend."

Many victims remembered the offender paying them special attention, beyond what would be expected, or normative, for a religious leader and a congregant. For example, Cindy remembered arriving at church on Sunday and seeing the priest in the processional line, preparing to lead worship: "He would break out of the line to come over and talk to me." Another time, the priest passed her in the aisle between services: "He asked if I had gotten a haircut. He didn't even know my name. It wasn't inappropriate but just an odd thing to say." In both cases, the behavior took place in the sanctuary, a sacred space. The behavior would not have seemed inappropriate in a casual relationship between peers, but it was outside the normative expectations of a religious leader's role during a worship service and so made Cindy feel "odd." Similarly, Kate remembers her anxiety when her pastor asked her to come into his office on Sunday mornings—alone—before he gave the sermon. Then he started calling her at home. At the time that these offended women received these various forms of unusual attention, it raised their sense of vigilance enough that they remembered it after the later experience of CSM. At the time, however, although they reported feeling wary, they dismissed it as their overreacting or misunderstanding their leaders' intentions.

Adding to their confusion was the fact that many of these behaviors took place in a public setting: the pastor publicly invited Kate to his study before worship, a time when church offices are bustling with people. The priest stepped out of the worship processional to have a conversation with Cindy and commented on her hair when he passed her in the church sanctuary full of worshipers. Kate's pastor called her at her home each Sunday morning, when her husband and children were there. In some ways, the fact that the behavior took place in front of others seemed to normalize it, and indeed, although some others also responded warily (for example, Kate's husband wondered why the pastor was calling his wife), no alarms were sounded. Consequently, the victim's view that "I'm making a mountain out of a molehill" or "I'm too sensitive; this is our pastor" was confirmed by both the public location for the special attention and the lack of response by other observers.

Whatever the offender's motivations for these overtures, no one openly questioned or objected to the offender's actions, resulting not only in the woman's alarm system being silenced, but also perhaps assuring the offender that his behavior must not be objectionable. After all, he called her when her husband was there; he invited her into his office when there were plenty of people around—and no one seemed to raise concerns. All the while, the offended and offender were forming a more intimate relationship that seemed to be accepted by the community, since it was being formed under the community's collective eyes.

Physical behaviors such as hugs and kisses are common in many Christian congregations, where sharing the peace in a worship service may include kisses on the cheek and embraces. More than half of the interviewees reported that their religious leaders hugged and kissed them in public. For example, Laura said that the minister at her church was "touchy-feely" with all the women, so when he started holding her hand, because the behavior took place in public, it took on an air of acceptability. He then wanted hugs from Laura in his office. Hugs in private can quickly take on a different meaning than hugs in a public setting, however. Rhonda remembered her rabbi's hug after a counseling session: "We both stood up, and he said, 'How about a hug?' He pulled me into a full-body embrace, for too long. I was uncomfortable and pulled away, and he said he would be praying for me."

The juxtaposition of the embrace and her awareness that he had an erection with the promise of prayer is confusing, suggesting that the inappropriate hug was part of his religious care.

A number of the offended were new to the faith community. Being new to a community is usually a time of heightened anxiety—as one interviewee said, "exciting and frightening at the same time." Being new means not yet knowing the community's norms. When a religious leader is engaging in non-normative behavior, these new community members would be least likely to identify that behavior as inappropriate, especially if others in the community seemed not to raise concerns.

The Culture of Niceness

By "nice," I mean overlooking or ignoring the behavior of others that we know to be socially inappropriate, rather than naming the behavior and risking embarrassing, angering, or hurting them. The offended whom I interviewed were living by this cultural norm, even in the face of offenders' blatantly inappropriate behavior. In other words, they were not simply normalizing the offenders' behavior and questioning their own perceptions; they recognized that the behavior was sexual and thus inappropriate, and still they did not object. Kate remembered the first time the offender kissed her:

> He kissed me, and I just figured it would be quick, but it wasn't. I remembered first feeling it was totally wrong. It felt like I was kissing an old man. I thought, "How am I going to tell him this? I don't want to hurt his feelings." I tried [to confront him], but I couldn't; it wasn't right. I desperately wanted to tell him that this was all wrong, but I couldn't hurt my closest friend with those words when he felt so deeply for me.

The norm of being "nice" was strengthened by some offenders giving gifts—books, jewelry, and cards—that were often religious in nature and so on the surface apparently appropriate, although the offender was singling out the congregant with this special attention. For example, each day Deena's pastor left spiritual readings in her mail slot that he had chosen specially for her; he then asked to meet with her daily to give her "spiritual direction." Giving gifts with a spiritual character made it more difficult for the offended to object to the special attention they were receiving. Moreover, gifts communicate the expectation of something in return.

A Lack of Accountability

Our world has increasingly privatized communication and consequently increased our ability to avoid oversight or accountability to others. Instead of letters in a family mailbox, where anyone in the family can see that a member has received a communication and from whom, letters come to private e-mail accounts out of sight of all who do not know the password. Instead of phones being located in a public space, such as on the kitchen wall, they are now in a purse or pocket and can be used anywhere, out of hearing of others. Such communication allows a relationship attachment to form and deepen, removed from observation. Many of those interviewed told of long and frequent conversations over the phone or through e-mail with their offenders. Lorie thought back on the frequency with which she communicated with her offender: "By the end of the summer, we had talked almost every day on the telephone."

These religious leaders evidently had no one to whom they were accountable for the use of their professional time, or for where they spend their time and with whom. It is common in small congregations for the pastor to be the only full-time staff person. If there are other secretarial or professional staff members with offices in the congregation's building, they are commonly supervised by and answer to the pastor or religious leader. Leaders are out and about in the community, calling on congregants in the hospital or at home, to offer comfort during times of stress or crisis or to work on congregational business.

Interviewees also reported that the offenders often used their church offices as places to engage them sexually. Kate knew the policies surrounding being in her pastor's office:

> Men and women were not supposed to counsel, but if it was necessary, there was a window in the door and it was required that the secretary be there. For the first period of time, he left the door open so she could see, but not hear. Over the span of a year, the door would be a little more closed, or she wouldn't be there. Then the door was shut and she wasn't there. He had covered the window with his jacket, and he closed the door all the way behind me.

The only observer of the pastor's schedule and compliance with the counseling policy was the part-time secretary, whom he supervised. Policies to prevent CSM can thus be put in place but easily broken if a leader is not accountable to anyone.

Overlapping and Multiple Roles

Most of the offended were in a formal counseling relationship with the religious leader. Others were meeting alone with their religious leader for what they called spiritual direction. They described this as a private meeting between the leader and congregant in which the congregant shared personal struggles and, in response, the leader provided guidance in the use of spiritual practices such as prayer and meditation.

In some cases, interactions differed from professional counseling relationships with other helping professionals, in that the direction of invitation was reversed. Instead of the congregant asking for help, the religious leader volunteered to provide the congregant with counseling. For example, Darla perceived her pastor to be a very powerful, charismatic speaker. He observed tears in her eyes while he was preaching and called her later that day, after worship, and said: "I saw your tears. Do we need to talk? Do you need counseling?" Touched that he was so observant and empathetic, Darla began seeing him for counseling, leading to sexual involvement. She learned later that he had used the same behavior with other women in the congregation.

In other cases, congregants themselves sought counseling from the religious leader. At the time of the offense, most of the offended had been experiencing a family crisis or loss—a deteriorating relationship with a parent, a teenager using drugs, a sequence of family deaths, the death of a young child, loss of a husband, divorce, or the end of a long-term romantic relationship.

These counseling relationships were not a one-time crisis intervention by a religious leader at a hospital bedside or before or after the funeral of a loved one. They often took on the characteristics of a psychotherapeutic relationship with multiple sessions, often extended over time, sometimes even at the initiative of the religious leader. Fifty-seven percent of the offended reported that in addition to being a religious leader and often a counselor or spiritual director as well, the offender was a friend or confidante, or seemed like a member of the family.

Trust in the Sanctuary

The congregation and its leaders are expected to be safe, a "sanctuary" where vulnerabilities will be protected. Congregants expect to be able to confess personal thoughts and struggles to their religious leaders without fearing that those confessions will be used to manipulate them. Leaders are supposed to be safe sources of guidance and forgiveness. Some offenders expressed admiration of the offended, sometimes in the form of compliments about the woman's spirituality. Dawn felt as though her offender was validating her relationship with God: "He could see good in me. It was intoxicating. I felt like God really loved me for the first time. I felt unburdened." The offender's admiration struck a chord with Dawn because it corresponded with her spiritual vulnerability. It is a significant boost to self-esteem to be favored by a powerful religious leader. Some offenders suggested to the offended that they would leave their marriages to start a new life of ministry with the offended. Tess spoke to her pastor frequently on the phone:

> He started talking to me about marriage and divorcing our spouses and working together in ministry because that is what God wanted. God had put us together for a reason. I believed him. He said, "Sometimes there's pain, but there is a reason for it." He talked about how he had thought about writing a book, and we would be good to write a book together. We were supposed to be together.

Implications for Prevention

These contextual dynamics of CSM suggest what might be helpful prevention and early intervention strategies. Community ignorance about the prevalence and characteristics of CSM leads to paralysis rather than action in the face of early warning signs. Education about the dynamics of CSM has been limited to seminary ethics courses and continuing education for pastors, neither of which reaches the lay governing bodies responsible for the actions of their leaders or the members who, if they were aware of these dynamics, might be more willing to trust their perceptions when a leader's behavior infringes on or shifts community norms.

The first question asked when I present these research findings to groups of laity is most often, "But don't women 'go after' their pastors?" My response is a qualified "probably." Pastors are often compassionate, highly personable, and powerful leaders. Women who are lonely, abused, and or spiritually needy may indeed want a relationship with them. Even when that happens, however, it is the responsibility of the religious leader to maintain safe boundaries. It is easier for the community to believe that the victims are to blame than that a beloved leader may have abused his or her power. In fact, many have undoubtedly experienced CSM happening in their own congregations and dismissed it by blaming the woman or excusing the pastor, forgiving him for the sexual relationship. That is the only way most people can understand or cope with an action that is so contrary to their perception of their religious leader. Moreover, it is often much easier to dismiss or excuse an affair than an abuse of power.

Positional power is a characteristic of roles carried not only by religious leaders but also by some congregants in the larger community, such as teachers, supervisors, employers, and parents. Therefore, addressing the ethical and moral use of power is an appropriate focus of religious education (Garland and Kabat 2010). Moreover, congregations educated about the dynamics of CSM may be more willing to wrestle with defining what is and what is not the role of the religious leader, as well as with creating a system of accountability that can protect both religious leaders and congregants from potential misconduct.

In response to our research findings, Helge and Toben (2009; see also the chapter by Toben and Helge in this volume) have crafted a model statute designed to withstand challenges on constitutional grounds of church-state separation. Such legislation could not only change attitudes about the nature of CSM but could also empower congregations and the offended to take action that removes offenders from positions of leadership where they can continue to do harm.

Conclusion

Whenever people are given power, they have the opportunity to abuse it, and some of them do. It is clear that religious leaders are not exceptions. In addition to religious leaders' responsibility to handle the power they are given in ways that protect rather than harm, it is also the responsibility of the community that gives them power to provide safeguards to protect against abuses, and to respond swiftly and compassionately when abuse happens.

Notes

1. With the permission of the editor of *Social Work & Christianity*, this article draws heavily on two articles published in that journal: Garland, "Wolves in Shepherds' Clothing: Helping Women Survive Clergy Sexual Abuse" (2006, 33 [1]: 1–35); and Garland and Argueta, "How Clergy Sexual Misconduct Happens: A Qualitative Study of First-Hand Accounts" (2010, 37 [1]: 1–27). I am grateful to Mark Chaves, my research partner in the quantitative study; to Christen Argueta, my partner in the qualitative study; and to the Ford Foundation, the Christian Life Commission of the Baptist General Convention of Texas, and the JES Edwards Foundation of Fort Worth, Texas, who provided financial support for this research project.

2. This case study is not an actual case but a composite, drawn from the cases of forty-six interviewees who as adults had experienced a sexual encounter or relationship with a religious leader (Garland and Argueta 2010).

3. This chapter deals only with clergy sexual misconduct with persons age eighteen or older, not with children.

4. I use the rather awkward but general term "offended" to describe those who are

targets of CSM, rather than the terms "victim" and "survivor." Moving from being a victim to becoming a survivor is a process of coping on the part of the target of CSM; here, the focus is on the religious leader's offensive behavior and its consequences, not the processes of coping and surviving. Because CSM may involve a range of leaders' intentionality and forethought, I have chosen to use terms related to the word "offense" because they do not imply intent or forethought on the part of the religious leader, nor necessarily the innocence or helplessness of the congregant.

References

Adam, E. 1998. "Echoes of Nalinika: A Monk in the Dock." *Journal of Buddhist Ethics* 5:261–76.

Anonymous. 1995. "Ghost in the Bedroom." *Canadian Baptist*, January, 17–18.

Carnes, P. J. 1997. *The Betrayal Bond: Breaking Free of Exploitative Relationships*. Deerfield Beach, FL: Health Communications.

Chaves, M., and D. Garland. 2009. "The Prevalence of Clergy Sexual Advances toward Adults in Their Congregations." *Journal for the Scientific Study of Religion* 48:817–24.

De Young, M., and J. A. Lowry. 1992. "Traumatic Bonding: Clinical Implications in Incest." *Child Welfare* 71:165–75.

Flynn, K. A. 2003. *The Sexual Abuse of Women by Members of the Clergy*. Jefferson, NC: McFarland.

Fortune, M. M. 1989. *Is Nothing Sacred? When Sex Invades the Pastoral Relationship*. New York: Harper and Row.

———. 1999. "Foreword." In *Victim to Survivor: Women Recovering from Clergy Sexual Abuse*, edited by N. W. Poling, i–xiv. Cleveland, OH: United Church.

Francis, P. C., and T. D. Baldo. 1998. "Narcissistic Measure of Lutheran Clergy Who Self-Reported Committing Clergy Sexual Misconduct." *Pastoral Psychology* 47 (2): 81–96.

Friberg, N. C., and M. R. Laaser. 1998. *Before the Fall: Preventing Pastoral Sexual Abuse*. Collegeville, MN: Liturgical.

Garland, D. R. 2006. "'Wolves in Shepherds' Clothing: Helping Women Survive Clergy Sexual Abuse." *Social Work & Christianity* 33 (1): 1–35.

Garland, D. R., and C. Argueta. 2010. "How Clergy Sexual Misconduct Happens: A Qualitative Study of First-Hand Accounts." *Social Work & Christianity* 37 (1): 1–27.

Garland, D. R., and V. M. Kabat. 2010. "Christians and Power: A Six-Session Bible Study Curriculum." Waco, TX: Baylor University Center for Family and Community Ministries. http://www.baylor.edu/social_work/cfcm/.

Gerdes, K. E., M. N. Beck, and H. Miller. 2002. "Betrayal of a Sacred Trust: 'Sanctuary Trauma' in Sexual Abuse Survivors." *Social Work Today* 27 (1): 6–11.

Goldfein, J. S. 2004. "The Stages of Trauma Recovery." *Psychotherapy Networker* 28 (1): 55.

Helge, K., and J. B. B. Toben. 2009. "Sexual Misconduct of Clergypersons with Congregants or Parishioners: Civil and Criminal Liabilities and Responsibilities." Unpublished paper. http://www.baylor.edu/clergysexualmisconduct/.

Hopkins, N. M. 1998. *The Congregational Response to Clergy Betrayals of Trust.* Collegeville, MN: Liturgical.

Hopkins, N. M., and M. Laaser, eds. 1995. *Restoring the Soul of a Church: Healing Congregations Wounded by Clergy Sexual Misconduct.* Collegeville, MN: Liturgical.

Horst, E. A. 1998. *Recovering the Lost Self: Shame-Healing for Victims of Clergy Sexual Abuse.* Collegeville MN: Order of St. Benedict.

———. 2000. *Questions and Answers about Clergy Sexual Misconduct.* Collegeville, MN: Liturgical.

Jackowski, K. 2004. *The Silence We Keep: A Nun's View of the Catholic Priest Scandal.* New York: Harmony.

Jacobs, J. 1984. "The Economy of Love in Religious Commitment: The Deconversion of Women from Nontraditional Religious Movements." *Journal for the Scientific Study of Religion* 23 (2): 155–71.

Jewell, J. 2006. "A Corrupt Salvation." *Christianity Today* 50 (3): 23–24.

Kennedy, M. 2003. "Sexual Abuse of Women by Priests and Ministers to Whom They Go for Pastoral Care and Support." *Feminist Theology* 11:226–36.

Liberty, P. L. 2001. "'It's Difficult to Explain'—The Compromise of Moral Agency for Victims of Abuse by Religious Leaders." *Journal of Religion & Abuse* 3 (3–4): 81–90.

Maris, M. 1995. "Preface." In *Restoring the Soul of a Church: Healing Congregations Wounded by Clergy Sexual Misconduct*, edited by N. M. Hopkins and M. Laaser, 3–22. Collegeville, MN: Liturgical.

Miller, D. A. 1993. *How Little We Knew: Collusion and Confusion with Sexual Misconduct.* Lafayette, LA: Prescott.

Oxenhandler, N. 2008. *The Wishing Year.* New York: Random House.

Poling, N. W. 1999. *Victim to Survivor: Women Recovering from Clergy Sexual Abuse.* Cleveland, OH: United Church.

Religion News Service. 2002. "Sex Abuse Report May Spark PCUSA Reforms." *Christian Century* 119 (21): 14.

Shupe, A. 1998. *Wolves within the Fold: Religious Leadership and Abuses of Power.* New Brunswick, NJ: Rutgers University Press.

———. 2007. *Spoils of the Kingdom: Clergy Misconduct and Religious Community.* Urbana: University of Illinois Press.

Simon, D. R., and D. S. Eitzen. 1982. *Elite Deviance.* Boston: Pearson/Allyn and Bacon.

Steinke, P. L. 1989. "Clergy Affairs." *Journal of Psychology and Christianity* 8 (4): 56–62.

Underwood, A. 2003. "Doing Justice in Cases of Clergy Abuse of Power: A Legal Perspective." *Journal of Religion & Abuse* 5 (1): 35–65.

Witherspoon, T. 2010. "Mistress Testifies That Matt Baker Told Her How He Killed His Wife." *Waco Tribune*, January 20.

Bradley Toben and Kris Helge

7 Clergyperson Sexual Misconduct with Congregants or Parishioners

Past Attempts to Impose Civil and Criminal Liabilities and a Proposed Criminal Law to Increase the Likelihood of Criminal Punishment of Perpetrators

Introduction

Recently, the media have made people cognizant of clergypersons who have allegedly committed sexual misconduct with children, with an intense focus on Catholic priests. Although less publicized, clergy sexual misconduct involving adults is also common. Very few states have been able to legally punish clergypersons who commit sexual misconduct against adults due to invalid laws or a lack of legal authority altogether. In this chapter, we propose a new criminal law that could be used to criminally punish a clergyperson who commits sexual misconduct with adults. For the purposes of this chapter, clergy sexual misconduct is defined as any sexual contact or action that is not consensual; it may consist of touching of the breasts or other sexual organs "or nonconsensual oral, vaginal or anal sex . . . that is initiated by a clergyperson against another non-consenting adult," to use the wording in Texas's law titled "Sexual Assault" (2010). The meaning of "nonconsensual" is a key concept and will be discussed in this chapter.

Ballotta's (1994) research demonstrates that, as noted, much recent media coverage has focused particularly on sexual misconduct of Roman Catholic priests with children and other minors, as well as on the response of dioceses and the Vatican to pedophilia in the ranks of the priesthood. The issue of clergyperson sexual misconduct with congregants or parishioners, however, is not limited to any particular denomination or faith tradition. According to recent studies, clergyperson sexual misconduct is a growing problem across an array of faith traditions. Christianity, Judaism, Islam, Buddhism, and Hinduism, as well as less prominent faith traditions, are affected by the misconduct. For example, in a study of the Church of England, Birchard (2000) demonstrated that 67 percent of clergypersons who responded to a survey had known a colleague who had engaged in sexual misconduct with a congregant. Another study indicated that 70 percent of Southern Baptist ministers knew of other ministers who had engaged in sexual misconduct with a congregant (White 2002). O'Reilly and Strasser (1994) further noted that American rabbis have been dismissed on account of sexual misconduct with congregants, and numerous Buddhist religious leaders have been accused of sexual misconduct. Accordingly, in this chapter, the term "clergyperson" will be used to refer to all of the principal leadership roles at the head of a congregation, synagogue, mosque, or parish, such as ministers, rabbis, imams, and priests. Moreover, as noted, clergyperson sexual misconduct extends beyond the abuse of children and minors. Most faith traditions also have dealt with the issue of such misconduct involving adults—typically female adults—who are congregants or parishioners. In these cases, the misconduct typically arises out of counseling relationships, but it may also arise within the context of other interactions between the clergyperson and congregants or parishioners (Cruz 1991).

No faith tradition or denomination can avoid the obligation to deal effectively with clergyperson sexual misconduct. This misconduct is a violation of the fundamental basis of the relationship of a clergyperson with those who look to him or her to provide guidance and instruction in spiritual matters regarded as falling within the special expertise of the clergy. Clergypersons occupy a distinctive role related to faith, morals, and higher matters that lie beyond the obvious and visible aspects of the human condition.

Most Clergy Sexual Misconduct Goes Legally Unpunished

Options Available to a Victim

Clergypersons need to be held legally accountable when they commit sexual misconduct against a congregant or parishioner. The current legal remedies available to the victim of clergy sexual misconduct are filing a civil lawsuit and reporting the misconduct to the police, in the hope that a prosecutor will file a criminal prosecution against the perpetrator.

When an individual commences a lawsuit in a civil court, he or she is usually asking for monetary relief from the perpetrator for his or her damages. These damages may include mental and emotional pain and suffering. A claim for emotional pain and suffering arises out of any emotional trauma experienced as a result of the perpetrator's behavior toward the victim. In a criminal matter, a victim initially files a report with the police or other governmental authority regarding a crime such as sexual misconduct. Then, based on this report, an attorney who works for the state or federal government may decide to commence a criminal action, asking a judge or jury to punish a perpetrator by requiring him or her to pay a fine and/or mandating his or her incarceration. A criminal prosecution is the process of putting an alleged perpetrator on trial, presenting all evidence against him or her, giving the alleged perpetrator a chance to rebut that evidence and put forth his or her own, and asking the judge or jury to declare the alleged perpetrator innocent or guilty.

Victims Fail to Report Sexual Misconduct

There are many reasons why clergyperson sexual misconduct may go unpunished. One is that victims are often hesitant to report the sexual misconduct. In most state criminal cases, the victim of a sexual offense must agree to cooperate with the state and press charges against an alleged perpetrator, before the prosecutor can pursue an action asking for punishment of the defendant. However, in the context of clergy sexual misconduct, prosecutions may not come to fruition because of the unwillingness of a victim to press charges against her or his own priest, pastor, or other religious leader. This unwillingness may be a result of the patriarchal nature of the church in which the sexual misconduct occurred, which subsequently influences a female victim to be hesitant to report such a crime. Also, many women's accusations of sexual abuse or misconduct are often discounted outright by such a patriarchally structured church. Other congregants may respond to such accusations with statements like "our priest wouldn't do that," which increases the victim's feelings of shame, embarrassment, and ostracism. Thus, female victims may remain silent due to the fear of possible negative perceptions of their fellow congregants or parishioners (Fortune 1998).

Victims Wait Too Long to Report Misconduct

Many of the victims who muster the courage to report clergyperson sexual misconduct do so too late. Most state laws mandate that a victim has to make an official complaint to legal authorities within a certain time period from when he or she knew the crime was committed. For example, in Minnesota, the "Actions for Damages Due to Sexual Abuse" (2010) statute ("statute" is a synonym for law) requires that a person subjected to a clergyperson's nonconsensual touching of a private body part has six years to make an official complaint from the time the victim knew or should have known the sexual offense occurred. If an alleged victim fails to make a complaint within that time period, state authorities cannot criminally prosecute and punish the alleged perpetrator.

Laws Are Inadequate

Sometimes a victim is not reticent about reporting misconduct or suing a clergyperson for sexual misconduct, but most states unfortunately do not have civil or criminal laws that specifically require clergyperson perpetrators to make monetary payments to a victim for damages caused, or that criminalize and punish sexual misconduct by clergypersons. Only thirteen states—Arkansas, Connecticut, Delaware, Iowa, Kansas, Minnesota, Mississippi, New Mexico, North Dakota, South Dakota, Texas, Utah, Wisconsin—and the District of Columbia have penal statutes (laws that punish; "penal" is synonymous with punitive) that, in at least some circumstances, support the criminal prosecution and punishment of clergypersons engaged in sexual misconduct with congregants or parishioners. These statutes turn on various linguistic formulations, most commonly specifying that the misconduct occurred within the confines of the counseling relationship. Also, the laws of each of the thirteen states and the District of Columbia define clergypersons as falling within the field of psychotherapy or counseling professionals (Falk 1998).

Only a handful of state penal statutes address clergyperson sexual misconduct outside of the context of the counseling relationship. Significantly, the sexual misconduct does not always occur within a counseling relationship. For example, it could occur while a pastor is recommending weekly hymns for service; or when a congregant meets with a clergyperson about recommended scripture readings for certain situations such as for the loss of a loved one, a marriage, or a financial crisis. Therefore, the majority of US states' legislatures have not passed laws that give adult citizens legal remedies when they have been sexually violated by a clergyperson.

Civil Lawsuits for Clergypersons' Sexual Misconduct with Adults

Two prefatory remarks are in order prior to considering civil suits against clergypersons for sexual misconduct with adults: the law addresses sexual misconduct with children differently than misconduct with adults and the now abolished "benefit of clergy" doctrine. In civil courts, children receive unquestioned legal protection from clergyperson sexual misconduct, but this chapter does not focus on the familiar cases of such misconduct involving children or other minors. The fundamental obligation of trust and care owed by an adult to a young person and the innocence and vulnerability of those who are under age and immature are well understood and accepted. The sexual abuse of children is criminalized in all fifty states and the District of Columbia. Its frequency is well documented, as is noted in the case *L.M. v. Karlson* (2002), which maintained that proven sexual abuse of a child is punished criminally per se because children are so young, vulnerable, and easily manipulated and cannot communicate well. There is no legal exception or recognized loophole that allows a clergyperson, or any adult perpetrator, who has been proven to have committed sexual misconduct with a child to elude criminal punishment. A recently decided case, *Roman Catholic Diocese of Jackson v. Morrison*, emphasizes that no legal exception exists for clergypersons who commit sexual misconduct with children because, as the court reasons, the United States Constitution does not prevent a suit against a Catholic Diocese stemming from accusation of child sexual abuse (2005,). In other words, if it is proven in a court of law that one has committed sexual misconduct with a child, then the perpetrator will face punishment from that court.

The "Benefit of Clergy" Doctrine

Civil and criminal laws that govern clergypersons in the United States have evolved over almost 250 years. For example, until around the mid-1800s, if a clergyperson committed a crime, he or she could invoke the "benefit of clergy" doctrine, which entitled the clergyperson to be given a special status by the courts. In some cases the clergyperson could avoid civil and criminal punishment altogether; in other cases, he or she would be required to reimburse a victim a lesser amount of money, or be sentenced to a lesser criminal punishment, than was prescribed by law for other offenders. However, this doctrine was abolished by all states around the mid-1800s (Sawyer 1990). Therefore, all clergypersons in the United States may now be fined and be required to pay another entity money in a civil court of law, or be judged guilty and assigned a punishment in a criminal court of law. Such punishment may consist of a fine, time spent in prison, community service, or some other form of penalty.

Clergy and Professional Malpractice

Today, without the "benefit of clergy" doctrine for protection, if a clergyperson is sued in a civil court for sexual misconduct, the court may force the offender, if convicted, to pay money for damages to the person filing the suit. Damages may consist of emotional distress, embarrassment, medical treatment, and other factors arising from the sexual misconduct. An action to collect money for these damages is often called "clergy malpractice." In general, clergy malpractice is defined as a clergy member's performing an action outside of his or her normal professional role as clergy that harms someone directly or indirectly. Therefore, when commencing a clergy malpractice lawsuit, a victim is essentially arguing that a clergyperson owed him or her a specific duty, such as to care for him or her, not betray his or her trust, or not to take advantage of his or her vulnerabilities. Furthermore, the victim is alleging that the clergyperson failed to grant this duty of care to the victim by committing some misconduct to betray the victim's trust, care, or vulnerabilities, such as by committing sexual misconduct. *Fortin v. Roman Catholic Bishop of Portland* (2005) illustrates that clergy malpractice cases have decided that the standard of care for clergy is one of exercising the level of care and diligence that a reasonable clergyperson of a particular sect would exercise, given the specific education and training offered or required by that entity.

This type of clergy malpractice lawsuit may also be termed a lawsuit for professional malpractice that seeks to hold a counselor or clergyperson liable (that is, legally responsible) for not upholding a duty owed to a client, such as not violating a client's trust. Again, professional malpractice may be defined as a professional's performing an action outside of his or her normal professional roles that directly or indirectly harms another person. One manner in which a client's trust may be violated is when the professional commits sexual misconduct against a client. This type of professional malpractice legal theory holds that a fiduciary duty is owed by the clergyperson to the client. A fiduciary duty is defined as an obligation owed to another person when a relationship of trust or confidence has been created between two or more individuals. For example, a clergyperson owes the fiduciary duty of confidentiality to a congregant or parishioner when that individual discusses a personal matter with the clergyperson: the clergyperson cannot tell others about the personal matter. According to *Webb v. West Virginia Board of Medicine* (2002), the factors that characterize a fiduciary relationship—trust, reliance, emotional intimacy, and vulnerability—between a counselor (the fiduciary) and a client (the person to whom the fiduciary duty is owed) are such that civil liability is imposed even if the client freely consents to having sexual contact with a clergyperson, and is imposed even if the wrongdoer is not a clergyperson (Lupu and Tuttle 2004).

Therefore, as *In re Phillips* (2008) and *Moses v. Diocese of Colorado* (1993) discuss, the determination of a clergyperson's liability for sexual misconduct with an adult in a civil court of law generally turns on the following factors: (1) the existence of a concept of duty such as one of trust, owed by the counselor (or clergyperson) to a client to provide a prescribed standard of care, and a determination that the counselor has failed to perform this duty; or (2) the existence of a fiduciary relationship between the counselor (or clergyperson) and a client that calls for the fiduciary (the counselor) to fully subordinate his or her interests to the interests of the client. By subordinating his or her interests, the counselor as fiduciary is thereby prohibited from sexually violating the client, even if the client reacts positively to sexual advances.

Legal Theories' Failure to Deter Clergy Sexual Misconduct

When the counseling has a religious or spiritual dimension the First Amendment of the US Constitution may, for the reasons discussed below, prevent victims or their representatives from successfully suing clergyperson perpetrators in a civil court of law using the previously mentioned legal theories, unless the secular nature of the clergy relationship with the congregant or parishioner can be defined with reasonable sharpness, which is possible under certain circumstances. Most often it is difficult, if not impossible, to separate the secular aspects of counseling (such as attempting to implement behavior change via a particular secular psychological theory—for example, Adlerian psychoanalytic behavior change) by a clergyperson from any religious or spiritual components (such as using prayer or scriptural interpretation to augment behavior change) of the same interaction. Only when a clergyperson functions as a counselor in a secular practice setting, so that his or her religious identity and expression become both inconsequential and dormant, does the counselor differentiate his or her identity as a secular therapist from his or her identity as a member of the clergy, thereby setting aside First Amendment issues.

The First Amendment as a Barrier to Civil Lawsuits

Individuals are prevented from pursuing civil lawsuits against clergypersons for sexual misconduct if the law used to sue the perpetrator violates the First

Amendment of the US Constitution. The Supreme Court created a test called the "*Lemon* test" to determine whether a law violates the First Amendment and is therefore invalid, and thus whether a clergyperson may be sued under a particular civil law or prosecuted under certain criminal laws (Nowak and Rotunda 2001). This test, described in *Lemon v. Kurtzman* (1971), requires that: (1) the law in question must have a secular purpose—that is, its purpose cannot focus on religious matters; (2) the law must not have the primary effect of either advancing or inhibiting religion—that is, its effect cannot impede one Christian denomination or other religion or advance another; and (3) the law must not result in an excessive entanglement between government and religion.

Excessive Entanglement and the Establishment Clause

Excessive entanglement (the third prong of the *Lemon* test) in the context of clergyperson sexual misconduct means that a law cannot require a court to determine the liability of a clergyperson's actions by interpreting church policy, practice, customs, liturgy, doctrine, or other denominational or religious matters. If any law used to sue a clergyperson requires a court to interpret any of these religious issues, then a court is likely to declare the law unconstitutional as a violation of the First Amendment's Establishment Clause, and the victim's lawsuit will be dismissed. The Establishment Clause basically states that Congress may not establish a national religion, and it may not give preference to one religion or sect over another. For example, if a victim files a lawsuit in civil court alleging that clergyperson sexual misconduct occurred during a counseling session, and the law used to sue or criminally punish a clergyperson requires the court to determine whether a denominational tradition of kissing and hugging between a clergyperson and a client during a counseling session is acceptable or unacceptable, then this law violates the Establishment Clause and is deemed unconstitutional. Such a law, therefore, cannot be used to sue a clergyperson perpetrator, because it is mandating a court (a governmental entity) to interpret and possibly reshape a church (a religious entity) or a denomination's culture, practices, or counseling policy. In addition, the law might be interpreted as showing a preference for one religion or denomination over another by forcing one religion or denomination to change its policy, while not requiring other religions or denominations to do so. Such a mandate equals "excessive entanglement," requiring a governmental entity (the court) to make policy decisions for a religious entity (the church). In other words, a government entity (such as a court) cannot create, shape, or modify policy, dogma, or beliefs of a religious entity (a church) because such action would violate the First Amendment and be unconstitutional (Nowak and Rotunda 2001).

Examples of Denials of Civil Actions

If a law fails to meet all three requirements of the *Lemon* test, it cannot be used to sue a clergyperson because it is unconstitutional. To be sure, the components of the *Lemon* test are linked and cannot be viewed in isolation. The Supreme Court has looked particularly at the effect of a statute to determine whether it creates an excessive entanglement between government and religion, as is exemplified in *Agostini v. Felton* (1997). In examining the effect, the Court examines the character and purpose of the institution benefited or inhibited, as is stated in *Waltz v. Tax Commission of the City of New York* (1970). Further, according to *Lemon v. Kurtzman* (1971), the Court also scrutinizes the resulting relationship between the government and religious authority. In other words, is the government placed in a position of having to make important denominational or church policy decisions that a government is prohibited from doing by the First Amendment?

Notwithstanding the holistic approach usually taken in considering the *Lemon* test, the third prong of the test—regarding whether the law creates excessive entanglement between government and religion—is the most important component and principally determines whether a court will be able to hear a civil lawsuit. Under the previously described theories regarding clergyperson sexual misconduct in the counseling context or any other context involving a congregant or parishioner, the first two prongs of the *Lemon* test are met. This follows from the fact that the imposition of civil liability for sexual misconduct with a client by a mental health therapist, including a clergyperson engaged in counseling as a therapist, has a clear secular purpose (the first prong of the *Lemon* test): penalizing the misuse of a professional mental health counseling relationship for sexual gratification. And the primary effect of imposing liability is to protect the integrity of such counseling relationships and not to advance or inhibit religion (which meets the second prong of the *Lemon* test).

In considering the applicability of the third prong of the *Lemon* test, if a civil lawsuit is brought pursuant to a theory that calls for the court, a governmental entity, to become "excessively entangled" with the interpretation or specification of religious practice, standards, or custom, the court would deem this unconstitutional based on the First Amendment. In other words, if the issue is whether the religiously or spiritually based counseling aspects of the relationship between the clergyperson and the congregant or parishioner were a factor in the victim's inability to effectively consent to sexual contact, then—based on the First Amendment—the court is constitutionally prevented from examining, or predicating liability on, such religious or spiritual components of the relationship, due to the excessive entanglement prong in the *Lemon* test.

To illustrate the doctrine's application with respect to other civil theories of liability, *Ayon v. Gourley* has stated that the "First Amendment bars claims of negligent hiring, negligent supervision, and outrageous conduct . . . [against an archdiocese] because such claims require inquiry into church policy and doctrine" (1999, 1250). Each of these theories in general holds that a church would be liable because it should have known a clergyperson it hired or supervised would have committed a malicious act against a congregant or parishioner. Such a requirement of inquiry and the consequent possible direction of church policy and doctrine by the court are deemed as excessive entanglement between a court as a governmental entity and a church as a religious institution. Similarly, *Schmidt v. Bishop* (1991) also decided that the First Amendment bars breach of fiduciary duty claims against pastors due to excessive entanglement of the courts in religion if required to articulate a generalized standard of care for clergymen.

Accordingly, it is almost legally impossible to bring a claim of clergy malpractice in the context of counseling relationships with a congregant or a parishioner, whether the action is premised on a theory of breach of duty of care (as measured by a reasonable standard of care) or on a theory of breach of a fiduciary duty, because it requires a court to interpret and possibly alter church policy. More specifically, a civil lawsuit advocating such claims would require a court to articulate or interpret church doctrine, liturgy, procedures, and other church matters and then further intervene in the inner workings of religious institutions, which is what occurred in the case of *Nally v. Grace Community Church* (1988). Duty of care claims call for a determination of whether the alleged wrongdoer failed to carry out the duty to afford the victim the "reasonable standard of care" within the given profession. For example, a reasonable standard of care for a certified public accountant would be filing a client's tax return using the best-known available tax deductions. Because such an action against a clergyperson calls for a determination of what a reasonable standard of care is for a clergyperson rendering religious or spiritual guidance within a given religious tradition—Would it be carrying out his or her duty of trust to the client? Or giving the best possible spiritual advice?—the courts have generally declined to hear such actions because of the First Amendment prohibitions explained above (see *Roman Catholic Diocese of Jackson v. Morrison* 2005).

Other courts have likewise declined relief in cases in which a claimant premised clergy liability for religious or spiritual counseling on the concept of breach of a fiduciary obligation owed by a clergyperson to a congregant or parishioner. In *Langford v. Roman Catholic Diocese of Brooklyn* (2000), the court, while denying relief on a breach of fiduciary theory, noted the following elements of proof that a fiduciary relationship had been established and that a breach of duty that arises from such a relationship within a specific religious setting had occurred: the vulnerability of one party to the other, which results in the empowerment of the stronger party by the weaker, which empowerment has been solicited or accepted by the stronger party, and prevents the weaker party from effectively protecting itself. This is also exemplified in *Moses v. Diocese of Colorado* (1993). These cases involve the problematic analysis of whether the parties are in a fiduciary relationship, a fact-sensitive inquiry that calls for an assessment of the perceptions of the clergyperson or the congregant or parishioner (or both) of the character of the counseling relationship and that may involve the court in constitutionally impermissible prescriptions of the character of a religiously based counseling relationship. Even if a fiduciary relationship is assumed, as in *Lowery v. Cook* (2007), the standard of fiduciary care within a religious setting must be prescribed. Hence, just as it is impermissible for the court to determine a proper standard of care for counseling for clergy in a religious setting, it is impermissible for the court to define the standard for breach of the fiduciary duty for clergy, because that would require the court to interpret church policy, dogma, and other church matters.

As a result, the imposition of civil liability on clergy, whether the theory is breach of the duty of care or breach of fiduciary duty, inevitably calls for judicial (court-mandated) determination of religious and spiritual issues that lie beyond the competency of the court. Therefore, if a clergyperson acting in his capacity as such and not as a secular counselor has sexual contact with a congregant or parishioner, by the estimation of most courts, the entanglement problem precludes any basis for civil liability.

Criminal Liability of Clergypersons for Sexual Misconduct

Unquestioned Bases of Liability with Children and Minors

As we stated above, state criminal laws uniformly punish sexual contact with children (see, for instance, the Michigan law "Sexual Conduct Definitions"

[2004] and the Colorado law "Unlawful Sexual Behavior" [2010]). Because of the minor's incapacity to consent (especially considering such factors as trust, reliance, emotional intimacy, and vulnerability), the nature of the relationship between the perpetrator and the child victim is of no consequence in establishing criminal liability, except in cases in which the perpetrator's relationship to the minor is otherwise used to identify certain classes of perpetrators for the purposes of differential punishment. For example, some criminal laws regarding sexual conduct, such as a law in Alaska titled "Sexual Abuse of a Minor" (2010) and one in Connecticut called "Sexual Offenses" (2007), identify specific perpetrators as being in positions of authority, such as coaches, teachers, and other juvenile authorities. People in these positions of authority—by virtue of their inherent trust, reliance, emotional intimacy, and vulnerability—have the potential to exercise undue influence over children or minors with whom they have an unusually close association. Thus, these individuals who commit sexual misconduct may be more severely punished by a court due to their position of authority over children. This consideration of the effect of a "position of authority," albeit in a different context, will play a part in developing a model statute, to be discussed shortly, with which one may criminally punish clergypersons who commit sexual misconduct outside of any counseling relationship with an adult congregant or parishioner. For now, suffice it to say that the societal interest in safeguarding the welfare of children supersedes any claim that might be advanced by a clergyperson that the clergy's constitutional religious exercise prerogatives extend to sexual relations with children.

Incapacity to Give Effective Consent

In the same broad policy vein, aside from the cases involving the incapability of a child's giving valid consent to a sexual act, all states have laws that likewise deem mentally disabled, unconscious, or intoxicated persons as incapable of rendering valid consent. Again, consent means to consciously agree to commit to an action, such as a sexual act. Also, as noted in a California law, "Crimes against the Person Involving Sexual Assault" (2008), some state laws render specific individuals as incapable of consenting to certain actions due to mental disorder or developmental or physical disability. And all states criminalize various forms of sexual contact, including intentional intimate contact without the effective consent of the victim. Furthermore, sexual contact that is coerced or induced and sexual contact accomplished by fraud are illegal in all states, as exemplified in the New Hampshire law, "Aggravated Felonious Sexual Assault" (2010). Even some consensual forms of sexual conduct are criminalized for public policy reasons, including incest and bigamy. Thus, in all fifty states and the District of Columbia, nonconsensual sexual contact is punishable by criminal law.

Secular-Based Counseling to Congregants or Parishioners

In some instances sexual contact is punished by courts, even if consent is not necessary. Just as therapists (or clergypersons) can be held liable in civil courts in a secular counseling context, nearly all state criminal laws also explicitly treat as criminal sexual acts or contacts between those who render secular counseling and their clients. For example, the following state laws punish therapists (or clergypersons) if they commit sexual acts or participate in sexual contact with a client: "Sexual Assault" (2010), in Texas; "Sexual Exploitation by a Therapist" (2010), in Wisconsin; and "Sex Offenses by Psychotherapists" (2006), in South Dakota.

In regard to criminal law, the issue to be resolved in the case of a clergyperson having sexual contact with a congregant or parishioner is whether the characteristics of a relationship with a child can also characterize a clergyperson's relationship with some adult congregants or parishioners, given appropriate circumstances surrounding the emotional content of the relationship. In other words, does the clergyperson project a position of power and authority over his or her congregants or parishioners to the extent that consent might not be independently given by an adult congregant or parishioner?

The providers of secular counseling services are most typically referred to in the text of laws as "psychotherapists," "psychologists," or "medical professionals." Some laws also may include language describing other providers (including clergypersons) of mental health services that fall well beyond the ambit of what is regarded as classical psychology, which has a fairly narrow definition in the law. For example, the Texas law "Sexual Assault" (2010) defines a mental health provider as a person who represents him- or herself to the public by a title or description of services provided that includes the word "psychological," "psychologist," or "psychology"; who provides or offers to provide psychological services to individuals, groups, organizations, or the public; who is a psychologist or psychological associate employed as described by another psychologist who offers or provides psychological services, other than lecture services, to the public for consideration separate from the salary that the person receives for performing the person's regular duties; or who is employed as a psychologist or psychological associate by an organization that sells psychological services, other than lecture services, to the public for consideration. In other words, the legal definition of a psychologist can be very broad, and it can be a challenge to accurately specify in a criminal law all the types of practitioners who perform secular counseling, given that the meaning of "psychotherapy" extends well beyond the ambit of traditional practice by psychiatrists and psychologists.

The American Psychological Association is so concerned about possible patient sexual abuse that it has issued the following statement on its website: Patients may not be aware of the discipline of their treating clinician; furthermore, they deserve protection from professional misconduct, regardless of the discipline of the offender. It is undesirable to characterize mental health professionals as

> psychotherapists or to confine a criminal law to those practicing psychotherapy, as opposed to somatic treatments. It is not necessary to rely on transference and other psychological mechanisms to explain the special vulnerability of patients. While these concepts offer a valuable way of understanding and describing certain instances of sexual misconduct, the justification for criminal sanctions does not rest upon any particular theory of psychotherapy or the mode of practice of the mental health professional. The justification for criminalization is found in the high frequency of patients who are harmed as a consequence, and the morally repugnant nature of the exploitative behavior. (American Psychological Association 2011)

However, if a clergyperson is charged with sexual misconduct in what can be characterized as a secular-based counseling relationship, the application of the penal laws criminalizing sexual contact by a clergyperson does not appear to violate the First Amendment because there is no excessive entanglement: a government entity (a court) does not need to tell a religious organization or entity how to act, or how to interpret its own policy or doctrine. Therefore, unlike when a clergyperson is sued for sexual misconduct in a civil court, criminal punishment of sexual misconduct does not prevent enforcement of the public interest as expressed through the penal laws, irrespective of any asserted religious practice or motivation, because there is no need for inquiry into any standard of care or obligation of a fiduciary duty. As in the case of sexual assault of a minor, public policy alone will categorize the behavior as penal.

Less Well-Established Bases of Liability

But what about the case of two consenting adults having sexual contact? Sexual contact between legitimately consenting adults (in the absence of factors such as fraud, bigamy, or incest) is not generally criminalized. Hence, a sexual contact relationship between a member of the clergy and a congregant or parishioner (again, in most such cases the victim is an adult female), would appear, as discussed above, to be criminal only if it is determined that, in like circumstances, outside the religious context in which the adults involved occupy the roles of clergy and congregant or parishioner, the sexual contact between the adults would also be punished by a criminal law—as in the case of a clergyperson rendering what is, in setting and contact, a solely secular form of therapy.

Given this fact, and in the absence of a theory of criminal liability that does not turn on a counseling relationship, if sexual contact between a clergyperson and a congregant or parishioner unfolds in a relationship in which no counseling of any sort occurs, or in which counseling is restricted solely to purely theological advice. For example, a clergyperson may advise a congregant or parishioner that "this is an approach that you may want to consider in interpreting scripture" or religiously related guidance (for example, " this sort of choral anthem may be appropriate for the season of the Epiphany") without engaging the factors that would extend the relationship to the level that encompasses an amalgam of relational factors that characterize a counseling relationship—trust, reliance, emotional intimacy, and vulnerability, or the phenomenon of transference. In these cases, criminal liability for the sexual contact does not arise. Moreover, when the counseling of a congregant or parishioner is mixed in character (both secular and religious), but the inducement to sex arises solely from spiritual, religious, or theological advice or guidance, the First Amendment is relevant if a clergyperson is prosecuted in a criminal court because the entanglement doctrine may be invoked as a constitutional impediment to prosecution. Once again, a governmental entity (a criminal court) would be telling a religious entity (a church) how to interpret doctrine, redevelop church policy, or decipher some other church information.

The Criminal Legal Theory of Positional Authority

But is there a theory of abuse of positional authority that can premise criminal liability not on the secular counseling characteristics of the underlying relationship, but instead on the reality of unequal positional power and influence between the parties, linked with the emotional fragility or vulnerability of the victim? Such a criminal law theory would offer the possibility of reaching clergyperson sexual misconduct with a congregant or parishioner that is outside the secular counseling relationship. There ought to be a way to reach a sexually offending clergyperson, even if he or she does not use a secular counseling relationship as a conduit to sex, or if the counseling is restricted solely to theological advice (not relevant to any sexual relationship). That is, a clergyperson who, by virtue of occupying a position of authority—as perceived by the congregant or parishioner—and who, because of that position, has knowledge or notice of the emotional dependence or vulnerability of an adult congregant or parishioner, can take advantage of the position of authority and engage in sexual acts or contacts with the congregant or parishioner. A theory of abuse of positional authority would provide a viable basis for the imposition of criminal liability and punishment in such a circumstance by drawing on positional authority and its characteristics to negate what may appear to be—but which the law does not hold to be—consent. Moreover, the theory, by eschewing any focus on religious or faith-based artifacts of the relationship, would not involve a violation of the First Amendment because a governmental entity would not be ordering a church to change its policy, liturgy, procedures, or other church activities.

The impropriety of clergyperson sexual contact in such circumstances arises not from a failure to perform a professional duty of the clergyperson qua psychotherapist or counselor, and not from the duties of a clergyperson as a legitimate spiritual advisor. Rather, it comes from a misuse of the clergyperson's peculiar position of authority in a realm in which his or her intentions consist of preying on the emotionally vulnerable who are susceptible to inappropriate sexual manipulation. This basis of criminal liability for sexual contact is akin to the state laws (such as those concerning fraud or, in the case of children, their legal incapacity to consent) that criminalize sexual contact by removing what appears to be the consent given to sexual contact. The phrase "position of authority" is used in certain current criminal laws to describe—usually in reference to those accused of sexual misconduct with a child or other minor—a group of persons who are regarded as being in a position that calls for greater responsibility, such as the group "teacher, coach, or juvenile authority" in a California criminal law, "Crimes against the Person Involving Sexual Assault" (2008).

The theory of positional authority as a trigger for the criminalization of sexual contact with a congregant or parishioner by a clergyperson appears viable, especially with the support of a recent Supreme Court case, *Lawrence v. Texas* (2003). In *Lawrence* the Court ruled that a state may not generally criminalize sexual contact between consenting adults in the privacy of their home, given that such sexual conduct is protected under the Fourteenth Amendment of the Constitution. However, the Court implied that this general rule may not apply in cases where the consent may have been forced, coerced, or received by fraud in some manner, mentioning cases involving "minors," "persons who might be injured or coerced," and persons who are "situated in relationships where consent might not easily be refused." This last category appears, relying on a concept of positional authority, to open the door for laws that would criminalize and punish sexual misconduct by clergy outside of a counseling relationship. One of the justices in this case writes that *Lawrence* does not involve persons who might be injured or coerced or who are "situated in relationships where consent might not easily be refused." Again, this reiteration indicates that the Court might find a person naturally subordinated to another individual due to specific circumstances such as emotional instability, and who is interacting with a clergyperson, might not be able to legally give consent to sexual contact or conduct.

Crafting a Model Statute

Outside the counseling relationship, then, the criminalization of sexual contact must rest on a law that prescribes a relationship in which sexual contact occurs in a circumstance in which the victim is a person who is "situated in a relationship where consent might not easily be refused." Such a statute should focus on the position and authority of the actor and the consequent vulnerability or susceptibility of the alleged victim as the predicates for the sexual misconduct.

Proposed Model Criminal Law

The following phraseology appears to be appropriate for a model law, based on the discussion above and the policy, case law, and constitutional issues related to the criminalization of sexual misconduct by a clergyperson with a congregant or parishioner. The model statute language below is not presented as the only possible wording. There are also other sources of law that may be invoked to prevent such misconduct—although these sources typically are ineffective for various reasons.

A person commits an offense when . . . The law must explain what sexual conduct is and that it is subject to criminal sanction. Provisions describing forms of sexual contact appear in a broad array of laws in the various states that have been mentioned in this chapter. The operative provisions generally address: (1) conduct involving the intentional, coerced, or induced touching of intimate parts of the body of the victim by the perpetrator or by another person acting at the instigation of the perpetrator; (2) the forced, coerced, or induced touching of intimate parts of the body of the perpetrator or another person by the victim acting at the instigation of the perpetrator; or (3) the forced, coerced, or induced penetration of a bodily orifice (for example, the vagina, anus, or mouth) of the perpetrator, another person, or the complainant by the perpetrator, another person acting at the instigation of the perpetrator, the complainant, or an object used by one of these parties. The penetration language is intended to encompass forced, coerced, or induced acts of sexual intercourse, cunnilingus, fellatio, and anal intercourse, involving any intrusion, however slight, as well as other sexual conduct involving penetration by objects. The language included in the law should address the nature of consent and related concepts such as force, coercion, and inducement; mental impairment or incapacitation; physical helplessness; fraud; and other concepts bearing on the character of consent, as well as many other concepts—including matters of age, relationship, and aggravating circumstances—that bear on the range of punishment for an act. The language of a model law addressing clergyperson sexual misconduct should be adapted in any particular state, territory, or federal jurisdiction to the overall structure of the jurisdiction's laws that address sexual crimes.

"Psychotherapist" or "mental health professional" includes . . . minister, priest . . ., etc. For circumstances involving counseling, the statute should include clergypersons within the definition of "psychotherapist" or "mental health professional," or any other terminology used to define the actor in the case of prohibited sexual conduct within the context of a counseling relationship.

A sexual offense is without consent if the actor is a member of the clergy, and in such capacity is in a position of trust or authority over the victim and uses this position of trust or authority to exploit the victim's emotional dependency on the member of the clergy to engage in forced, coerced, or induced acts of sexual intercourse, cunnilingus, fellatio, or anal intercourse, involving any intrusion, however slight, as well as other sexual conduct involving penetration by objects with the victim. This is the provision that extends criminal liability to circumstances outside of the counseling relationship when a clergyperson engages in sexual misconduct with a congregant or parishioner. As mentioned above, only thirteen states and the District of Columbia have criminal laws that, in at least some circumstances, support the criminal prosecution of clergypersons engaged in sexual misconduct with adult congregants or parishioners. Only two of those jurisdictions have language that is designed to make such conduct illegal by clergypersons outside of the counseling context: Arkansas, with a law titled "Sexual Assault in the Fourth Degree" (2009), and Texas, with a law titled "Sexual Assault" (2010). Note that the model statute includes the notation that the conduct is without consent. This characterizes the conduct as nonconsensual even if it appears to be consensual. The sexual conduct of clergypersons with congregants or parishioners that is criminalized by this language is deemed to be without consent by virtue of the relationship of the parties and the circumstances in which the sexual conduct occurs, as is the case with mental impairment or incapacitation and the physically helpless.

A Similar Statute in Arkansas

The language of the proposed model statute is supported by a similar statute that was promulgated by the Arkansas legislature. Like the proposed model law, the Arkansas statute provides that a person commits a sex crime if the person is a "member of the clergy and is in a position of trust or authority over the victim and uses the position of trust or authority to engage in sexual intercourse or deviate sexual activity (defined terms)" ("Sexual Assault in the Fourth Degree" 2009, § 5-14-126). The Arkansas statute contemplates a clergyperson taking advantage of the emotional deference of another person (presumably a congregant or parishioner) and parlaying that deference into a sexual encounter. The statute does not further describe what characterizes a "position of authority," but the elements of trust, reliance, emotional intimacy, and vulnerability would necessarily be involved.

The Arkansas statute is not likely to be deemed to excessively entangle government regulation with religion because it does not require a court to tell a church how to interpret church doctrine. The statute does not require: (1) that the clergyperson be a spiritual or religious advisor to the congregant or parishioner; (2) that the congregant be seeking spiritual advice or theological guidance from the clergyperson; or (3) that the relationship between a clergyperson and the congregant that leads to the sexual engagement pertain at all to religious or spiritual matters. Instead, the statute requires only that the clergyperson be in a position of trust or authority over the victim and use that trust or authority to engage in prohibited sexual contact by taking advantage of the trust, reliance, emotional intimacy, and vulnerability that arise between the clergyperson and the victim by virtue of the relationship.

Dissimilar Laws with Improper Phrasing

In focusing solely on positional authority and not requiring that the prohibited conduct occur in the context of the clergyperson rendering spiritual or theological advice or otherwise acting in a pastoral capacity, the Arkansas statute deftly avoids the issue of entanglement and the First Amendment. The statutes and pending laws of the other jurisdictions that have criminalized clergyperson sexual contact with a congregant or parishioner outside of a counseling relationship have inadvisably used phraseology that invites inquiry into whether the statute is criminalizing conduct in circumstances that call for the court to act beyond its competence and run into First Amendment problems. In Kansas, a proposed bill required that a member of the clergy engaging in the prohibited sexual contact "[act] as a member of the clergy carrying out the clergy member's pastoral duties" (H.R. 2100, 2009 Leg. Sess. Kan. 2009, Section 1. K.S.A. 21-3520). And the Texas statute requires that the actor be a clergyperson who is "exploiting the other person's emotional dependency on the clergyman in the clergyman's professional character as spiritual advisor" ("Sexual Assault" 2010, § 22.011). The emphasis in these formulations on the need for the clergyperson to be discharging "pastoral duties" or acting as a "spiritual advisor" invites inquiry into theological and spiritual matters that might involve a government entity (the court) telling a church how to act. Although statutes of other states do not purport to address sexual misconduct outside of the counseling relationship, they nonetheless fall over this same line and into the territory governed by the entanglement doctrine. A Delaware statute requires that the actor be engaged in "pastoral counseling" ("Definition of Sexual Offenses" 2010, § 761). A District of Columbia statute requires a professional relationship of trust combined with counseling, "whether legal, spiritual, or otherwise" ("First Degree Sexual Abuse of a Patient or Client" 2007, § 22-3015). A New Mexico statute requires the clergyperson to be "acting in his or her roles as a pastoral counselor" ("Definition Sexual Offenses" 2010, § 30-9-10). Hence, the model statute must not raise the issue of the victim seeking or receiving spiritual or religious advice, aid, or comfort from the clergyperson in an encounter or during the period of the criminalized conduct; it must also avoid the analogous reference to the clergyperson acting in a pastoral capacity or as a spiritual advisor.

The Minnesota statute "Criminal Sexual Contact in the Third Degree" (2003) is also an example of the manner in which such language can lead to a violation of the Constitution due to the entanglement doctrine. The relevant part of this statute provides that "a person who engages in sexual penetration with another person is guilty of criminal sexual conduct in the third degree if the actor is or purports to be a member of the clergy, the complainant is not married to the actor, and the sexual penetration occurred during the course of a meeting in which the complainant sought or received religious or spiritual advice, aid, or comfort from the actor in private; or the sexual penetration occurred during a period of time in which the complainant was meeting on an ongoing basis with the actor to seek or receive religious or spiritual advice, aid, or comfort in private" (§ 609.344). Consistent with the concept that the statute is criminalizing conduct that is consensual on its face, the statute specifically provides that consent by the complainant is not a defense.

The Minnesota statute was determined to be unconstitutional by a court reasoning that the provision violated the entanglement doctrine and the First Amendment. *State v. Bussman* (2007) determined that the statute did not have a secular purpose and fostered an excessive government entanglement with religion. The court reasoned that an unmarried clergyperson who dated a congregant and had sexual contact would be guilty of the crime if the two were also discussing spiritual and religious matters on an ongoing basis. Likewise, a parishioner who initiated and persistently pursued a sexual relationship with a member of the clergy would nevertheless be deemed to be incapable of effectively consenting to that relationship so long as the two discussed spiritual or religious issues, however disconnected with the sexual contact that discussion may have been. The court further declared that the absence of a clear secular purpose to enact the law supported the conclusion that the statute encroached into constitutionally illegitimate territory.

Like the Minnesota statute, the Texas statute "Sexual Assault" (2010) is not a suitable model for criminalizing sexual misconduct of clergypersons with congregants or parishioners. As noted above, this statute provides that sexual assault is without consent if "the actor is a clergyman who causes the other person to submit or participate by exploiting the other person's emotional dependency on the clergyman in the clergyman's professional character as spiritual advisor" (§ 22.011). The language about "the clergyman's professional character as spiritual advisor" may be deemed excessive entanglement with religion, similar to the wording in the Minnesota statute. This dimension of the law is deemed excessive entanglement because the law requires Texas courts to tell a clergyperson how to act as spiritual advisor, while he or she is interpreting church doctrine, directing liturgy, or performing other church-related duties. Nevertheless, the Texas statute has not yet been challenged on constitutional grounds.

Avoiding First Amendment Issues with Secular Language

In an Arkansas case, *Talbert v. State* (2006), the defendant raised objections to language in the Arkansas statute regarding position of authority. The language appears not to run afoul of the same pitfalls as the Minnesota and Texas statutes because it does not refer to the misconduct occurring in circumstances in which pastoral duties—including the rendering of religious or spiritual advice—were involved. As noted above, the Arkansas statute provides that a person commits a sex crime if the person engages in a sexual criminal act and is "a member of the clergy and is in a position of trust or authority over the victim and uses the position of trust or authority to engage in sexual intercourse or deviate sexual activity." In *Talbert* the statute was alleged to be unconstitutional, not on entanglement grounds (apparently because of the adept use of language), but because it treated people unequally and violated individuals' privacy. The defendant, a minister, was convicted under the statute for having used a position of trust and authority to have sexual intercourse with a congregant who had confided in him and for whom he was "someone she could turn to for help." Against the contention based on *Lawrence v. Texas* (2003), the defendant on appeal argued that the state cannot infringe on an adult's right to engage in private, consensual sex with other adults. The court answered that the statute in *Lawrence* criminalized consensual sex between adults when each participant freely consented to the relationship. This was a different situation than that in the defendant's case, because the defendant instead abused his position of trust and authority to entice the victim into having sexual intercourse with him. Moreover, the court found no legal right that allowed a clergyperson to abuse his or her position of authority in order to obtain a sexual favor.

The defendant also contended that the statute was constitutionally invalid because the statute forced the court to treat him differently than other individuals because he was a minister, as well as imposing a sanction on him for engaging in consensual sex with other adults. The Fourteenth Amendment to the Constitution states that courts cannot deny any person equal protection of the laws. For example, a court cannot give preferential treatment to one individual over another based on his or her race. The court in *Talbert* stated that the law had a rational basis to prevent clergypersons from using their positions of authority to take advantage of vulnerable congregants or parishioners for their own sexual gratification. Furthermore, the court found that there was a rational basis for holding clergypersons accountable for a breach of a position of trust and authority leading to sexual relations with congregants or parishioners: clergypersons are held in high regard and esteem and, as with professional mental health providers, people seek out clergypersons in time of need, being led to them on account of reliance and trust in their ability to give needed and sound guidance and counsel. Thus, the court declared the law valid and reiterated that the defendant was not unlawfully being treated differently from others due to his peculiar position of authority.

The defendant in *Talbert* also asserted that the statute violated his right to privacy, in that he could not act as he pleased in private dwellings or other private locations. The court disagreed, declaring that there could be no right of privacy just to obtain sex from emotionally vulnerable persons with disparate bargaining power. The assertion that the statute violated the Constitution was rejected by the court, which observed that the defendant's conduct fell clearly within the purview of the statute in regard to having a relationship of trust and authority as well as in regard to the law's description of prohibited conduct. In any event, associational rights are for the mutual benefit of those in the relationship of association. In this case, the statute is aimed at protecting someone who is emotionally vulnerable; the relationship involves parties in disparate positions of power vis-à-vis one another. Thus, the current statute in Arkansas and the model statute presented here are examples jurisdictions can use to craft a criminal statute that can protect congregants and parishioners from predatory clergypersons.

Political and Special-Interest Barriers to Legislation

Even though the Arkansas statute and the proposed model statute provide guidance for crafting a valid law, the enactment of such a law faces stiff opposition from political and special interest groups. According to the "Exempt Organizations" section (2012) in the Internal Revenue Code, for taxing purposes churches are classified as 501(c)3 entities and are therefore not supposed to influence legislation as a substantial part of their activities. Yet some churches skirt this mandate and overly promote or denounce specific political agendas or proposed legislation. Therefore, although many states would benefit from legislation that curtails and punishes the sexual misconduct of clergypersons, political and special interests groups—including churches—often influence legislatures, preventing proposed bills from becoming laws or drastically altering the original content of the proposed bills.

These political and special interests permeate the law-making process at various stages. For example, for a law to be enacted, first an individual, usually a state senator or a state representative, must propose a bill. Then the contents of a bill are debated in both houses of the legislature and may be subjected to various committee debates and hearings. During each of these steps, legislators may propose amendments to a bill, altering its original intent, or quash it altogether. Amendments may be guided by the desires of special interest groups. A bill may be subjected to different amendments in both chambers of the legislature. Ultimately, both chambers must pass the same version of the bill, which must then be signed by the governor before it becomes law. As a result of this legislative process, a bill proposed to inhibit the sexual misconduct of clergypersons could be weakened due to the influence of special interest groups over legislatures. Even if such a bill becomes law, special interest groups may influence the legislature in the future to amend the law, repeal it, or submit the law to popular referendum vote, which could result in its being repealed. Thus, enacting a proposed bill and keeping its original intent intact requires political agility to deftly navigate through special interest hoops.

Current examples of special interest groups—including religious cadres—that influence the proposal, amendment, and ultimate fate of bills include nondenominational African American churches, Catholic churches, and the Church of Jesus Christ of Latter-day Saints (Bernstein and Jakobsen 2010). All of these groups recently influenced state legislatures' votes on same-sex marriage initiatives in Maryland (Tavernise 2012) and California (Sherkat, Mattias de Vries, and Creek 2010). Such special interest influence changed the original intent of both states' bills, and in Maryland this political pressure resulted in a referendum vote that could repeal the law.

History includes many examples of religiously affiliated groups influencing federal and state legislation. For example, the so-called moral majority and conservative Christian coalitions influenced legislative outcomes during the late 1970s and 1980s at both the state and federal level (Wilcox, Linzey, and Jelen 1991). From the late 1980s until 2000, many clergy and congregants of Protestant churches also played an influential role in the legislative debate regarding legalizing gambling in South Carolina (Olson, Guth, and Guth 2003). Thus, it is imperative to understand that special interest groups are likely to resist any attempt by the legislature in most states to enact legislation that would effectively penalize clergy who commit sexual misconduct. Additionally, if such a bill became law, it could be altered or repealed by future legislatures or a referendum vote.

Conclusion

Although the media have recently focused on clergyperson sexual misconduct against children, an overwhelming number of adult congregants and parishioners, primarily women, have been victimized by that misconduct as well.

The large majority of these instances remain unreported and/or unpunished in courts of law. For various reasons discussed in this chapter, it is also difficult to bring a successful civil suit against a clergyperson for sexual misconduct with a congregant or a parishioner. Many victims are simply too scared of the consequences of bringing such a lawsuit, which include being embarrassed or shunned by their congregation or parish, along with the time and emotional pain involved in bringing such a suit. Other victims wait too long and then are legally barred from suing the offender. For example, in Minnesota, if a victim does not commence a lawsuit for sexual abuse within six years, then he or she is barred from obtaining justice through the courts. Unfortunately, the large majority of states do not even have laws that allow an adult victim to bring a lawsuit against a clergyperson for sexual misconduct. In jurisdictions whose laws do permit such suits, the laws often mandate that a court interpret religious doctrine, policy, liturgy, or other church practice, thereby violating the First Amendment of the Constitution. Consequently, when an alleged victim uses such a law to sue a clergyperson for sexual misconduct, the suit is typically dismissed because of a constitutional violation.

As noted above, clergy sexual misconduct may not be properly penalized in a criminal court because a congregant or parishioner does not report it by the legal deadline, or at all. Yet a large amount of onus must be put on state legislatures for not promulgating laws that properly define sexual misconduct as a criminal behavior in a manner that does not violate the First Amendment and that prescribe an appropriate punishment. Many attempts have been made to criminally prosecute clergypersons for sexual misconduct that occurred during secular-based counseling or during counseling that appeared to blend a secular approach with a religious overtone. These attempts typically fail due to entanglement issues and violations of the First Amendment when the counseling includes religious overtones, or because a substantial proportion of clergyperson sexual misconduct occurs outside of a counseling setting, such as when a congregant or parishioner meets with a clergyperson to discuss appropriate music for the Advent season.

Thus, a need exists for a model criminal statute that can be implemented to prosecute and penalize clergypersons who commit sexual misconduct primarily based on their position of authority over their congregant or parishioner victim, in situations where the victim's consent might not be easily refused due to his or her vulnerable state and the level of trust placed in the clergyperson. The model criminal statute proposed in this chapter focuses solely on a clergyperson who commits sexual misconduct against a congregant or parishioner when the clergyperson is deemed to have positional power over the victim, which avoids entanglement and First Amendment barriers to prosecution.

One must keep in mind that politically powerful special interest groups are likely to influence a state legislature to amend or quash such a proposed statute. Yet legislatures need to persistently attempt to promulgate laws similar to the model statute proposed in this chapter. Numerous state legislatures, such as Kansas and Texas, have recently proposed bills or enacted laws to address this sexual misconduct problem. However, most of these bills or laws include language that requires a court to interpret church policy or doctrine. Thus, they are likely to run afoul of entanglement issues. Instead, in drafting statutes to address this problem, legislatures should use phraseology that focuses solely on clergypersons' positional authority and should not use language that would require a court to examine religious doctrine. Such a focus on positional authority would prevent constitutional conflicts and equip governmental authorities with appropriate tools to effectively respond to clergyperson sexual predators.

References

Actions for Damages Due to Sexual Abuse, 33 Minn. Stat. Ann. § 541.073 (2010).

Aggravated Felonious Sexual Assault, 62 N.H. Rev. Stat. Ann. § 632-A:2 (Supp. 2010).

Agostini v. Felton, 521 U.S. 203, 233 (1997), rev'g 519 U.S. 1093 (1997).

American Psychological Association. 2011. "Sexual Abuse." http://www.apa.org.

Ayon v. Gourley, 47 F. Supp. 2d 1246, 1249–50 (D. Colo. 1998), aff'd on other grounds, 185 F.3d 873 (10th Cir. 1999).

Ballotta, K. A. 1994. "Losing Its Soul: How the Cipolla Case Limits the Catholic Church's Ability to Discipline Sexually Abusive Priests." *Emory Law Journal* 43 (4): 1431–66.

Bernstein, E., and J. R. Jakobsen. 2010. "Sex, Secularism and Religious Influence in US Politics." *Third World Quarterly* 31 (6): 1023–39.

Birchard, T. 2000. "Clergy Sexual Misconduct: Frequency and Causation." *Sexual and Relationship Therapy* 15 (2): 127–39.

Crimes against the Person Involving Sexual Assault, 45 Cal. Penal Code § 261 (2008).

Criminal Sexual Contact in the Third Degree, 40A Minn. Stat. Ann. § 609.344 (2003).

Cruz, E. 1991. "When the Shepherd Preys on the Flock: Clergy Sexual Exploitation and the Search for Solutions." *Florida State University Law Review* 19 (2): 499–524.

Exempt Organizations, 26 I.R.C. § 501(c)3 (2012).

Falk, P. J. (1998). "Rape and Fraud by Coercion." *Brooklyn Law Review* 64 (1): 39–180.

"First Degree Sexual Abuse of a Patient or Client." 2007. District of Columbia Code §22-3015.

Fortin v. Roman Catholic Bishop of Portland, 871 A.2d 1208 (Me. 2005).

Fortune, M. M. 1998. "Reporting Child Abuse: An Ethical Mandate for Ministry." In *Abuse and Religion: When Praying Isn't Enough*, edited by A. L. Horton and J. A. Williamson, 189–97. Lanham, MD: Lexington.

In re Phillips, 867 N.Y.S.2d 20 (N.Y. App. Div. 2008).

Langford v. Roman Catholic Diocese of Brooklyn, 677 N.Y.S.2d 436, 899–900 (N.Y. Sup. Ct. 1998), aff'd 705 N.Y.S.2d 661 (N.Y. App. Div. 2000).

Lawrence v. Texas, 539 U.S. 558, 578 (2003), rev'g, 537 U.S. 1044 (2002).

Lemon v. Kurtzman, 403 U.S. 602 (1971).

L.M. v. Karlson, 646 N.W.2d 537, 543 (Minn. Ct. App. 2002).

Lowery v. Cook, No. 20061086-CA, 2007 WL 772782, at *1 (Utah Ct. App. Mar. 15, 2007) (mem. op.).

Lupu, I. C., and R. W. Tuttle. 2004. "Sexual Misconduct and Ecclesiastical Immunity." *Brigham Young University Law Review* 2004 (5): 1789–896.

Moses v. Diocese of Colorado, 863 P.2d 310, 321 n.13 (Colo. 1993).

Nally v. Grace Community Church, 763 P.2d 948 (Cal. 1988).

Nowak, J. E., and R. D. Rotunda. 2001. *Constitutional Law*. Eagan, MN: West.

Olson, L. R., K. V. Guth, and J. L. Guth. 2003. "The Lotto and the Lord: Religious Influences on the Adoption of a Lottery in South Carolina." *Sociology of Religion* 64 (1): 87–110.

O'Reilly, J. T., and J. M. Strasser. 1994. "Clergy Sexual Misconduct: Confronting the Difficult Constitutional and Institutional Liability Issues." *St. Thomas Law Review* 7 (1): 31–74.

Roman Catholic Diocese of Jackson v. Morrison, 905 So.2d 1213 (Minn. 2005).

Sawyer, J. K. 1990. "Benefit of Clergy in Maryland and Virginia." *American Journal of Legal History* 34 (1): 49–68.

Schmidt v. Bishop, 779 F. Supp. 321 (S.D.N.Y. 1991).

Sex Offenses by Psychotherapists, 14 S.D. Codified Laws § 22–22–27 (2006).

Sexual Abuse of a Minor, 3 Alaska Stat. §§ 11.41.434–440 (2010).

Sexual Assault, 2 Tex. Penal Code Ann. § 22.011 (Supp. 2010).

Sexual Assault in the Fourth Degree, 3A Ark. Code Ann. § 5–14–126 (Supp. 2009).

Sexual Conduct Definitions, A44 Mich. Comp. Laws Serv. § 750.520a (2004).

Sexual Exploitation by a Therapist, Wisc. Stat. Ann. § 895.441 (Supp. 2010).

Sexual Offenses, 28A Conn. Gen. Stat. Ann. § 53a-71 (2007).

Sherkat, D. E., K. Mattias de Vries, and S. Creek. 2010. "Race, Religion, and Opposition to Same-Sex Marriage." *Social Science Quarterly* 91 (1): 80–98.

State v. Bussmann, 741 N.W.2d 79, 99–100 (Minn. 2007).

Talbert v. State, No. CR05–1279, 2006 Ark. LEXIS 446, at *8–11 (Ark. Ct. App. Sept. 21, 2006) (not designated for publication).

Tavernise, S. 2012. "Gay Marriage a Tough Sell for Blacks in Maryland." *New York Times*, February 15.

Unlawful Sexual Behavior, 18 Colo. Rev. Stat. Ann. § 18–3-401 (2010).

Waltz v. Tax Commission of the City of New York, 397 U.S. 661 (1970).
Webb v. West Virginia Board of Medicine, 569 S.E.2d 225, 238 (W. Va. 2002).
White, G. 2002. "Sexual Misconduct: Keeping Vigil: How Various Faiths Protect the Innocent in Their Flocks." *Atlanta Journal-Constitution*, September 14.
Wilcox, C., S. Linzey, and T. G. Jelen. 1991. "Reluctant Warriors: Premillennialism and Politics in the Moral Majority." *Journal for the Scientific Study of Religion* 30 (3): 245–58.

About the Contributors

Diana Garland is the inaugural dean of the School of Social Work at Baylor University, where she has served on the faculty since 1997. Her newest book is *Family Ministry: A Comprehensive Guide*, a revised edition of her 1999 book that received the Book of the Year Award of the Academy of Parish Clergy at Princeton Seminary. She is author, co-author, or editor of eighteen other books, including *Inside Out Families: Living the Faith Together* and *Flawed Families of the Bible: Stories You Didn't Learn in Sunday School*. She has also published more than 100 professional articles and book chapters. In addition, she has raised more than $7.5 million in research and program grants since coming to Baylor, from organizations such as the Lilly Endowment, Pew Charitable Trusts, the Annie E. Casey Foundation, the Henry Luce Foundation, and the Ford Foundation. She is known for her leadership with congregations and religious organizations in family and community ministry and for her research on the faith life of families.

John C. Gonsiorek received his PhD in clinical psychology from the University of Minnesota in 1978 and holds a Diplomate in Clinical Psychology from the American Board of Professional Psychology. He is a past president of the American Psychological Association's Division 44, and he has published widely in such areas as professional misconduct and impaired professionals, sexual orientation and identity, and professional ethics. He is a fellow of Divisions 9, 12, 29, 36, and 44 of the American Psychological Association. For many years, he provided expert witness evaluation and testimony regarding impaired clergy and professionals, standards of care, and psychological damages; he has also provided training and consultation to a variety of religious denominations and organizations. He is a consulting editor for *Professional Psychology: Research and Practice*. His major publications include *Breach of Trust: Sexual Exploitation by Health Care Professionals and Clergy*; *Homosexuality: Research Implications for Public Policy* (with James D. Weinrich); *Male Sexual Abuse: A Trilogy of Intervention Strategies* (with Walter H. Bera and Donald LeTourneau); and *Homosexuality and Psychotherapy: A Practitioner's Handbook of Affirmative Models*.

Kris Helge became the scholarly communications librarian at the University of North Texas in October 2012. He previously served as a librarian and faculty member at Texas

Wesleyan University School of Law and Baylor Law School. He holds a BA from Baylor University, a JD from South Texas College of Law, and an MLS from the University of North Texas. He is currently pursuing a PhD in information science at the University of North Texas.

Claire M. Renzetti holds the Judi Conway Patton Endowed Chair in the Center for Research on Violence against Women and is also a professor of sociology, both at the University of Kentucky. She is editor of the international, interdisciplinary journal *Violence Against Women*; coeditor, with Jeffrey Edleson, of the Interpersonal Violence book series for Oxford University Press; and editor of the Gender, Crime, and Law book series for Northeastern University Press. She has authored or edited sixteen books as well as numerous book chapters and articles in professional journals. Much of her research has focused on the violent victimization experiences of socially and economically marginalized women. Her current research includes an ethnography of a faith-based organization involved in work against human trafficking; a national web-based survey examining the effects of religiosity on the quality of and conflict within intimate relationships; and an empowerment education project with the Women's Justice Programs, in the Cook County (Chicago), Illinois, Sheriff's Office.

Paul D. Steele is a professor of sociology and criminology and the director of the Center for Justice Studies at Morehead State University. He was a member of the Sociology Department faculty of the University of New Mexico for several years, and is an emeritus professor there, but he left the university for a time to serve as director of research at the Vera Institute of Justice. After returning to New Mexico, he was appointed by the governor to be the director of the New Mexico Criminal Justice Analysis Center, the statistical analysis center for that state.

Karen J. Terry is a professor in the Department of Criminal Justice at John Jay College of Criminal Justice, City University of New York. She holds a doctorate in criminology from Cambridge University. Her research focuses on sexual abuse and victimization, and she has published widely on the management and supervision of sex offenders. Most recently, she was the principal investigator for two national studies on the sexual abuse of minors by Catholic priests.

Bradley Toben has been dean of the Baylor Law School since 1991. He received a BA from the University of Missouri, a JD from Baylor Law School, and an LLM from Harvard Law School. He joined the Baylor Law School faculty in 1983, having previously served on the faculty at Indiana University School of Law. The holder of the M. C. and Mattie Caston Chair of Law at Baylor, he has been honored by the Texas Trial Lawyers Association for "exemplary service and commitment as a guiding light in legal scholarship and the pursuit of justice."

Sandra Yocum received her doctorate in theology from Marquette University. Her research focuses on the intersections between theology and culture in US Catholic life and thought. She has taught in the Religious Studies Department at the University of Dayton since the fall of 1992, where she has served as the department's director of graduate studies and chair. She has published articles in edited collections, encyclopedias, and several journals, including *Theological Studies*, *Horizons*, *Church History*, and *U.S. Catholic Historian*. She coedited *American Catholic Traditions: Resources for Renewal* (1997) with William Portier. She also wrote *Joining the Revolution in Theology: The College Theology Society, 1954–2004* (2007). She is currently completing a project on the entry of Catholic women into the field of contemporary theological studies.

Index